GREAT PLAINS

ACKNOWLEDGMENTS

We gratefully acknowledge the help of our representatives for their efficient and perceptive inspections of the lodgings listed. Forbes Travel Guide is also grateful to the talented writers who contributed to this book.

GREAT PLAINS ★★★★★

ISBN: 9-780841-61417-8   Manufactured in the USA

10 9 8 7 6 5 4 3 2 1

TABLE OF CONTENTS

GREAT PLAINS ★★★★★

STAR ATTRACTIONS

If you've been a reader of Mobil Travel Guide, you will have heard that this historic brand partnered with another storied media name, Forbes, in 2009 to create a new entity, Forbes Travel Guide. For more than 50 years, Mobil Travel Guide assisted travelers in making smart decisions about where to stay and dine when traveling. With this new partnership, our mission has not changed: We're committed to the same rigorous inspections of hotels, restaurants and spas—the most comprehensive in the industry with more than 500 standards tested at each property we visit—to help you cut through the clutter and make easy and informed decisions on where to spend your time and travel budget. Our team of anonymous inspectors are constantly on the road, sleeping in hotels, eating in restaurants and making spa appointments, evaluating those exacting standards to determine a property's rating.

What kind of standards are we looking for when we visit a proprety? We're looking for more than just high-thread count sheets, pristine spa treatment rooms and white linen-topped tables. We look for service that's attentive, individualized and unforgettable. We note how long it takes to be greeted when you sit down at your table, or to be served when you order room service, or whether the hotel staff can confidently help you when you've forgotten that one essential item that will make or break your trip. Unlike other travel ratings entities, we visit the places we rate, testing hundreds of attributes to compile our ratings, and our ratings cannot be bought or influenced. The Forbes Five Star rating is the most prestigious achievement in hospitality—while we rate more than 8,000 properties in the U.S., Canada, Hong Kong, Macau and Beijing, for 2010, we have awarded Five Star designations to only 53 hotels, 21 restaurants and 18 spas. When you travel with Forbes, you can travel with confidence, knowing that you'll get the very best experience, no matter who you are.

We understand the importance of making the most of your time. That's why the most trusted name in travel is now Forbes Travel Guide.

STAR RATED HOTELS

Whether you're looking for the ultimate in luxury or the best value for your travel budget, we have a hotel recommendation for you. To help you pinpoint properties that meet your needs, Forbes Travel Guide classifies each lodging by type according to the following characteristics:

★★★★★These exceptional properties provide a memorable experience through virtually flawless service and the finest of amenities. Staff are intuitive, engaging and passionate, and eagerly deliver service above and beyond the guests' expectations. The hotel was designed with the guest's comfort in mind, with particular attention paid to craftsmanship and quality of product. A Five Star property is a destination unto itself.

★★★★These properties provide a distinctive setting, and a guest will find many interesting and inviting elements to enjoy throughout the property. Attention to detail is prominent throughout the property, from design concept to quality of products provided. Staff are accommodating and take pride in catering to the guest's specific needs throughout their stay.

★★★These well-appointed establishments have enhanced amenities that provide travelers with a strong sense of location, whether for style or function. They may have a distinguishing style and ambience in both the public spaces and guest rooms; or they may be more focused on functionality, providing guests with easy access to local events, meetings or tourism highlights.

★★The Two Star hotel is considered a clean, comfortable and reliable establishment that has expanded amenities, such as a full-service restaurant.

★The One Star lodging is a limited-service hotel or inn that is considered a clean, comfortable and reliable establishment.

For every property, we also provide pricing information. All prices quoted are accurate at the time of publication; however, prices cannot be guaranteed.

STAR RATED RESTAURANTS

Every restaurant in this book comes highly recommended as an outstanding dining experience.

★★★★★Forbes Five Star restaurants deliver a truly unique and distinctive dining experience. A Five Star restaurant consistently provides exceptional food, superlative service and elegant décor. An emphasis is placed on originality and personalized, attentive and discreet service. Every detail that surrounds the experience is attended to by a warm and gracious dining room team.

★★★★These are exciting restaurants with often well-known chefs that feature creative and complex foods and emphasize various culinary techniques and a focus on seasonality. A highly-trained dining room staff provides refined personal service and attention.

★★★Three Star restaurants offer skillfully-prepared food with a focus on a specific style or cuisine. The dining room staff provides warm and professional service in a comfortable atmosphere. The décor is well-coordinated with quality fixtures and decorative items, and promotes a comfortable ambience.

★★The Two Star restaurant serves fresh food in a clean setting with efficient service. Value is considered in this category, as is family friendliness.

★The One Star restaurant provides a distinctive experience through culinary specialty, local flair or individual atmosphere.

Because menu prices can fluctuate, we list a pricing range rather than specific prices. The pricing ranges are per diner, and assume that you order an appetizer or dessert, an entrée and one drink.

STAR RATED SPAS

Forbes Travel Guide's spa ratings are based on objective evaluations of more than 450 attributes. About half of these criteria assess basic expectations, such as staff courtesy, the technical proficiency and skill of the employees and whether the facility is clean and maintained properly. Several standards address issues that impact a guest's physical comfort and convenience, as well as the staff's ability to impart a sense of personalized service. Additional criteria measure the spa's ability to create a completely calming ambience.

★★★★★Stepping foot in a Five Star spa will result in an exceptional experience with no detail overlooked. These properties wow their guests with extraordinary design and facilities, and uncompromising service. Expert staff cater to your every whim and pamper you with the most advanced treatments and skin care lines available. These spas often offer exclusive treatments and may emphasize local elements.

★★★★Four Star spas provide a wonderful experience in an inviting and serene environment. A sense of personalized service is evident from the moment you check in and receive your robe and slippers. The guest's comfort is always of utmost concern to the well-trained staff.

★★★These spas offer well-appointed facilities with a full complement of staff to ensure that guests' needs are met. The spa facilities include clean and appealing treatment rooms, changing areas and a welcoming reception desk.

IOWA

PROBABLY MORE THAN ANY OTHER HEARTLAND STATE, IOWA CONJURES UP IMAGES OF table-top-flat cornfields dotted with silos and farmhouses. And while in some parts of the state you will find yourself driving through a sea of corn that stretches to the horizon (Iowa grows more of it than any state but Illinois), with a bit of exploring, you'll find ski slopes, towering bluffs above the Mississippi River, six wildlife refuges: one harboring wetlands and fields that teem with birds during migration season, another that showcases Iowa's prairie heritage, with native grasses and wild flowers and the chance to encounter buffalo and elk, and another where you can climb up and down hills left untouched by the glaciers that chiseled and flattened the land elsewhere thousands of years ago.

The Sioux called Iowa the "Beautiful Land" and it's a name that fits. Every region of the state has a loop of Scenic Byways, well-marked routes that reveal the beauty of the countryside. Iowa has miles of bike trails, many built on the gentle grades of old railroad lines. Hikers can retreat into the tranquility of nature preserve trails that retrace historical journeys such as those of Louis and Clark or the Mormons as they moved west.

History abounds in Iowa. This is the birthplace of Buffalo Bill Cody, John Wayne and Herbert Hoover. In Des Moines, visitors to the State Historical Museum are greeted by a 16,000-year-old Hebior mammoth, while airplanes "buzz" overhead in the atrium. To the northeast, in Dubuque, freshwater creatures and habitats get their due, in the National River Museum and Aquarium. Down the road, in Eldon, see the house that inspired the background for Iowa native Grant Wood's most famous painting, "American Gothic." And in the southeast, the Amana colonies—seven historic villages formed by German immigrants as a religious communal society—offer attractions than can easily fill a day, or even a week.

You won't need a guidebook to discover Iowa's essential charm, the friendly character of people who are by heritage tied to the land and the value of work. To find this, sit down in a local café in a small town at lunchtime. Or, in the summer, make your way to one of the fairs held in each of the 99 counties. Buy yourself a corn dog and head to the agricultural barn where kids display their meticulously groomed cows, pigs and sheep. From the dedication and pride you'll see in these young people's faces, you'll learn what Iowa is about.

AMANA COLONIES

See also Cedar Rapids, Iowa City

The history of this religious community goes back to the 1714 founding in Germany of the Inspirationists, a Lutheran separatist group. Members migrated to America and settled near Buffalo, New York. Later they bought 25,000 acres of prairie land in Iowa and moved west. Their first Iowa village was called Amana, a Biblical name meaning "remain faithful." Five more villages were built (West, High, Middle, East and South Amana). The village of Homestead was purchased outright so that the towns could use its railroad terminal.

FROM THE BRIDGES OF MADISON COUNTY TO THE LOESS HILLS

Surrounded by wooded hills, Winterset, originally a Quaker settlement, is the hub of several short-side trips to the six covered bridges made famous by the Robert Waller's novel The Bridges of Madison County. If you want to make the full circuit, pick up a free brochure and map to all the bridges from local businesses (most are on remote county roads). If you don't have time for the full tour, one of the bridges is now preserved in Winterset's city park. The Madison County Historical Complex is an 18-acre park with a number of historic buildings, including a limestone barn and the old Winterset train depot.

Quaker-founded Winterset was a station along the Underground Railroad. A painted brick house, now in the Winterset Art Center, served as a temporary home for hundreds of displaced slaves during the 1850s and 1860s, including scholar George Washington Carver, who lived here after experiencing discrimination elsewhere in the Midwest. Winterset is also the birthplace of actor John Wayne, who was born Marion Robert Morrison. His family home is open to visitors.

Drive south on Highway 169 and turn west on Highway 34 to Creston, an old railroading center with an impressive core of late Victorian homes and storefronts. The town's McKinley Park houses the Union County Historical Museum, with remnants of Creston's heyday in the 1880s. Continue on Highway 34 to the village of Corning, once home to the Icarian Colony, the longest operating nonreligious utopian community in the United States. Founded in 1850, the 80-member community disbanded in 1900 after establishing vineyards, lilac hedges and stands of rhubarb in the area. (Rhubarb pie is still a favorite in local cafés.)

Follow Highway 34 across the prairies to Red Oak and then go south on Highway 59 to Shenandoah, originally a Mormon settlement. From Shenandoah, turn west on Highway 2 toward Sidney, a village in Iowa's famous Loess Hills. These green, heavily eroded hills were formed at the end of the last Ice Age. The Missouri River brought silt-rich waters from the north, where massive glaciers were busy grinding rock into till. As the silt deposits dried, winds blew the fine sand into dunes hundreds of feet high. Now covered with virgin prairie grasslands and upland forests, the Loess Hills are home to wildlife such as coyotes, deer, bald eagles and prairie dogs, and were considered for national park status during the Clinton administration.

While in Sidney, be sure to stop at the Penn Drug Store. Built in 1865, the store is still operated by the Penn family; it is the oldest family-owned business in the state and features an old-fashioned soda fountain. From Sidney, two scenic back roads, the Pleasant Overview Loop and the Spring Valley Loop, wind into the Loess Hills. Approximately 205 miles.

At first, the members of the Amana Colonies lived a simple, communal life. Families were assigned living quarters with common kitchen and dining facilities and everything was shared equally. Farming was (and still is) a mainstay of the group. In 1932, common property was dissolved and redistributed on a stock basis. The new corporation, encouraging individual skills and vigor, prospered mostly because of the quality work of its artisans. Today, nearly every family owns its own house.

WHAT TO SEE
AMANA HERITAGE SITES

Highways 151 and 220, Amana, 319-622-3567; www.amanaheritage.org
This community has a furniture factory that offers tours of the production area; a woolen mill with salesroom; woodworking shops, a meat shop, a gen-

eral store, a brewery, wineries, restaurants and shops. The residence of the late Christian Metz, former leader of Amana Colonies, is here.

AMANA HERITAGE MUSEUM

4310 220th Trail, Amana, 319-622-3567; www.amanaheritage.org

Exhibits include a schoolhouse, crafts, lithographs and documents. An audio-visual presentation explains the history of the Amanas.

Admission: adults $7, children free with adult admission. Daily.

OLD CREAMERY THEATRE COMPANY

Price Creek Stage, 39 38th Ave., Amana, 319-622-6194, 800-352-6262, 319-622-6034; www.oldcreamery.com

Iowa's oldest professional theater company puts on a variety of productions. April-mid-December, Wednesday-Sunday.

WHERE TO STAY
★★HOLIDAY INN

2211 U. Ave., Williamsburg, 319-668-1175, 800-633-9244; www.holiday-inn.com

Connected to the Wasserbahn Waterpark, this hotel carries on the German heritage and mid-western hospitality of the area. Little Amana complex is adjacent with an old-time general store and winery.

155 rooms. Restaurant, bar. Fitness center. Pool. Pets accepted. $60 and under

★SUPER 8

1708 N. Highland St., Williamsburg, 319-668-9718; www.super8.com

This intimate hotel offers a great location close to many of the attractions around the Amana Colonies including the Tanger Outlet Mall. Each suite has a different theme so ask for one that suites your taste.

33 rooms. Complimentary breakfast. Fitness center. Pool. Pets accepted. $60 and under

WHERE TO EAT
★★BRICK HAUS

728 47th Ave., Amana, 319-622-3278

Go hungry as the portions are huge at this hearty comfort food spot. The restaurant is decorated with photos on the wall detailing the history of village so receive a history lesson while filling up on the seemingly never ending side dishes.

German, American. Breakfast, lunch, dinner. Children's menu. $16-35

★★COLONY VILLAGE

I-80 at Exit 225, Little Amana, 319-668-1223; www.colonyvillage.com

Colony Village serves everything from a classic Reuben sandwich to traditional wiener schnitzel. The pickled Amana ham is a well-known dish that is not to be missed.

American, German. Breakfast, lunch, dinner. Children's menu. Bar. $16-35

★★OX YOKE INN
4420 220th Trail, Amana, 319-622-3441; www.oxyokeinn.com
This family run family style restaurant has been dishing up delicious eats since 1940. They now serve smaller portions by request so you can save room to enjoy their famous pie fresh from the oven.
German, American. Lunch, dinner, Sunday brunch. Children's menu. Bar. $16-35

★★RONNEBURG
4408 220th Trail, Amana, 319-622-3641; www.ronneburgrestaurant.com
Grab a stein of beer and sing a sing in the lively beer garden before heading inside for authentic German food at this family style restaurant that traces its roots to a religious movement in the early 1700's.
German. Breakfast, lunch, dinner, brunch. Bar. $16-35

AMES
See also Boone
Located near the geographical center of the state, Ames beats to the pulse of Iowa State University. The town is named in honor of a Massachusetts congressman, Oakes Ames, who was financially interested in a local railroad project.

WHAT TO SEE
IOWA ARBORETUM
1875 Peach Ave., Madrid, 515-795-3216; www.iowaarboretum.org
This arboretum includes 340 acres of trees, shrubs and gardens. Trails, horticultural plantings, scenic overlooks, ravines, streams.
Admission: Donation. Daily 8:30 a.m.-4:30 p.m.

IOWA STATE UNIVERSITY
117 Beardshear Hall, Ames, 515-294-4777, 515-294-4111; www.iastate.edu
One of the oldest land-grant universities in the United States, founded in 1858, ISU is known for its spacious, green central campus with sculptures and fountains by artist Christian Petersen and for its many historic buildings. The school is also the birthplace of the electronic digital computer, built by John V. Atanasoff in the basement of the Physics Building in the late 1930s.

GRANT WOOD MURALS
Parks Library, Morrill Road, Ames
Considered among the best works of this Iowa artist, the nine murals began as a Works Projects Administration project during the Great Depression. They depict various academic divisions of the school as well as the breaking of sod by pioneer farmers.

MAMIE DOUD EISENHOWER BIRTHPLACE
709 Carroll St., Boone, 515-432-1907; www.mamiesbirthplace.homestead.com/
This one-story frame house includes period furnishings such as the bed in which Mamie Eisenhower was born.
Admission: adults $4, children 6-17 $1. June-October, Monday-Saturday, 10 a.m.-5 p.m.

WHERE TO STAY
★BAYMONT INN & SUITES

1745 S.E. Marshall St., Boone, 515-296-2500, 866-999-1111; www.baymontinns.com

The clean, comfortable and spacious rooms at this hotel make this the perfect place to stay while visiting the Ames area. Great locations minutes away from all the area has to offer.

89 rooms. Complimentary breakfast. Pool. Pets accepted. $60 and under

★★THE HOTEL AT GATEWAY CENTER

2100 Green Hills Drive, Ames, 515-292-8600, 800-367-2637; www.gatewayames.com

Located next door to the Iowa State University, this full service hotel is walking distance from the restaurants and other cultural events. Be sure to view the over 300 original works of art throughout the hotel and the on site Audubon restaurant.

188 rooms. Restaurant, bar. Business center. Fitness Center. Pool. Pets accepted. $60 and under

WHERE TO EAT
★HICKORY PARK RESTAURANT CO

1404 S. D, Ames, 515-232-8940; www.hickorypark-bbq.com

This charming restaurant, with old advertising memorabilia decorating the walls, is an Ames tradition. With over 100 items including their signature smoked meats on the menu, it is easy to find something you will enjoy.

American. Lunch, dinner. Children's menu. $16-35

★LUCULLANS

400 Main St., Ames, 515-232-8484; www.lucullans.com

This Italian restaurant offers a rich selection of authentic food including hearty pastas, grilled steaks and fresh-baked breads. Go with a large group and order the Cajun pasta, it is not to be missed.

Italian. Dinner. Closed Monday. Children's menu. Bar. $16-35

BETTENDORF

See also Clinton, Davenport

Bettendorf began as a quiet rural village called Gilbert. In 1903, the town's future changed with the arrival of the Bettendorf Axle and Wagon Company, which became the largest manufacturer of railroad cars west of the Mississippi. The growing city changed its name in honor of the company. Today Bettendorf, on the Mississippi River, is part of the Quad Cities metropolitan area.

WHAT TO SEE
BUFFALO BILL CODY HOMESTEAD

28050 230th Ave., Princeton, 563-225-2981; www.scottcountyiowa.com

Restored and furnished boyhood home of Buffalo Bill Cody, built by his father in 1847. Buffalo and long horn cattle graze on the grounds surrounding the property.

Admission: adults $2, children 16 and under free. April-October, daily 9 a.m.-5 p.m.

FAMILY MUSEUM OF ARTS & SCIENCE

2900 Learning Campus Drive, Bettendorf, 563-344-4106; www.familymuseum.org
This interactive museum features hands-on exhibits as well as a traveling exhibit gallery for kids and adults alike.
Admission: adults $6, Children under 2 free. Monday-Thursday 9 a.m.-8 p.m., Friday-Saturday 9 a.m.-5 p.m., Sunday noon-5 p.m.

WHERE TO STAY
★★HOLIDAY INN

909 Middle Road, Bettendorf, 563-355-4761, 800-626-0780; www.holiday-inn.com
Recently renovated, this classic Holiday Inn is located minutes away from many of the Quad Cities attractions.
150 rooms. Restaurant, bar. Fitness center. Pool. $61-150

★★THE LODGE

900 Spruce Hills Drive, Bettendorf, 563-359-7141, 800-285-8637; www.lodgehotel.com
The hotel sets itself apart with its unique charm and 14 different room styles to choose from. Be sure to enjoy the onsite restaurant's Sunday Brunch as it is one of the largest in the area.
210 rooms. Restaurant, bar. Fitness center. Pool. Spa. Pets accepted. $61-150

★RAMADA BETTENDORF/DAVENPORT

3020 Utica Ridge Road, Bettendorf, 563-355-7575; www.ramada.com
With a convenient location only seven miles from the airport, this hotel has recently remolded rooms and a brand new indoor family fun pool. This is a great location and plenty of activities for the kids.
119 rooms. Complimentary breakfast. Business center. Fitness center. Pool. Pets accepted. $61-150

WHERE TO EAT
★★★THE FAITHFUL PILOT CAFÉ

117 N. Cody Road, Le Claire, 563-289-4156; www.faithfulpilotcafe.com
This restaurant features progressive American cuisine served in an elegant, modern dining room. Menu highlights include rack of lamb over minted wild rice and grilled beef tenderloin with rosemary potatoes.
American. Dinner (Monday-Saturday), Sunday brunch. $16-35

★★★THE LODGE RESTAURANT

900 Spruce Hills Drive, Bettendorf, 563-359-1607; www.lodgehotel.com
This restaurant features an extensive collection of American and German fare. Specialties include Regensburg goulash, chicken von jumer and rack of lamb. The bourbon pork chop is not to be missed.
American, German. Lunch, dinner, Sunday brunch. Children's menu. Bar. $16-35

CEDAR FALLS
See also Waterloo
Named after the river that flows through the city, Cedar Falls was once one

of the most important milling centers in the state. Today Cedar Falls is a university town, home to the University of Northern Iowa, one of Iowa's three state universities.

WHAT TO SEE
CEDAR FALLS HISTORICAL SOCIETY VICTORIAN HOME MUSEUM
308 W. Third St., Cedar Falls, 319-266-5149;
This Victorian house is furnished in period style. The Carriage House Museum contains a library, archives, fashions, Lenoir train exhibit and memorabilia of the first permanent settlement in Black Hawk County.
Admission: donation. Wednesday-Saturday 10 a.m.-4 p.m., Sunday 1-4 p.m.

GEORGE WYTH HOUSE
303 Franklin St., Cedar Falls, 319-266-5149; www.cedarfallshistorical.org
The residence of George Wyth, founder of the Viking Pump Company, was built in 1907. It's now furnished in the Art Deco style of the 1920s and includes pieces by Gilbert Rhode. The Viking Pump Company museum is housed on the third floor.
Admission: donation. Tours: May-September, Sunday; also by appointment.

ISLE OF CAPRI CASINO
777 Isle Parkway, Bettendorf, 563-359-7280, 800-724-5825;
www.isleofcapricasino.com
This casino features over 35,000 square feet of gaming options as well as various entertainment choices and three onsite restaurants.

LITTLE RED SCHOOL
First and Clay streets, Cedar Falls, 319-266-5149; www.cedarfallshistorical.org
This country school has been authentically furnished to reflect turn-of-the-century education.
Admission: donation. May-October, Wednesday, Saturday-Sunday.

UNIVERSITY OF NORTHERN IOWA
1222 W. 27th St., Cedar Falls, 319-273-2311, 319-273-2838; www.uni.edu
This campus of 14,000 students, founded in 1876, features a campanile built in Italian Renaissance style that chimes daily. Also on campus is a museum with exhibits on geology and natural history.

SPECIAL EVENT
CEDAR FALLS MUNICIPAL BAND
Overman Park, Second and Franklin streets, Cedar Falls, 319-266-1253;
www.cedarnet.org/cfband
The Cedar Falls Municipal Band, the oldest concert band in the state, entertains crowds each summer outdoors at a modern band shell. Bring a lawn chair or blanket and relax as these 45 musicians perform.
June-August, Tuesday.

WHERE TO STAY
★★HOLIDAY INN
5826 University Ave., Cedar Falls, 319-277-2230; www.holiday-inn.com
Conveniently located hotel with a lobby that opens on to the indoor pool and waterfall. The hotel also offers an open game room and a computer for guest's use.
181 rooms. Restaurant, bar. Fitness center. Pool. $61-150

CEDAR RAPIDS
See also Amana Colonies, Iowa City
This vibrant smaller city has all the amenities you need for a cosmopolitan lifestyle that rivals other Midwestern cities twice its size. From dining and shopping to the arts and nightlife, this city has it all in a comfortable and very livable atmosphere.

WHAT TO SEE
CEDAR RAPIDS MUSEUM OF ART
410 Third Ave. S.E., Cedar Rapids, 319-366-7503; www.crma.org
Housed here is an extensive collection of works by Grant Wood, Marvin Cone and Mauricio Lasansky.
Admission: adults $5, children 18 and under free. Free Thursday 4 p.m.-8 p.m. Tuesday-Saturday 10 a.m.-4 p.m., Thursday 10 a.m.-8 p.m., Sunday noon-4 p.m.

CZECH VILLAGE
48 16th Ave. S.W., Cedar Rapids, 319-362-2846; www.czechvillageiowa.com
Near downtown, this is an intriguing area with shops, restaurants and businesses celebrating the cultural history of the area. A bakery, a meat market, gift shops, restaurants and historic structures preserving Czech heritage are featured here.

INDIAN CREEK NATURE CENTER
6665 Otis Road S.E., Cedar Rapids, 319-362-0664; www.indiancreeknaturecenter.org
On this 210-acre nature preserve is an observatory and museum offering changing exhibits in a remodeled dairy barn as well as hiking trails.
Admission: donation. Monday-Friday.

MASONIC LIBRARY
813 First Ave. S.E., Cedar Rapids, 319-365-1438; www.gl-iowa.org
This library houses the most complete Masonic collection in the United States. The building is a Vermont-marble structure with bas-relief decoration and stained-glass windows.
Monday-Friday.

PALISADES-KEPLER STATE PARK
700 Kepler Drive, Mount Vernon, 319-895-6039; www.iowadnr.gov/parks
This 970-acre park includes limestone palisades that rise 75 feet above the Cedar River; timbered valleys, wildflowers. Fishing, boating; nature and hiking trails; snowmobiling; picnicking, lodge, camping, cabins.

PARAMOUNT THEATRE

123 Third Ave. S.E., Cedar Rapids, 319-398-5211; www.uscellularcenter.com

A restored theater built in the 1920s, the Paramount hosts stage productions, films and Broadway series, and is the home of the Cedar Rapids Symphony.

SCIENCE STATION

427 First St. S.E., Cedar Rapids, 319-363-4629; www.sciencestation.org

Science and technology museum features unusual hands-on exhibits including a working hot air balloon and giant kaleidoscope.
Mid-April-May, Tuesday-Sunday; June-August 30, daily; August 31-mid-April, Tuesday-Saturday.

US CELLULAR CENTER

370 First Ave. N.E., Cedar Rapids, 319-398-5211; www.uscellularcenter.com

This 10,000-seat entertainment center features sports events, concerts, exhibits, rodeos, ice shows and more.

SPECIAL EVENTS
FREEDOM FESTIVAL

Cedar Rapids Freedom Festival, 1857 Second Ave. S.E., Cedar Rapids, 319-365-8313; www.freedomfestival.com

Eighty events are held citywide, topped off by a large fireworks display. Two weeks preceding and including July 4.

HOUBY DAYS

30 16th Ave. S.W., Czech Village, Cedar Rapids, 319-362-8500

Features Czech fine arts, folk arts and customs, music, dancing, food; mushroom hunt contests and races.
Weekend after Mother's Day.

16

WHERE TO STAY
★★BEST WESTERN COOPER'S MILL HOTEL

100 F Ave. N.W., Cedar Rapids, 319-366-5323, 800-858-5511; www.bestwestern.com

Located on the site of a former flour mill, this hotel is along the banks of the Cedar River and just blocks from downtown.
86 rooms. Restaurant, bar. Complimentary breakfast. Pool. Pets accepted.
$60 and under

★★★CROWNE PLAZA

350 First Ave. N.E., Cedar Rapids, 319-363-8161, 800-227-6963; www.crowneplaza.com

Located in downtown Cedar Rapids, this hotel is near shopping, restaurants, and entertainment. In inclement weather, the convenient 12 block skywalk system leads to many great local restaurants.
275 rooms. Restaurant, bar. Business center. Fitness center. Pool. $60-150

★HAMPTON INN

3265 Sixth St. S.W., Cedar Rapids, 319-364-8144, 800-426-7866; www.hamptoninn.com

This newly renovated hotel is close to both the airport and downtown and is surrounded by restaurants for either delivery or eating out.
106 rooms. Restaurant, bar. Complimentary breakfast. Fitness center. Pool.
$60 and under

★★MARRIOTT CEDAR RAPIDS
1200 Collins Road N.E., Cedar Rapids, 319-393-6600; www.marriott.com
While staying at this hotel, be sure to check out the expansive open atrium and two-story water marble feature. Conveniently located close to everything you need including shopping, spas, golf and the airport.
221 rooms. Restaurant, bar. Business center. Fitness center. Pool. $61-150

CLEAR LAKE
See also Mason City
Scene of a Native American uprising in 1854, Clear Lake challenged Mason City for honors as the county seat, but lost out because it was not in the geographic center of the area. Taking its name from the nearby lake, this is an ancient Native American fishing and hunting ground and a popular resort town.

WHAT TO SEE
CLEAR LAKE STATE PARK
2730 S. Lakeview Drive, Clear Lake, 641-357-4212; www.iowadnr.gov/parks
Swimming, fishing, boating, snowmobiling, picnicking, camping are all available at this park.

SURF BALLROOM
460 North Shore Drive, Clear Lake, 641-357-6151; www.surfballroom.com
This was the site of Buddy Holly's last concert before Holly, Ritchie Valens and J. P. Richardson (the Big Bopper) died in a plane crash nearby on February 2, 1959. The ballroom features entertainment on weekends and a museum of musical history. Tours are available.

SPECIAL EVENT
BUDDY HOLLY TRIBUTE
Surf Ballroom, 460 North Shore Drive, Clear Lake, 641-357-6151;
www.surfballroom.com
An event to commemorate Holly's last concert, this tribute features local and national entertainers.
First weekend in February.

WHERE TO STAY
★★BEST WESTERN HOLIDAY LODGE
2023 Seventh Ave. N., Clear Lake, 641-357-5253, 800-606-3552;
www.bestwestern.com
The thoughtful staff at this hotel provides fresh baked cookies daily after 3:00 p.m. with seasonal beverages including lemonade in the summer and hot apple cider in the fall. The hotel is conveniently located near the 2,600 acre Clear Lake.

138 rooms. Restaurant. Complimentary breakfast. Pool. Pets accepted. $60 and under

CLINTON
See also Bettendorf
Agriculture, industry and business are blended in this city of wide streets and modern buildings on the Mississippi River. First called New York, it was later renamed after DeWitt Clinton, former governor of New York. Once the largest lumber-producing city in the world, Clinton today is famous for its prime beef production.

WHAT TO SEE
EAGLE POINT PARK
Highway 67 N., 563-242-0622;
This park features flower gardens, picnicking shelters, a lodge, playground, observation tower, children's nature center and petting zoo.
Mid-April-late October, daily.

LILLIAN RUSSELL THEATRE
311 Riverview Drive, Clinton, 563-242-6760; www.summer-stock.org
This theater is located aboard paddle wheel showboat the City of Clinton.
June-August.

MISSISSIPPI BELLE II
Showboat Landing, 311 Riverview Drive, Clinton, 563-243-9000, 800-457-9975;
www.clintonia.com
You can gamble along the Mississippi River all year at this casino boat.

SPECIAL EVENTS
RIVERBOAT DAYS
115 Fourth Ave. S., Clinton, 800-395-7277; www.riverboatdays.org
Pageant, events, tractor pulls, entertainment, shows, carnival.
July Fourth weekend.

WHERE TO STAY
★★BEST WESTERN FRONTIER MOTOR INN
2300 Lincoln Way St., Clinton, 563-242-7112, 800-728-7112; www.bestwestern.com
113 rooms. Restaurant, bar. Complimentary breakfast. Fitness center. Pool.
Pets accepted. $151-250

★COUNTRY INN & SUITES
2224 Lincoln Way, Clinton, 563-244-9922, 888-201-1746; www.countryinns.com
63 rooms. Complimentary breakfast. Pool. Pets accepted. $61-150

COUNCIL BLUFFS
See also Missouri Valley; also see Omaha, NE
The Lewis and Clark expedition stopped in Council Bluffs in 1804 to rest and hold their first "council bluff" with local Native American tribes. Council

Bluffs was settled in 1846 by Mormons fleeing religious persecution. They called the town Kanesville, but the city officially took the name Council Bluffs in 1853. The town subsequently became a booming hub of commerce as the nation's fifth-largest rail center.

WHAT TO SEE
GOLDEN SPIKE MONUMENT
S. 21st Street and Ninth Avenue, Council Bluffs; www.cbparksandrec.org
Erected in 1939, this 56-foot golden concrete spike commemorates the junction of the Union Pacific and Central Pacific railroads in Council Bluffs.

HISTORIC GENERAL DODGE HOUSE
605 Third St., Council Bluffs, 712-322-2406; www.dodgehouse.org
Guided tours are given of this restored Victorian house built by Grenville M. Dodge, chief construction engineer for the Union Pacific Railroad and a general in the Civil War.
Admission: adults $7, seniors $5, students 6-16 $3, children under 6 free.
Tuesday-Saturday 10 a.m.-5 p.m., Sunday 1-5 p.m.

HISTORIC POTTAWATTAMIE COUNTY SQUIRREL CAGE JAIL
226 Pearl St., Council Bluffs, 712-323-2509; www.thehistoricalsociety.org
This unique three-story rotary jail is sometimes referred to as the "human squirrel cage" or "lazy Susan jail."
Admission: adults $7, seniors $6, children 6-12 $5, children 5 and under free. April-October, Wednesday-Saturday, 10 a.m.-4 p.m., Sunday 1-4 p.m.

LEWIS AND CLARK MONUMENT
19962 Monument Road, Council Bluffs, 712-328-4650
A shaft of native stone on the bluffs depicts Lewis and Clark holding council with the Oto and Missouri tribes.

LINCOLN MONUMENT
323 Lafayette Ave., Council Bluffs; www.parksandrec.councilbluffs-ia.gov
This granite shaft marks the spot from which Lincoln designated the town as the eastern terminus of the Union Pacific Railroad. Erected in 1911.

RAILSWEST RAILROAD MUSEUM
16th Avenue and S. Main Street, Council Bluffs, 712-323-5182
The historic Rock Island depot was built in 1899. Displayed here are railroad memorabilia and HO gauge model trains.
Admission: adults $6, seniors $5, children 6-16 $4, children 5 and under, free. April-October, Wednesday-Saturday 10 a.m.-4 p.m., Sunday 1-4 p.m.

WESTERN HISTORIC TRAILS CENTER
3434 Richard Downing Ave., Council Bluffs, 712-366-4900; www.iowahistory.org
Explore preserved and restored sites along the Lewis and Clark, Mormon Pioneer, California and Oregon trails. Discover the history of Native American tribes and trails heritage in the region.
Admission: free. Daily.

WHERE TO STAY

★★AMERISTAR CASINO HOTEL

2200 River Road, Council Bluffs, 712-328-8888, 877-462-7827;
www.ameristarcasinos.com

This upscale property is adjoined by the Ameristar Casino, which is Iowa's largest riverboat. Expect to find extensive gaming and on-site entertainment options. 160 rooms. Restaurant, bar. Fitness center. Pool. $150-250

★FAIRFIELD INN

520 30th Ave., Council Bluffs, 712-366-1330, 800-228-2800; www.fairfieldinn.com

This hotel offers updated clean and modern rooms in a convenient location for both business and leisure travelers.
62 rooms. Complimentary breakfast. Fitness center. Pool. $60 and under

★HEARTLAND INN COUNCIL BLUFFS

1000 Woodbury Ave., Council Bluffs, 712-322-8400, 800-334-3277;
www.heartlandinns.com

This comfortable hotel offers easy access to the nearby zoo and other area attractions. Guests have a choice of two room sizes with the deluxe room offering 30% more space.
87 rooms. Complimentary breakfast. Business center. Fitness center. Pool. $60 and under

WHERE TO EAT

★CHRISTY CRÉME

2853 N. Broadway, Council Bluffs, 712-322-2778; www.christycreme.com

Locals love this favorite spot for their daily fix of homemade ice cream sherbet and hot from the grill specials including hamburgers and legendary French fries. Do not miss the Unfloat, an original mix of 7-Up and sherbet. American. Lunch, dinner. Closed December-January. Outdoor seating. Children's menu. $15 and under

★PINK POODLE STEAKHOUSE

633 N. Old Lincoln Highway, Crescent, 712-545-3744; www.pinkpoodlesteakhouse.com

This quaint small town favorite is known for its prime rib but also offers chicken, pork and pasta entrees. Each diner comes with unlimited soup and salad refills.
American. Dinner. Closed Monday. $16-35

DAVENPORT

See also Bettendorf

Stretching five miles along the Mississippi River, Davenport is part of the Quad Cities metropolitan area. Davenport's Palmer College of Chiropractic is the fountainhead of that practice in the United States. The city is named for its founder, a former U.S. Army officer who explored this bank of the river while stationed on Rock Island. The state's first railroad came here when tracks were put across the Mississippi at this point in 1854. In pre-Civil War days, Dred Scott claimed the town as his home, and John Brown camped here before his attack on Harpers Ferry.

A WALK THROUGH DAVENPORT

Davenport is one of the Quad Cities, a four-city metropolitan area that straddles the Mississippi and includes Moline and Rock Island in Illinois, plus Bettendorf, just upriver from Davenport. Begin this walk on Credit Island Park, the site of a turn-of-the-century amusement park. Scenic trails loop around the island, and number of public art pieces are found here, part of the Quad Cities Art in the Park project.

Cross over to the Iowa mainland from the east end of Credit Island Park and walk along the Mississippi through two more riverside parks. Centennial Park features riverside walkways past sports fields and stadiums. Atop the bluff on Division Street is Museum Hill, home of the Putnam Museum of Science and Natural History *(1717 W. 12th St.)* and the Davenport Museum of Art *(1737 W. 12th St.)*. The Putnam houses two permanent exhibits about the Mississippi River. The art museum's permanent collection includes works by Midwestern painters, including Thomas Hart Benton and Grant Wood, an Iowa native famous for his painting *American Gothic*. Just to the east is LeClaire Park, home to summer outdoor events and concerts.

The Davenport Downtown Levee includes a riverboat casino, restaurants, nightclubs and the renovated Union Station railroad depot, which houses the Quad Cities Convention and Visitors Center. A local Farmers' Market is also held here on Wednesday and Saturday mornings from May through October.

Just downstream from the historic Government Bridge, Dam 15 provides a navigational pool for commercial shipping on the Mississippi. Lock 15 allows boats to transfer between the rivers pools. Cross Government Bridge to Arsenal Island, which was acquired by the U.S. Government in 1804 under a treaty with the Sauk and Fox Indians. Fort Armstrong was established in 1816 on the tip of the island, where a replica now stands. Manufacturing began on the island in 1840, and in 1869 it became home to the Rock Island Arsenal, a major military manufacturing facility. The island contains a number of historic homes and structures, including the Rock Island Arsenal Museum; the restored Colonel George Davenport Mansion, filled with furnishings from the mid-1800s; and the Mississippi River Visitors Center, with exhibits about the history of navigation on the river. A Confederate Soldiers Cemetery and National Military Cemetery date back to the 1800s. Hikers and bikers can enjoy a five-mile trail around the island.

WHAT TO SEE

DAN NAGLE WALNUT GROVE PIONEER VILLAGE

18817 290th St., Long Grove, 563-328-3283; www.scottcountyiowa.com

This 3-acre walk-through site contains 18 historic buildings moved from various locations in the county. Visitors can explore a blacksmith shop, schoolhouse, pioneer family home; also St. Anne's Church.
Admission: free. April-October, daily 9 a.m.-6 p.m.

FIGGE ART MUSEUM

1737 W. 12th St., Davenport, 563-326-7804; www.figgeartmuseum.org

Rotating displays from a permanent collection of 19th- and 20th-century paintings, Mexican Colonial, Asian and native Haitian art are displayed here, as well as works by regional artists Grant Wood and Thomas Hart Benton. Admission: adults $7, seniors $6, children ages 3-12 $4. Tuesday-Sunday.

PUTNAM MUSEUM OF HISTORY & NATURAL SCIENCE

1717 W. 12th St., Davenport, 563-324-1933; www.putnam.org

Permanent and changing exhibits of regional history, natural science and world -cultures. Daily.

Admission: adults $6, seniors $5, children ages 3-12 $4. Exhibit Hall hours: Monday-Saturday 10 a.m.-5 p.m., Sunday noon-5 p.m.

SCOTT COUNTY PARK

19251 290th St., Long Grove, 563-285-9656

More than 1,000 acres with a pioneer village and nature center. Swimming, fishing, ball fields, 18-hole golf, skiing, tobogganing, ice-skating, picnicking, camping and trailer sites.

Daily.

SPECIAL EVENT
BIX BEIDERBECKE MEMORIAL JAZZ FESTIVAL

LeClaire Park, 311 N. Ripley St., Davenport, 563-324-7170; www.bixsociety.org

Join the crowd at a jazz festival to honor the Davenport-born musician.

Mid-July.

WHERE TO STAY
★LA QUINTA INN

3330 E. Kimberly Road, Davenport, 563-359-3921; www.lq.com

This hotel is conveniently located for those who are looking for convenient access to downtown but do not want to pay the higher prices. One of the area's largest golf courses and the Mississippi River is only two blocks away.

129 rooms. Complimentary breakfast. Fitness center. Pool. Pets accepted. $61-150

★SUPER 8

410 E. 65th St., Davenport, 563-388-9810, 800-800-8000; www.super8.com

This efficient value orientated hotel has all the amenities you need for a quick stay at a good price.

61 rooms. Complimentary breakfast. Pets accepted. $60 and under

WHERE TO EAT
★IOWA MACHINE SHED

7250 N.W. Blvd., Davenport, 563-391-2427; www.machineshed.com

This local restaurant chain offers fresh hearty food highlighting the meat and produce from surrounding Midwest farms. The restaurant is open for all day dining so stop in anytime.

American. Breakfast, lunch, dinner. Children's menu. Bar. $15-35

★★THUNDER BAY GRILLE

6511 Brady St., Davenport, 563-386-2722; www.thunderbaygrille.com

Grab a seat by the large fireplace and enjoy the great outdoors influenced atmosphere at this cozy restaurant. The spicy jambalaya is a specialty along with grilled steaks.

American. Lunch, dinner, Sunday brunch. Children's menu. Bar. $16-35

DECORAH

A center of Norwegian culture in the United States, Decorah is the seat of Winneshiek County and located in one of the state's most picturesque areas.

Within a short distance are Siewers and Twin Springs and towering spires of limestone along the Upper Iowa River. The town is named for a Native American chief who aided settlers during the Black Hawk War.

WHAT TO SEE
THE BILY CLOCKS MUSEUM
323 N. Main St., Spillville, 563-562-3569; www.bilyclocks.org
A beautiful collection of hard-carved antique clocks created from unique wood gathered from around the world.
Admission: adults $6, seniors $5, children free. April and November, Saturday 10 a.m.-4 p.m., Sunday noon-4 p.m.; May-October, Monday-Saturday 9 a.m.-5 p.m., Sunday noon-4 p.m. Closed December-March.

FORT ATKINSON STATE PRESERVE
10225 Ivy Road, Decorah, 563-425-4161; www.iowadnr.com/parks
Fort was built in 1840 as federal protection for the Winnebago from the Sac, Fox and Sioux. Restored buildings include barracks, a blockhouse and magazine. Museum exhibits Native American and pioneer relics.
Admission: free. Mid-May-mid-October, daily.

SEED SAVERS HERITAGE FARM
3094 N. Winn Road, Decorah, 563-382-5990; www.seedsavers.org
This 173-acre farm features displays of endangered vegetables, apples, grapes and ancient White Park cattle. Preservation Gardens house 15,000 rare vegetable varieties; Cultural History Garden displays old-time flowers and vegetables. Historic Orchard has 650 19th-century apples and 160 hardy grapes.
Admission: Donation. April-December, daily.

VESTERHEIM NORWEGIAN-AMERICAN MUSEUM
523 W. Water St., Decorah, 563-382-9681; www.vesterheim.org
Extensive exhibits relate history of Norwegians in America and Norway. Pioneer objects, handicrafts, ship gallery, arts displayed in a complex of 13 historic buildings with a restored mill.
Admission: adults $7, seniors and children ages 7-18 $5. Free Thursday. Daily.

SPECIAL EVENT
NORDIC FEST
507 W. Water St., Decorah, 563-382-3990, 800-382-3378; www.nordicfest.com
Parades, dancing, pioneer tool display; demonstrations of cooking, needlework and rosemaling.
Last full weekend in July.

WHERE TO STAY
★★★HOTEL WINNESHIEK
104 E. Water St., Decorah, 563-382-4164; www.hotelwinn.com
The Hotel Winneshiek is a gem: an elegantly restored 1905 hotel in the heart of downtown. Guests are greeted at a concierge desk in an entryway decorated

with fresh flowers and displays of antique glassware and porcelain figurines. The lobby has an octagonal three-story atrium, set under a large stained-glass skylight. Rooms are simple but decorated with antique reproductions.
31 rooms. Restaurant, bar. Complimentary breakfast. $61-150

WHERE TO EAT
★MILTY'S
200 Main St., Lansing, 563-538-4585; www.miltys.net
This no frills bar and grill serves simple food ranging from baskets of fried chicken strips to more elaborate steak and pork dinners. Stop by on Friday for their weekly fish fry.
American. Lunch, dinner. Closed Monday. $15 and under

★★STONE HEARTH INN
811 Commerce Drive, Decorah, 563-382-4614
Visit this restaurant for their prime rib, but stay for a night cap in their lower level sports bar.
American. Lunch, dinner. Closed Sunday. Children's menu. Bar. $16-35

DES MOINES
Des Moines is the capital of Iowa and largest city in the state. This city is the industrial, retail, financial and political hub of Iowa. A military garrison established Fort Des Moines at a point on the Raccoon and Des Moines rivers in 1843. Two years later the territory was opened to settlers and the town of Fort Des Moines was chosen as the county seat. The word "fort" was abandoned when the community became a city in 1857; the next year it became the state capital. Today more than 60 insurance companies have their home offices here, as does media giant Meredith Corporation, publishers of *Better Homes & Gardens* and *Ladies' Home Journal*.

WHAT TO SEE
ADVENTURELAND PARK
305 34th Ave. N.W., Altoona, 515-266-2121,800-532-1286;
www.adventurelandpark.com
This amusement park has more than 100 rides, shows and attractions.
Admission: adults $31, seniors and children ages 4-9 $27, children 3 and under free. June-late August, daily; May and September, Saturday-Sunday.

BLANK PARK ZOO
7401 S.W. Ninth St., Des Moines, 515-285-4722, 515-323-8383;
www.blankparkzoo.com
The animal and bird habitats at this zoo are designed for close viewing. It includes Australian and African walk-through displays, a farm animal contact area, camel rides and an Old West train ride.
Admission: adults $9.95, seniors $7.95, children 3-12 $4.95, children 2 and under free. Daily.

DES MOINES ART CENTER

4700 Grand Ave., Des Moines, 515-277-4405; www.desmoinesartcenter.org

Exhibits of 19th- and 20th-century paintings and sculptures are displayed in a contemporary building designed by Eliel Saarinen, with additions by Richard Meier and I.M. Pei.

Admission: free. Tuesday-Sunday.

DES MOINES BOTANICAL CENTER

909 Robert D. Ray Drive, Des Moines, 515-323-6290; www.botanicalcenter.com

Displays of nearly 1,500 species from around the world are located here along with seasonal floral displays.

Admission: adults $4, seniors and children 6-17 $2, children 5 and under free. Daily 10 a.m.-5 p.m.

DRAKE UNIVERSITY

2507 University Ave., Des Moines, 515-271-2011; www.drake.edu

This small private university has many buildings designed by distinguished architects, including Eliel and Eero Saarinen, Harry Weese and Associates, Borg and Skiles and Ludwig Mies van der Rohe.

HERITAGE VILLAGE

State Fairgrounds, East 30th Street and University Avenue, Des Moines, 515-262-3111; www.iowastatefair.org

Featured here are a century-old barn, exposition hall with displays of early farm machinery, an authentically furnished country school and replicas of an 1834 church.

Tours mid-April-mid-October, by appointment.

HOYT SHERMAN PLACE

1501 Woodland Ave., Des Moines, 515-244-0507; www.hoytsherman.org

This 1877 house was once the home of General William Tecumseh Sherman's brother. It now features the city's oldest art gallery, including artifacts, antique furniture and art collection.

Tours by appointment. Monday-Friday 9 a.m.-4 p.m.

IOWA HISTORICAL BUILDING

Capitol Complex, 600 E. Locust, Des Moines, 515-281-5111; www.iowahistory.org

Modern cultural center houses state historical museum. Displays portray Iowa history and heritage. Library contains county, state and family history materials; rare books and manuscripts about Iowa; census records and newspapers. Monday-Saturday 9 a.m.-4:30 p.m., Sunday noon-4:30 p.m.

LIVING HISTORY FARMS

11121 Hickman Road, Urbandale, 515-278-5286; www.lhf.org

This complex has four farms and a town set on 600 acres. A Native American settlement includes gardens, shelters and crafts of the Ioway tribe. The pioneer farm of 1850 features a log cabin and outbuildings. The horse-powered farm of 1900 depicts farm and household chores typical of period. The 1875 town of Walnut Hill includes a Victorian mansion, schoolhouse, pottery,

THE DES MOINES RIVER VALLEY

This route travels through picture-perfect farming communities founded by European settlers, then along the lower Des Moines River, where historic towns have changed little since the riverboat era. From Des Moines, drive east on Highway 163 toward Pella. Founded in 1847 by Dutch settlers who came to this valley to escape religious persecution in Holland, Pella retains a sense of Dutch orderliness and is filled with trim historic homes and tulip-filled public parks.

East on Highway 163 through rolling hills is Oskaloosa, a farming town settled by Quakers. The town's past is retold at Nelson Pioneer Farm and Craft Museum, which preserves a farm community from the 1850s. From Oskaloosa, follow Highway 163 to Ottumwa, a busy industrial center.

Continuing on, turn east on Highway 34, and then turn south on Highway 16, which closely follows the Des Moines River. One of the earliest settled regions of Iowa, this section of the Des Moines valley is lined with tiny towns founded in the 1830s when the river was the only avenue for travel. Bypassed by the rail lines and the freeway system, these towns were forgotten by the forward rush of time. Today, they have handsome period architecture, newly refurbished small hotels and inns, historical museums and antique stores.

The town of Eldon contains one of the most archetypal structures in the Midwest: At the corner of Gothic and Burton streets is the house painted by Grant Wood as the backdrop to his famous portrait American Gothic. The rustic couple in the painting were the painter's sister and his dentist. Keosauqua is home to the oldest courthouse in the state, as well as the imposing Manning Hotel, 150 years old and still in operation. Farther downstream, the entire village of Bentonsport, once a sizable river port, is a National Historic District. The Mason House Hotel, built by Mormon craftsmen in the 1840s, is open for tours and for paying guests. At the town of Bonaparte, the original grist and woolen mills have been preserved.

From Bonaparte, follow Highway 81 south to Farmington, with the oldest Congregational Church west of the Mississippi River and a stone carriage factory. Continue east to Highway 218 and turn south to Keokuk, at the confluence of the Des Moines and Mississippi rivers. Keokuk was head of steamboat navigation on the Mississippi before Lock Number 19, the largest on the river system, was built in 1913. The lock is part of Keokuk Dam, which was the world's largest hydroelectric dam until the 1930s. Approximately 185 miles.

blacksmith and carpentry shops, veterinary infirmary, church, bank, newspaper, doctor's offices and a general store.

Admission: adults $11.50, seniors $10.50, children 4-12 $7. May-mid-September, daily; September-October, Wednesday-Sunday.

PRAIRIE MEADOWS RACETRACK AND CASINO

1 Prairie Meadows Drive, Altoona, 800-325-9015; www.prairiemeadows.com

Live Thoroughbred, quarter horse and harness racing occurs late April to October. Also featured are simulcasts of Thoroughbred and greyhound racing; a 24-hour casino with more than 1,500 slots, a poker room and video poker machines.

Daily.

SCIENCE CENTER OF IOWA

Science Center of Iowa, 401 W. Martin Luther King, Jr. Parkway, Des Moines,
515-274-6868, 515-274-4138; www.sciowa.org

Natural and physical science exhibits are the draw at this center, as are live demonstrations, Digistar planetarium shows and laser shows. Admission: adults $9, seniors $8, children 2-12 $7. Daily.

STATE CAPITOL
1005 Grand Ave., Des Moines, 515-281-5591; www.legis.state.ia.us
The towering central dome of this 1871 building is covered with 23-karat gold leaf; four smaller domes have golden seam marks. State offices, Supreme Court, House and Senate chamber, law library. Paintings, mosaics, collection of war flags.
Daily.

TERRACE HILL
2300 Grand Ave., Des Moines, 515-281-3604; www.terracehill.org
This extravagant Italianate/Second Empire mansion, now the residence of Iowa governors, is situated on a commanding knoll above downtown. The restored house is an outstanding example of Victorian residential architecture. Tours include first and second floors, carriage house and gardens.
March-December, Tuesday-Saturday 10 a.m.-1:30 p.m.

SPECIAL EVENTS
DRAKE RELAYS
Drake University, 2507 University Ave., Des Moines, 515-271-3647;
www.godrakebulldogs.com
One of the most prestigious intercollegiate track and field events in the country; more than 5,000 athletes compete.
Last week in April.

IOWA STATE FAIR
Fairgrounds, East 30th Street and University Avenue, Des Moines, 515-262-3111;
www.iowastatefair.com
One of the oldest and largest fairs in the country, it includes 20 acres of farm machinery, fine arts, a giant midway, grandstand stage and track events, free entertainment and contests.
August.

WHERE TO STAY
★★ADVENTURELAND INN
3200 Adventureland Drive, Altoona, 515-265-7321, 800-910-5382;
www.adventurelandpark.com
Located next to Adventureland Park, this newly renovated inn provides complimentary shuttle service to and from the park. Guests can enjoy the fun of Adventureland then return to the comforts of the inn, with a tropical pool and live entertainment.
187 rooms. Restaurant, bar. Pool. $61-150

★★★DES MOINES MARRIOTT DOWNTOWN
700 Grand Ave., Des Moines, 515-245-5500, 800-228-9290; www.marriott.com
Connected to the Iowa Events Center by skywalk, this downtown hotel is close to the city's top shopping and restaurants. Rooms have been up-

dated with the chain's luxury bedding, including down duvets and pillow-top mattresses.
415 rooms. Restaurant. Pool. Pets accepted. $61-150

★★EMBASSY SUITES
101 E. Locust St., Des Moines, 515-244-1700, 800-362-2779;
www.embassysuitesdesmoines.com
This all-suites hotel is located right on the river and steps away from the best downtown Des Moines has to offer. The complimentary cooked to order breakfast and nightly manager's reception adds to the appeal of this hotel.
234 rooms. Restaurant, bar. Complimentary breakfast. Business center. Fitness center. Pool. $151-250

★★BEST WESTERN DES MOINES AIRPORT HOTEL
1810 Army Post Road, Des Moines, 515-287-6464, 800-368-7764;
www.fbestwestern.com
Recently renovated in French country décor, this hotel is perfectly situated for those who need convenient access to the airport.
140 rooms. Restaurant, bar. Complimentary breakfast. Business center. Fitness center. Pool. Spa. Pets accepted. $61-150

★★HOTEL FORT DES MOINES
1000 Walnut St., Des Moines, 515-243-1161, 800-532-1466;
www.hotelfortdesmoines.com
Nearly a century old, this classic hotel as housed many famous faces over the years. The hotel's French restaurant, Django, is a must stop for fresh oysters and steak frites.
242 rooms. Restaurant, bar. Fitness room. Pool. Pets accepted. $61-150

★WILDWOOD LODGE
11431 Forest Ave., Clive, 515-222-9876, 800-728-1223; www.thewildwoodlodge.com
This Northwoods lodge decorated hotel has a unique indoor pool with three-story waterfall. The location is convenient for business travelers as it is near many business parks in the western part of Des Moines.
100 rooms. Bar. Complimentary breakfast. Fitness room. Pool. $61-150

WHERE TO EAT
★★★CHRISTOPHER'S
2816 Beaver Ave., Des Moines, 515-274-3694; www.christophers-restaurant.com
Italian-American food, including pastas, steaks and seafood, and a casual atmosphere have made this dining room a local favorite for many years.
American, Italian. Dinner. Closed Sunday. Children's menu. Bar. $16-35

★★★TROSTEL'S GREENBRIAR
5810 Merle Hay Road, Johnston, 515-253-0124; www.greenbriartrostels.com
The menu at this main-street restaurant offers a broad selection of seafood, chicken, pasta and specialty prime rib.
American. Lunch (Monday, Wednesday-Friday), dinner. Closed Sunday. Outdoor seating. Children's menu. $16-35

★JESSE'S EMBERS
4810 86th St., Urbandale, 515-251-7175; www.jessesembers.com
This dimly lit clubby restaurant is the place to get a grilled steak in Des Moines. If steak is not your thing, stop by on Friday for a lunch of their signature clam chowder.
Seafood, steak. Lunch, dinner. Closed Sunday. Bar. $36-85

★THE MACHINE SHED
11151 Hickman Road, Urbandale, 515-270-6818; www.machineshed.com
This local restaurant chain offers fresh hearty food highlighting meat and produce from surrounding Midwest farms. The restaurant is open for all day dining so stop in anytime.
American. Breakfast, lunch, dinner. Children's menu. Bar. $16-35

★OHANA STEAKHOUSE
2900 University Ave., West Des Moines, 515-225-3325; www.ohanasteakhouse.com
This Japanese steakhouse is great for those who can't decide between the theatre and dinner. The highly trained chefs prepare your meal right before your eyes with their teppanyaki-style dining.
Japanese, steak. Dinner. Closed Monday. Children's menu. Bar. $16-35

★SPAGHETTI WORKS
310 Court Ave., Des Moines, 515-243-2195
Choose from one of the signature sauces and design your own pasta entrée at this casual and cozy Italian restaurant located within a restored 19th century building.
American, Italian. Dinner. Outdoor seating. Children's menu. Bar. $16-35

★WATERFRONT SEAFOOD MARKET
2900 University Ave., West Des Moines, 515-223-5106
Head to this fresh seafood restaurant and order from the extensive selections at the oyster and sushi bars or off the menu. Before heading home, be sure to grab some seafood to go for tomorrow night's dinner.
Seafood. Lunch, dinner. Closed Sunday. Children's menu. Bar. $16-35

DUBUQUE
Facing both Wisconsin and Illinois across the broad Mississippi River, Dubuque became the first known European settlement in Iowa when Julien Dubuque, a French Canadian, came from Quebec in 1788 and leased land from the Native Americans to mine lead. After his death, Native Americans barred settlement until 1833 when the territory was opened under a treaty with Chief Black Hawk. Once a boisterous river and mining town, Dubuque had the first bank and newspaper in what is now Iowa. Its downtown has been extensively rejuvenated in recent years, with a number of restaurants opening in restored buildings.

WHAT TO SEE
BELLEVUE STATE PARK
24668 Highway 52, Dubuque, 563-872-4019; www.iowadnr.com/parks
Approximately 540 acres on a high bluff above the Mississippi. Native

American mounds, rugged woodlands, hiking trails, snowmobiling, picnicking, camping, nature center.

CATHEDRAL SQUARE

Second and Bluff streets, Dubuque, 563-582-7646
Surrounding the square are stylized figures of a lead miner, farmer, farmer's wife, priest and river hand. Opposite the square is the architecturally and historically significant St. Raphael's Cathedral.

CRYSTAL LAKE CAVE

7699 Crystal Lake Cave Drive, Dubuque, 563-556-6451; www.crystallakecave.com
A network of passageways carved by underground streams surrounds a lake with glittering stalactites and stalagmites, with water that really is crystal clear. Guided tours.
Admission: adults $12, children 4-11 $6, children 3 and under free. Memorial Day-late October, daily; May, Saturday-Sunday.

DUBUQUE ARBORETUM AND BOTANICAL GARDENS

3800 Arboretum Drive, Dubuque, 563-556-2100; www.dubuquearboretum.com
These gardens feature annual and perennial gardens, rose, water, formal gardens; ornamental trees, woodland and a prairie wildflower walk.
Admission: free. Daily.

DUBUQUE COUNTY COURTHOUSE

720 Central Ave., Dubuque, 563-589-4445; www.dubuquecounty.org
This gold-domed courthouse is on the National Historic Register of Places. Monday-Friday.

DUBUQUE MUSEUM OF ART/OLD COUNTY JAIL

701 Locust St., Dubuque, 563-557-1851
This museum is housed in a brand-new facility. The gallery is an example of Egyptian Revival architecture.
Tuesday-Sunday.

EAGLE POINT PARK

2200 Bunker Hill Road, Dubuque, 563-589-4263; www.dbq.com
On a high bluff above the Mississippi, this 164-acre park overlooks three states. A Works Progress Administration project, the park's Prairie School pavilions and naturalistic landscaping were designed by Alfred Caldwell, who studied under Frank Lloyd Wright.
Mid-May-mid-October, daily.

FENELON PLACE ELEVATOR

512 Fenelon Place, Dubuque, 563-582-6496; www.dbq.com/fenplco
In operation since 1882, one of the world's shortest, steepest incline railways connects Fenelon Place with Fourth Street, providing a three-state view. Accepts bicycles.
Admission: adults $2 (roundtrip), children 5-12 $1, children 4 and under free. April-November, daily 8 a.m.-10 p.m.

FIELD OF DREAMS MOVIE SITE

28995 Lansing Road, Dyersville, 563-875-8404; www.fieldofdreamsmoviesite.com

If you're a fan of the movie *Field of Dreams* or just a baseball fan, you'll want to make a stop here in Dyersville to check out the field featured in the movie. Hang out on the bleachers or play a little ball.

April-November, daily 9 a.m.-6 p.m.

FIVE FLAGS THEATER

405 Main St., Dubuque, 563-589-4254; www.fiveflagscenter.com

Designed by Rapp and Rapp, premier theater architects of their day, the Five Flags was modeled after Parisian music halls.

Tours by appointment.

GENERAL ZEBULON PIKE LOCK AND DAM

3000 Lock and Dam Road, Dubuque, 563-582-1204

A steady stream of barges and other river traffic moves through lock.

GRAND OPERA HOUSE

135 Eighth St., Dubuque, 563-588-1305; www.thegrandoperahouse.com

This century-old opera house was recently restored and offers a variety of entertainment throughout the year.

HERITAGE TRAIL

13606 Swiss Valley Road, Dubuque, 563-556-6745; www.dubuquecounty.com

This trail provides 26 miles of scenic hiking, biking and cross-country skiing on an old railroad along rugged Little Maquoketa River valley. Level, sur-faced trails cross from wooded, hilly, "driftless" areas to rolling prairie near Dyersville. Self-guided tour identifies railroad landmarks, includes water-powered mill sites.

Daily.

JULIEN DUBUQUE MONUMENT

Grandview Avenue and Julien Dubuque Drive, Dubuque, 563-556-0620

Tower built in 1897 at the site of Julien Dubuque's mine and the spot where Native Americans buried him in 1810. Provides an excellent view of the Mississippi River.

MATHIAS HAM HOUSE HISTORIC SITE

2241 Lincoln Ave., Dubuque, 563-583-2812

An 1857 Italianate/Victorian mansion with a cupola, this house has spectacu-lar views of the Mississippi River. Built by lead miner Mathias Ham. Also Iowa's oldest log cabin and one-room schoolhouse.

Admission: adults $5, children $3.50, children 6 and under free. June-Octo-ber, daily; May, Saturday-Sunday.

NATIONAL MISSISSIPPI RIVER MUSEUM AND AQUARIUM

350 E. Third St., Dubuque, 563-557-9545; www.mississippirivermuseum.com

Complex of six Dubuque County Historical Society museums, all emphasizing the city's river history.

Admission: adults $10.50, seniors $9.50, youth 7-17 $8, children 3-6 $4.50. Daily.

SUNDOWN MOUNTAIN SKI AREA

16991 Asbury Road, Dubuque, 563-556-6676, 888-786-3696; www.sundownmtn.com

Skiing in Iowa? Yep. And at this spot, the lodge is at the top of the run. Five chairlifts, tow rope, patrol, school, rentals, snowmaking. Twenty-one runs; longest run 1/2 mile; vertical drop 475 feet.

Late November-mid-March, daily.

WOODWARD DISCOVERY CENTER

350 E. Third St., Ice Harbor, Dubuque, 563-557-9545; www.mississippirivermuseum.org

Dramatizes 300 years of Mississippi River history: Native Americans, explorers, lead miners, boat builders and steamboat captains; lead mines; pilothouse and log raft displays. The aquarium may be the nation's most significant display of river and freshwater creatures, with five huge tanks and live-animal exhibits. This is one of the region's outstanding attractions.

SPECIAL EVENT
DUBUQUE COUNTY FAIR

Dubuque County Fairgrounds, 14569 Olde Highway Road, Dubuque, 563-588-1406

Recently the fair has had a knack for booking country and contemporary rock acts just as they are hitting it big.

Late July.

WHERE TO STAY
★★BEST WESTERN MIDWAY HOTEL

3100 Dodge St., Dubuque, 563-557-8000, 800-336-4392; www.bestwesterniowa.com

This recently renovated hotel offers modern rooms in a convenient location close to the Mississippi River and the Port of Dubuque. The quiet atmosphere is a nice retreat from the activities nearby.

149 rooms. Complimentary breakfast. Restaurant, bar. Fitness center. Pool. Pets accepted. $60 and under

★★DAYS INN

1111 Dodge St., Dubuque, 563-583-3297, 800-772-3297; www.daysinn.com

If you're heading to Dubuque for a little riverboat gambling, you might want to gamble on the Days Inn first. Located 20 minutes from Sundown Mountain and 30 minutes from the *Field of Dreams* movie site (located in Dyersville), the Days Inn Dubuque is just 5 to 10 minutes from the riverboat gambling cruises and offers free transportation for all guests.

155 rooms. Restaurant, bar. Complimentary breakfast. Fitness room. Pool. Pets accepted. $61-150

★★THE GRAND HARBOR RESORT AND WATERPARK

350 Bell St., Dubuque, 563-690-4000, 888-690-4006; www.grandharborresort.com

Families love The Grand Harbor Resort and Water Park, not just for its attached, one-of-a-kind watery theme park, but also for its video arcade (approximately 150 games keep kids busy), weekend children's programs, and family-friendly room service menu of buckets of chicken and pizza. There's also plenty of fun for grown-ups, including two giant hot tubs and a fitness room. And in case you want more water, every room has a view of the Mississippi River.

193 rooms. Restaurant, bar. Fitness room. Pool. $61-150

★★HOLIDAY INN

450 Main St., Dubuque, 563-556-2000, 800-465-4329; www.holiday-inn.com

A beautiful, airy lobby greets guests in this family-friendly downtown hotel. High ceilings, pillars, and lush flower arrangements provide a feeling of grandeur, but several conversation areas of small wooden coffee tables, sofas, and curved chairs make the open space seem cozy and interesting. Porter's Restaurant, tucked behind closed doors, has a "patio" that spills out onto the lobby.

193 rooms. Restaurant, bar. Business center. Fitness center. Pool. Pets accepted. $61-150

★★JULIEN INN

200 Main St., Dubuque, 563-556-4200, 800-798-7098; www.julieninn.com

This historic site has housed a hotel since 1839; the present hotel was built in 1914, after a fire ravaged the hotel that had been there since 1854. The Julien has an auspicious history; not only did Al Capone escape here when things in Chicago got hot, but he owned the inn during Prohibition and even built an underground garage to hide his car. The Riverboat Lounge, with its piano bar and ornamental iron work, is designed to replicate the saloons of the Mississippi steamers of yesteryear.

137 rooms. Restaurant, bar. Fitness room. $61-150

★★THE REDSTONE INN

504 Bluff St., Dubuque, 563-582-1894; www.theredstoneinn.com

This restored 1890s Victorian mansion was built by a prominent Dubuque industrialist as a wedding gift for his daughter.

14 rooms. Complimentary breakfast. Pets accepted. $251-350

WHERE TO EAT

★★CAFÉ MISSISSIPPI

431 S. River Park Drive, Guttenberg, 563-252-4405, 866-595-4093; www.cafemississippi.net

Stop by this casual cafe for a leisurely lunch overlooking the Mississippi. The food provides a good value but the view is what sets this place apart.

American. Lunch, dinner, brunch. Bar. $16-35

★★MARIO'S

13th and Main Street, Dubuque, 563-556-9424; www.mariosdubuque.com

This family run authentic Italian experience has been around for many years and continues to satisfy with the hearty fare. The items range from pizzas to fresh pasta to grilled steaks.

Italian, American. Lunch, dinner. Closed Sunday. Bar. $16-35

★YEN CHING

926 Main St., Dubuque, 563-556-2574

Stop by this casual sit-down Chinese restaurant for some of the best egg rolls and spicy chicken in the area.

Chinese. Lunch, dinner. Closed Sunday. $15 and under

GRINNELL

See also Newton

When Horace Greeley said "Go west, young man, go west and grow up with the country!" he was talking to Josiah Bushnell Grinnell, who took the advice, went west to a bit of prairie between the Iowa and Skunk rivers, and established the town of Grinnell. Today, Grinnell is a thriving small college town.

WHAT TO SEE
GRINNELL COLLEGE

1121 Park St., Grinnell, 641-269-3400; www.grinnell.edu

Considered one of the top liberal arts colleges in the United States, this school was founded in 1846 and has fewer than 1,500 students.

Tours by appointment.

GRINNELL HISTORICAL MUSEUM

1125 Broad St., Grinnell, 641-236-3732; grinnellmuseum.org

Historical furnishings; relics, documents of J. B. Grinnell and aviator Billy Robinson housed in a late Victorian house.

Admission: donation. June-August, Tuesday-Sunday; rest of year, Saturday-Sunday or by appointment.

WELLS FARGO BANK OF IOWA—POWESHIEK COUNTY

Downtown, Grinnell

The second in the series of "jewel box" banks that architect Louis Henri Sullivan designed late in his career, this building was constructed in 1914. This unique structure, one of the more important designs in the series, has been restored within the confines of a working bank environment.

Monday-Friday.

IOWA CITY

See also Amana Colonies, Cedar Rapids

Referred to as "the river city," Iowa City is the home of the University of Iowa and the state's first capital. In its early days, Iowa City boomed as a backwoods metropolis, with the Territorial Legislative Assembly meeting here for the first time in 1841. A Doric stone capitol was erected, but with the shift of population, the legislators moved to Des Moines in 1857. As a conciliatory gesture to Iowa City, they selected it as the site of the new university, the University of Iowa. The city has a small-town feel accented by the kind of cultural amenities and adventurous restaurants that a university presence delivers. In the fall, the town is mesmerized by football when the Hawkeyes are playing at home on Saturdays.

WHAT TO SEE

CORALVILLE LAKE

2850 Prairie du Chien Road, Iowa City, 319-338-3543; www.mvr.usace.army.mil

This 5,400-acre lake offers swimming, boating and fishing. Flooding that occurred during the summer of 1993 eroded a 15-foot-deep channel exposing the underlying bedrock. Now called Devonian Fossil Gorge, it offers a rare opportunity to view Iowa's geological past. The site is an Army Corps of Engineers project.
Daily.

HERBERT HOOVER NATIONAL HISTORIC SITE

110 Parkside Drive, West Branch, 319-643-2541; www.nps.gov/heho

The 187-acre park includes the restored house in which President Hoover was born, the Quaker meeting house where he worshipped as a boy, a school, a blacksmith shop and the graves of President and Lou Henry Hoover.
Daily.

HERBERT HOOVER PRESIDENTIAL LIBRARY-MUSEUM

210 Parkside Drive, West Branch, 319-643-5301; www.hoover.nara.gov

Administered by the National Archives and Records Administration. Features a museum with recreated historic settings in China, Belgium, Washington and other places prominent in Hoover's 50 years of public service. Research library: by appointment. Admission: adults $6, seniors $3, children 16 and under free. Daily 9 a.m.-5 p.m.

IOWA CHILDREN'S MUSEUM

1451 Coral Ridge Ave., Coralville, 319-625-5500; www.theicm.org

This museum has interactive exhibits for kids.
Admission: adults and children $6. Tuesday-Thursday 10 a.m.-6 p.m., Friday-Saturday 10 a.m.-8 p.m., Sunday 11 a.m.-6 p.m.

KALONA HISTORICAL VILLAGE

411 Ninth St., Kalona, 319-656-2519; www.kalonaiowa.org

Amish traditions and lifestyle are preserved in this village containing the Wahl Museum, the Mennonite Museum and Archives, and an implement building, restored 110-year-old depot, log house, one-room school, country store, Victorian house, working windmill, post office and church.
Monday-Saturday.

PLUM GROVE

1030 Carroll St., Iowa City, 319-337-6846; www.uiowa.edu

The 1844 residence of the territory's first governor, Robert Lucas, has been restored and furnished with period furniture.
Memorial Day-October, Wednesday-Sunday 1-5 p.m.

UNIVERSITY OF IOWA

IMU Madison and Jefferson streets, Iowa City, 319-335-0557, 319-335-3500;
www.uiowa.edu

This major state university has more than 28,000 students, 100 major buildings on 1,900 acres, 11 colleges, six schools and 82 departments. Big Ten basketball is played at the Carver-Hawkeye Arena, and Hawkeye football is an annual Iowa City obsession.

SPECIAL EVENT
IOWA ARTS FESTIVAL
408 S. First Ave., Iowa City, 319-337-7944; www.iowacityjazzfestival.com
Celebration of the arts.
Mid-June.

WHERE TO STAY
★★HAMPTON INN
1200 First Ave., Coralville, 319-351-6600, 800-426-7666; www.hamptoninn.com
Close to 41 public parks throughout the area, this hotel is a great place to relax after exploring the nearby outdoor experiences offered.
115 rooms. Restaurant. Complimentary breakfast. Business center. Fitness center. Pool. $61-150

★★HOLIDAY INN
1220 First Ave., Coralville, 319-351-5049, 800-252-7466; www.holiday-inn.com
This standard hotel is close to the interstate so great for those looking for a convenient location and easy access to other parts of the area.
96 rooms. Restaurant. Complimentary breakfast. Fitness center. Pool. Pets accepted. $61-150

★★★SHERATON IOWA CITY HOTEL
210 S. Dubuque St., Iowa City, 319-337-4058, 800-848-1335;
www.starwoodhotels.com
Located one block from the University of Iowa, rooms at this hotel have been updated with the chain's signature luxury beds and soaking tubs. The many area bars and restaurants offer a variety of options for a night out.
236 rooms. Restaurant, bar. Fitness room. Pool. Pets accepted. $61-150

MARQUETTE
First known as North McGregor, this town was later renamed for Father Jacques Marquette. He and Louis Jolliet were the first to see Iowa territory from the mouth of the Wisconsin River in 1673. Within a 15-mile radius of the town are hundreds of effigy mounds, fortifications and earthworks.

WHAT TO SEE
EFFIGY MOUNDS NATIONAL MONUMENT
151 Highway 76, Harpers Ferry, 563-873-3491; www.nps.gov
Preserves traces of indigenous civilization from 2,500 years ago. Mounds built in shapes of animals, birds and other forms. Area divided by Yellow River; Great Bear Mound is the largest known bear effigy in the state, 70 feet across the shoulders, 137 feet long and five feet high. Footpath leads from headquarters to Fire Point Mound Group, to scenic viewpoints overlooking the Mississippi and Yellow rivers.
Admission: adults $3 or $5 per car. Daily.

PIKES PEAK STATE PARK

15316 Great River Road, McGregor, 563-873-2341; www.iowadnr.gov

Set on 970 acres on bluffs overlooking the Mississippi River. Native American mounds, colored sandstone outcroppings, woods and wildflowers. A trail leads across rugged terrain to Bridal Veil Falls.

SPOOK CAVE AND CAMPGROUND

13299 Spook Cave Road, McGregor, 563-873-2144; www.spookcave.com

Guided 35-minute tour of underground cavern via power boat. Campground has swimming beach, lake fishing, hiking trails and picnic areas. Admission: adults $10, children 4-12 $7, children 3 and under free. May-October, daily.

WHERE TO STAY
★HOLIDAY SHORES

110 Front St., McGregor, 563-873-3449; www.holidayshoresmotel.com

While the hotel is a little dated in décor, the rooms are clean and well kept and the view over the Mississippi River makes up for any shortcomings. 33 rooms. Pool. $61-150

MASON CITY

See also Clear Lake

A Native American uprising slowed growth of the city after the first settlement, but pioneers, many of whom were Masons, gradually returned. The town was first known as Shibboleth, later as Masonic Grove. This is the seat of Cerro Gordo County and was the inspiration for the classic musical *The Music Man*.

WHAT TO SEE
FRANK LLOYD WRIGHT STOCKMAN HOUSE

530 First St. N.E., Mason City, 641-421-3666; www.stockmanhouse.org

The only Prairie School house in Iowa designed by Frank Lloyd Wright, this 1908 structure is one of the few houses built by Wright during this period to address middle-class housing needs.

Admission: adults $5, children 10 and under $1. Late May-August, Thursday-Sunday; September-October, Saturday-Sunday.

MEREDITH WILSON BOYHOOD HOME

314 S. Pennsylvania Ave., Mason City, 641-423-3534

Birthplace of the author of *The Music Man*.

Admission: adults $4, children 12 and under $2. May-October, daily; November-April, Saturday-Sunday.

WHERE TO STAY
★COMFORT INN

410 Fifth St. S.W., Mason City, 641-423-4444, 800-228-5150; www.comfortinn.com

The location is the best amenity this hotel offers as it is walking distance to the city-like Music Man Square. Other attractions include Frank Lloyd Wright's historic prairie homes.

60 rooms. Complimentary breakfast. Pool. $61-150

NEWTON

See also Grinnell

The washing machine industry was born here in 1898, and for years the Maytag Company was the dominant business in the city.

WHAT TO SEE

FRED MAYTAG PARK

301 S. 11th Ave. West, Newton, 641-792-1470

Donated by the founder of the Maytag Company. Tennis, picnicking, playground, amphitheater, log cabin.

Daily. June-August, daily.

JASPER COUNTY HISTORICAL MUSEUM

I-80 Exit 164, Newton, Iowa, 641-792-9118;

Local historical displays include a bas-relief sculpture of the natural history of the county, Victorian home, schoolroom, chapel and tool/farm equipment collections. There's also a Maytag historical display of washing machines. Admission: donation. May-September, afternoons.

WHERE TO STAY

★★★LA CORSETTE MAISON INN

629 First Ave. E., Newton, 641-792-6833; www.lacorsette.com

This family run historic mission-style mansion from 1909 is decorated with stained glass and oak. Guest suites are unique in styles and have French furnishings and wood-burning fireplaces. The on-site restaurant is a destination in its own right.

5 rooms. Restaurant. Complimentary breakfast. $151-250

WHERE TO EAT

★★★LA CORSETTE MAISON INN

629 First Ave. E., Newton, 641-792-6833; www.lacorsette.com

Located inside La Corsette Maison Inn, guests are served by tuxedoed waiters and entertained with music from the baby grand piano. Entrées include creations such as roasted pork loin with prune chutney or orange roughy with walnut cream sauce. Many of the ingredients come from the surrounding Iowa farms.

American, French. Lunch, dinner. Reservations recommended. $36-85

OKOBOJI

Lake Okoboji, one of the Iowa great lakes, is a vacationer's paradise. Lake Okoboji and the surrounding area are among the most popular resort areas in Iowa. Visitors will find everything from golf to fishing to shopping and every expected water sport available.

WHAT TO SEE
ARNOLDS PARK AMUSEMENT PARK
37 Lake St., Arnolds Park, 712-332-2183; www.arnoldspark.com
Century-old amusement park with classic old rides and newer favorites, plus entertainment and games.
Admission: adults $20, children $16. Mid-June-mid-August, daily; May-mid-June and late August, Saturday-Sunday; hours vary.

GULL POINT STATE PARK
1500 Harpen St., Wahpeton, 712-337-3211; www.iowadnr.gov
Set on 165 acres on West Okoboji Lake, this park has swimming, fishing, boating, snowmobiling, hiking trails, picnicking and camping.

OTTUMWA PARK
105 E. Third St., Ottumwa, 641-682-1307
This 365-acre recreation area in the center of the city includes camping, fishing, tennis, volleyball, basketball courts, baseball diamond, horseshoes and bocce ball.
April-mid-October, daily.

OKOBOJI QUEEN II
37 Lake St., Arnolds Park, 712-332-5159
Several steamship cruises on West Okoboji Lake are offered in the summer, with a more limited schedule the rest of the year.

SPECIAL EVENT
OKOBOJI SUMMER THEATER
Highway 71, Okoboji, 712-332-7773; www.okoboji.com
This theater has a new play each week and is operated by Stephens College of Columbia, Missouri.
Mid-June-mid-August, Tuesday-Sunday.

WHERE TO STAY
★★★ARROWWOOD RESORT AND CONFERENCE CENTER BY CLUB-HOUSE
1405 Highway 71 N., Okoboji, 712-332-2161; www.arrowwood-okoboji.com
This spacious resort and conference center provides guests with a relaxed environment and a host of activities to choose from, including tennis, swimming or simply taking in the beautiful scenery along with a 27-hole golf course.
99 rooms. Restaurant, bar. Fitness center. Pool. Golf. Tennis. Pets accepted. $61-150

★★INN AT OKOBOJI
3301 Lake Shore Drive, Okoboji, 712-332-2113; www.theinnatokoboji.com
An inviting place for rest and relaxation, this inn is located on Lake Okoboji. It has two pools, a golf course, and a recreation area for kids. Guests can enjoy live entertainment, a café, and much more.
156 rooms. Restaurant, bar. Business center. Pool. Golf. Tennis. Closed October-April. $61-150

WHERE TO EAT
★★MINERVA'S RESTAURANT & BAR
1405 Highway 71 N., Okoboji, 712-332-2161; www.arrowwood-okoboji.com
This restaurant located within the Arrowwood Resort, offers pasta, steak and seafood specialties. The weekly interactive stations are a highlight such as the make your own pasta night.
American. Breakfast, lunch, dinner. $16-35

SIOUX CITY
At the heart of a tri-state region bordered by the Sioux and Missouri rivers, Sioux City has historically been a hub for shipping, transportation and agriculture. The Lewis and Clark expedition followed the Missouri River; the only fatality of that historic trek is commemorated here with the Sergeant Floyd Monument, the first registered historic landmark in the United States. Today, the Missouri River is important to the city from a recreational standpoint, with a developed riverfront with parks, a dance pavilion and a riverboat casino. Sioux City also has many theaters, parks, an art center, nature center, historical attractions and festivals and events throughout the year.

WHAT TO SEE
SERGEANT FLOYD MONUMENT
Glenn Avenue and Highway 75, Sioux City
This was the first registered national historic landmark in the United States. The 100-foot obelisk marks the burial place of Sergeant Charles Floyd, the only casualty of the Lewis and Clark expedition.

SIOUX CITY ART CENTER
225 Nebraska St., Sioux City, 712-279-6272; www.siouxcityartcenter.org
This art center features contemporary traveling exhibits, a permanent collection, a three-story glass atrium and special programs.
Admission: free. Tuesday-Wednesday, Friday-Saturday 10 a.m.-4 p.m., Thursday 10 a.m.-9 p.m., Sunday 1-4 p.m.

SIOUX CITY PUBLIC MUSEUM
2901 Jackson, Sioux City, 712-279-6174; www.siouxcitymuseum.org
Exhibits show Sioux City history and life in pioneer days; geological, archaeological and Native American materials. Located in a Romanesque 23-room mansion.
Tuesday-Saturday 9 a.m.-5 p.m., Sunday 1-5 p.m.

STONE STATE PARK
500 Talbot Road, Sioux City, 712-255-4698; www.iowadnr.com/parks
Set on 1,069 acres, the park overlooks the Missouri and Big Sioux River valleys and offers views of three states from Dakota Point Lookout near Big Sioux River. The 10-acre Dorothy Pecant Nature Center is also here.
Tuesday-Saturday 9 a.m.-5 p.m., Sunday 1-5 p.m.

WOODBURY COUNTY COURTHOUSE

620 Douglas St., Sioux City, 712-279-6601

This courthouse was the largest structure ever completed in the architectural style of Chicago's Prairie School. Designed by Purcell and Elmslie, long-time associates of Louis Sullivan, the city-block-long building was constructed in 1918 of Roman brick and ornamented with massive pieces of terra-cotta, stained glass and relief sculpture by Alfonso Ianelli, who also worked with Frank Lloyd Wright. Both the exterior and highly detailed interior are in near-pristine condition. Courtrooms still contain original architect-designed furniture and lighting fixtures.
Monday-Friday.

WHERE TO STAY
★RAMADA CITY CENTRE

130 Nebraska St., Sioux City, 712-277-1550, 800-272-6232; www.ramada.com

114 rooms. Bar. Complimentary breakfast. Business center. Fitness center. Pool. Pets accepted. $61-150

WHERE TO EAT
★GREEN GABLES

1800 Pierce St., Sioux City, 712-258-4246

Now run by the third generation family members of the restaurant's founder, this Sioux City classic has been around since 1929. The eclectic menu offers both matzo ball soup and ice cream sundaes.
Steak. Lunch, dinner, late-night. Children's menu. $16-35

WATERLOO

See also Cedar Falls

On both banks of the wide Cedar River, Waterloo has established park and picnic areas, docks and boating facilities along the shoreline. One of the largest tractor production facilities in the world is located here.

WHAT TO SEE
GEORGE WYTH MEMORIAL STATE PARK

3659 Wyth Road, Waterloo, 319-232-5505; www.iowadnr.gov

The 1,200-acre park includes several lakes. Swimming, fishing, boating, nature, hiking and bicycle trails, snowmobiling, picnicking and camping.

GROUT MUSEUM OF HISTORY AND SCIENCE

503 S. St., Waterloo, 319-234-6357; www.groutmuseumdistrict.org

Permanent and changing exhibits on regional history and science. Discovery Zone offers many hands-on activities. Pioneer Hall, photo history area, industrial hall; genealogy library. Planetarium shows.
Admission: $10. Tuesday-Saturday 9 a.m.-5 p.m.

WATERLOO COMMUNITY PLAYHOUSE

224 Commercial St., Waterloo, 319-235-0367; www.wcpbhct.org

Open since 1916, this theater offers seven productions yearly including comedies, dramas, mysteries and classics.

WATERLOO MUSEUM OF ART

225 Commercial St., Waterloo, 319-291-4490; www.waterloocenterforthearts.org

Permanent collections include Haitian, American and regional art plus Grant Wood drawings and changing exhibits. The gift shop offers works by Midwest artists.

Tuesday-Saturday 10 a.m.-5 p.m., Sunday 1-5 p.m.

SPECIAL EVENT
MY WATERLOO DAYS FESTIVAL

215 E. Fourth St., Waterloo, 319-233-8431

This citywide festival features air show, balloon rallies, parade, laser and fireworks show, music, renaissance fair and ood.

Four days beginning the Thursday after Memorial Day.

WHERE TO STAY
★HEARTLAND INN WATERLOO CROSSROADS

1809 LaPorte Road, Waterloo, 319-235-4461, 800-334-3277; www.heartlandinns.com

This hotel offers guests both complimentary snacks in the evening and a hot breakfast in the morning. The convenient location adds to the appeal.

112 rooms. Complimentary breakfast. Business center. Fitness center. Pool. $61-150

★HEARTLAND INN WATERLOO GREYHOUND PARK

3052 Marnie Ave., Waterloo, 319-232-7467, 800-334-3277; www.heartlandinns.com

With free coffee delivery in your room in the mornings and a convenient location near all the local attractions, this hotel is great for those early birds.

54 rooms. Complimentary breakfast. Business center. Pool. $61-150

KANSAS

IN THE MOVIE THE WIZARD OF OZ, KANSAS IS A DUSTY, EMPTY LANDSCAPE IN BLACK-AND-white. In real life, no one will deny Kansas has plenty of open space (the state has been using the slogan "As Big As You Think" to promote itself), but the curious visitor will find that Kansas is full of interesting places and natural attractions. And yes, it's in color: the gold and black of sunflowers growing by the thousands in a field, the green of vast swaths of native prairie grass (dappled with splashes of brightly colored wildflowers) and of course, the amber waves of grain—wheat—that is grown on so much of Kansas's ground.

You'll find colors of another kind at the annual Wah-Shun-Gah Days pow-wow in a Santa Fe Trail town, where tribal dancers in native costumes dip and sway to drums. Or if you like your colors loud and your timing is right, you can catch the spectacle of car racing at the NASCAR track in Kansas City.

Native Americans inhabited Kansas thousands of years before Spanish conquistador Francisco Vasquez de Coronado explored the territory in 1541. Other early explorers of Kansas were Meriwether Lewis and William Clark. Army Captain Zebulon Pike also explored the area, continuing westward to discover what is now known as Pikes Peak in Colorado.

By the 1840s, traders and immigrants had established the Santa Fe and Chisholm Trails across the region. Kansas's pre-Civil War activities included the exploits of John Brown, who operated part of the Underground Railroad for slaves escaping through Kansas. Many clashes occurred between anti-slavery and proslavery forces as Kansas was being admitted to the Union. The Abolitionists were determined that Kansas be a "free" state. As railroads expanded westward, the era of cattle drives made such towns as Abilene, Hays, Wichita and Dodge City centers of the legendary Old West, as did such men as Bat Masterson, Wyatt Earp, "Wild Bill" Hickok and the Dalton Gang.

Eastern Kansas is green, fertile and hilly, with woods, streams and lakes. Western Kansas is a part of the Great Plains, once the grass-covered haunt of the buffalo. In 1874, Mennonite immigrants from Russia introduced their Turkey Red wheat seed to Kansas soil, helping to establish Kansas as the breadbasket of the nation.

When you want to rub elbows with civilization, Topeka, the state's largest city with a 600,000 metro area population, has galleries and museums. Its historic Delano District, once known for its brothels and saloons, is a place to find martini lounges and jazz. If you're looking for the laid-back vibe of a college town, head to Lawrence, home of the University of Kansas. While it's now a place of coffeehouses, brewpubs and great ethnic restaurants, Lawrence was where the Abolitionists and pro-slavery forces clashed. More than 150 citizens were killed in the fiery Quantrill's Raiders attack. Finally, at the state's eastern edge, the Kansas City metro area is a bustling cluster of suburbs (including Overland Park, Shawnee, Bonner Springs, Lenexa, Olathe and Leawood) spilling over from the bigger Kansas City on the Missouri side of the border. It's a place full of shopping malls and outlet stores, and restaurants ranging from barbecue to gourmet.

ABILENE

See also Salina

Once famous as a Kansas "cow town," Abilene in 1867 was the terminal point of the Kansas Pacific (later Union Pacific) Railroad and the nearest railhead for the shipment of cattle brought north over the Chisholm Trail. The number of cattle shipped east from here between 1867 and 1871 has been estimated at more than a million, and often 500 cowboys were paid off at a time. City marshals Tom Smith and "Wild Bill" Hickok brought in law and order in the 1870s. Today, Abilene is a wheat center, perhaps best known as the boyhood home of Dwight D. Eisenhower.

WHAT TO SEE
ABILENE & SMOKY VALLEY RAIL ROAD
200 S. Fifth St., Abilene, 785-263-1077, 888-426-6687; www.asvrr.org
This 100-year-old wooden diner coach makes trips through the historic countryside.
Memorial Day-Labor Day, Wednesday-Saturday 9 a.m.-4 p.m., Sunday, 1-4 p.m.

DICKINSON COUNTY HISTORICAL MUSEUM
412 S. Campbell St., Abilene, 785-263-2681; www.heritagecenterdk.com
Exhibits at this museum depict life in early pioneer days and include antique toys and household items used at the turn of the century. Also onsite is a Heritage Center, carousel and log cabin.
Daily.

EISENHOWER CENTER
200 S.E. Fourth St., Abilene, 785-263-4751; www.dwightdeisenhower.com
President Dwight D. Eisenhower's birthplace is also the location of his presidential library. Visitors can tour the 1887 house where Eisenhower was raised; the interior and most furnishings are original. The museum houses changing exhibits of mementos, souvenirs and gifts received during Eisenhower's career. The library contains presidential papers. President and Mrs. Eisenhower are buried in the Meditation Chapel.
Admission: adults $8, seniors $6, children 8-15 $1. Daily.

LEBOLD MANSION
106 N. Vine St., Abilene, 785-263-4356; www.abilenekansas.org
A restored Victorian mansion with period furnishings, this house was built in 1880 by C. H. Lebold.
Admission: adults $10, children 6-16 $5. Tours: Tuesday-Sunday 10 a.m.-4 p.m.

SEELYE MANSION AND MUSEUM
1105 N. Buckeye Ave., Abilene, 785-263-1084; www.seelyemansion.org
This 25-room Georgian mansion is listed on the National Register of Historic Places. It was built in 1905 by A. B. Seelye, a patent medicine entrepreneur. The museum depicts a turn-of-the-century medicine business.
Admission: adults $10, children 6-12 $5. Daily.

WHERE TO EAT
★★BROOKVILLE HOTEL DINING ROOM
105 E. Lafayette, Abilene, 785-263-2244; www.brookvillehotel.com
American. Dinner. Closed Monday. $36-85

★★★KIRBY HOUSE
205 N.E. Third St., Abilene, 1-785-263-7336; www.kirby-house.com
Built as a home in 1885, this Victorian-style restaurant has a friendly atmosphere popular with large groups and anyone celebrating a special occasion. The menu features American classics like country fried steak.
American. Lunch, dinner. Closed Sunday. Children's menu. Bar. $16-35

COUNCIL GROVE
See also Emporia
As the last outfitting place on the Santa Fe Trail between the Missouri River and Santa Fe, Council Grove, now a National Historic Landmark, holds historic significance in the development of the West. The town grew up around a Native American campground in a grove of oaks near the Neosho River and has many turn-of-the-century buildings, several parks and two lakes.

WHAT TO SEE
COUNCIL OAK SHRINE
313 E. Main St., Council Grove
The treaty of 1825 was signed here between U.S. government commissioners and the Osage.

CUSTER'S ELM SHRINE
South Neosho Street, Council Grove
This elm trunk stands as a shrine to a tree that was 100 feet tall, 16 feet in circumference and reputedly sheltered the camp of General George Custer in 1867 when he was leading an expedition to western Kansas.

MADONNA OF THE TRAIL MONUMENT
Corner of Union and Main streets, Council Grove
One of 12 statues erected in each of the states through which the National Old Trails Roads passed. The Madonna pays tribute to pioneer mothers and commemorates the trails that opened the West.

POST OFFICE OAK
East Main Street, Council Grove
This mammoth oak tree with a cache at its base served as an unofficial post office for pack trains and caravans on the Santa Fe Trail from 1825-1847.

SPECIAL EVENT
WAH-SHUN-GAH DAYS
207 W. Main St., Council Grove, 620-767-5413
This event is the Kaw Intertribal Powwow and includes a Santa Fe Trail ride and supper, antique tractor pull and street dance.
Third weekend in June.

A WALK THROUGH THE OLD WEST

If you're looking for an authentic Old West town, journey to Council Grove, a once busy trading center on the Santa Fe Trail during the 1840s and 1850s. Council Grove contains some of the best-preserved frontier-era architecture in Kansas, and many of the buildings are still used for their original commercial purpose.

Begin your tour at the Kaw Mission State Historic Site (500 N. Mission St.). Methodist missionaries built this school for native Kaw children in 1851. Today the structure contains a museum dedicated to the Kaw, the Santa Fe Trail and early Council Grove. From here, walk south on Mission Street to Main Street, which follows the route of the Santa Fe Trail through town. The Cottage House Hotel (25 N. Neosho) is a beautifully maintained Victorian hotel still in operation with wraparound porches and striking Queen Anne turrets and gazebos. Across Main Street, the Farmers and Drovers Bank (201 W. Main St.) is a handsome landmark of red brick and limestone, with eclectic architectural features including Romanesque arches, stained-glass windows and a Byzantine dome.

One block east on Main Street is another historic structure, which is still in operation. The Hays House Restaurant (112 W. Main St.) is the oldest continuously operating restaurant west of the Mississippi. Since it was constructed in 1857, the restaurant has served the likes of General George Custer and Jesse James. The ambience is frontier-era, and peach pie is among the favorite offerings. Also on this block of Main Street is the stone Last Chance Store (also in operation since 1857) and the Council Grove National Bank Building.

Before crossing the Neosho River Bridge, turn south two blocks to the Seth Hays Home. Built in 1867, this home has been preserved and is open to visitors on Sundays and by appointment. Cross the Neosho River on Main Street. In a shelter along the riverbank you will find the remains of the Council Oak, a once-vast oak tree under which representatives of the United States and the Osage tribe signed a treaty in 1825 that guaranteed settlers safe passage across Indian territory. On the north corner of Main and Union streets is a small park containing the Madonna of the Trail, a statue of a pioneer mother and children erected in 1925 by the Daughters of the American Revolution. Along with a museum of frontier history, the park is home to the Post Office Oak, a 300-year-old burr oak that served as an unofficial post depository for travelers along the Santa Fe Trail. Continue east on Main to Durland Park (at Fifth Street) where Council Grove's first jail, constructed in 1849, still stands. Also in Durland Park are two 19th-century train depots.

WHERE TO EAT

★★HAYS HOUSE HISTORIC RESTAURANT AND TAVERN

112 W. Main St., Council Grove, 620-767-5911; www.hayshouse.com

This restaurant is the oldest continually operating restaurant West of the Mississippi River and is on the National Register of Historic Landmarks on the Santa Fe Trail.

American. Breakfast, lunch, dinner, Sunday brunch. Children's menu. Bar. $16-35

EL DORADO

See also Wichita

El Dorado, the seat of Butler County, is located on the western edge of the Flint Hills. The city's growth can be attributed to oil—two refineries are located here. Stapleton No. 1, the area's first gusher, tapped in 1915, is commemorated by a marker at the northwestern edge of the town.

HISTORIC DODGE CITY

Memorable for buffalo hunts, longhorn cattle and frontier marshals, Dodge City was laid out by construction crews of the Santa Fe Railroad and named for nearby Fort Dodge. Vast herds of buffalo—estimated at 24 million or more—which then covered the surrounding plains, had been hunted here for years. The railroad provided transportation to make the hides commercially profitable. A skilled hunter could earn $100 a day at the industry's height; by 1875 the herds were nearly exterminated. Cattle drives, also stimulated by the railroad, took the buffalo's place in the town's economy. In the 1870s, Dodge City became the cowboy capital of the region. Among its notable peace officers were Bat Masterson and Wyatt Earp. The prevalence of sudden and violent death resulted in the establishment of Boot Hill cemetery. In the mid-1880s the era of the cattle drives ended, and by 1890 much of the grazing land had been plowed for crops. Visitors to Doge City can get a peak into the Wild West's past by exploring the many preserved historic buildings, including those on restored historic Front Street.

WHAT TO SEE
EL DORADO STATE PARK

618 N.E. Bluestem Road, El Dorado, 316-321-7180

The largest of Kansas's state parks, El Dorado is made up of four areas totaling 4,000 acres. Rolling hills, wooded valleys and an open prairie make up the natural environment of the park. El Dorado Lake is also within the park. Daily.

KANSAS OIL MUSEUM

383 E. Central Ave., El Dorado, 316-321-9333; www.kansasoilmuseum.org

Displays at this museum depict the area's oil, ranching and agricultural history, including a model rotary drilling rig. Outdoor historic oil field exhibits include a restored cable-tool drilling rig, shotgun lease house and antique engines.

Admission: adults $4, seniors $3, students 6-16 $2. children 5 and under free. May-September, Monday-Saturday 9 a.m.-5 p.m.; October-April, Tuesday-Friday, 9 a.m.-5 p.m., Sunday noon-5 p.m.

WHERE TO STAY
★★BEST WESTERN RED COACH INN

2525 W. Central St., El Dorado, 316-321-6900, 800-362-2034; www.bestwestern.com

The exterior of the hotel is in the motor court style, but the rooms have been recently updated and have all the amenities to enhance your stay.

73 rooms. Restaurant. Fitness room. Pool. Pets accepted. $61-150

EMPORIA

See also Council Grove

This was the home of one of America's most famous newspaper editors, William Allen White. His *Emporia Gazette* editorials, written from the 1890s to the 1940s, attracted nationwide attention and earned White a Pulitzer Prize. Emporia is the seat of Lyon County and on the edge of the Flint Hills area.

WHAT TO SEE
DAVID TRAYLOR ZOO OF EMPORIA
75 Soden Road, Emporia, 620-341-4365; www.emporiazoo.org
This building houses William Allen White's widely-quoted newspaper. Located here is a small one-room museum that displays newspaper machinery used in White's time.

EMPORIA GAZETTE BUILDING
517 Merchant St., Emporia, 620-342-4800
This building houses William Allen White's widely-quoted newspaper. Located here is a small one-room museum that displays newspaper machinery used in White's time.

FLINT HILLS NATIONAL WILDLIFE REFUGE
530 W. Maple Ave., Hartford, 620-392-5553; www.fws.gov/flinthills
Consisting of 18,500 acres located on the upstream portion of John Redmond River, this park offers hiking and camping. Wild food gathering is permitted. Bald eagles can be spotted in fall and winter. Fishing and hunting in legal seasons.
Monday-Friday 8 a.m.-4:30 p.m.

NATIONAL TEACHERS HALL OF FAME
1200 Commercial, Emporia, 620-341-5660; www.nthf.org
This organization is committed to drawing the public's attention to exceptional teachers through a museum, teacher's resource center and an induction ceremony that recognizes five of the nation's most outstanding Pre-Kindergarten through Grade 12 educators each year.
Monday-Saturday.

WHERE TO STAY
★★BEST WESTERN HOSPITALITY HOUSE
3021 W. Highway 50, Emporia, 620-342-7587, 800-362-2036; www.bestwestern.com
If you are looking to experience the natural beauty of nearby Flint Hills, this is a great hotel to stay at. While not exploring the local historical monuments and the hills, the hotel offers a full service restaurant, lounge and indoor pool.
143 rooms. Restaurant. Bar. Complimentary breakfast. Business center. Fitness center. Pool. Pets accepted. $61-150

HAYS
Fort Hays, a former military post on the old frontier, gave this railroad town its name. Oil, grain, cattle, educational and medical facilities, and tourism are important to the area.

WHAT TO SEE
ELLIS COUNTY HISTORICAL SOCIETY MUSEUM
100 W. Seventh St., Hays, 785-628-2624; www.elliscountyhistoricalmuseum.org
More than 26,000 items are on display in this museum including antique toys and games, musical instruments and rotating exhibits including quilts from the 1800s to present. Also here are a one-room schoolhouse and the oldest

stone church in Ellis County.

Admission: adults $4, children 3-12 $1, children 2 and under free. June-August, Tuesday-Friday, Saturday; rest of year, Tuesday-Friday.

HISTORIC FORT HAYS

1472 Highway 183 Alternate, Hays, 785-625-6812; www.kshs.org/places/forthays

This former U.S. Army post was in use from 1865-1889 as a base for defending the railroad that ran through the area. Wild West legends Wild Bill Hickok and Buffalo Bill Cody are just some of the figures who passed through the fort.

Admission: adults $3, seniors and students $2, children 5 and under free. Tuesday-Saturday 9 a.m.-5 p.m., Sunday 1-5 p.m. Group tours by appointment.

STERNBERG MUSEUM OF NATURAL HISTORY

3000 Sternberg Drive, Hays, 785-628-4286; www.fhsu.edu/sternberg

This museum features natural history, paleontological and geological collections.

Admission: $6, seniors $4, children 4-12 $4. Tuesday-Sunday.

SPECIAL EVENTS
PIONEER DAYS AT HISTORIC FORT HAYS

1472 Highway 183 Alternate, Hays, 785-625-6812

Two full days are filled with demonstrations of butter churning, tatting, rope making, rug weaving, whittling and stone post cutting at this annual event. Third week in September.

WILD WEST FESTIVAL

Frontier Park, 2700 Vine St., Hays, 785-628-8202; www.wildwestfestival.com

This annual event features family-oriented activities, concerts, food booths and a fireworks display.

Early July.

WHERE TO STAY
★HAMPTON INN

4002 General Hays Road, Hays, 785-621-4444, 800-426-7866; www.hamptoninn.com

This family-run Mexican restaurant is the locals' favorite. You could not go wrong with one of their house specialties or a frozen margarita.

Mexican, American. Lunch, dinner. Children's menu. Bar. $16-35

WHERE TO EAT
★GUTIERREZ

1106 E. 27 St., Hays, 785-625-4402; www.thelocalsfavorite.com

This family-run Mexican restaurant is the locals' favorite. You could not go wrong with one of their house specialties or a frozen margarita.

Mexican, American. Lunch, dinner. Children's menu. Bar. $16-35

IOLA

Most of the expansion of this small eastern Kansas town happened after natural gas was discovered in the area in the 1900s. The town retains its historic feel with a preserved downtown with Victorian buildings.

WHAT TO SEE
OLD JAIL MUSEUM

203 N. Jefferson Ave., Iola, 620-365-3051; www.kansastravel.org

A historic building, this jail has been restored and is now open for tours. Admission: free. May-September, Tuesday-Saturday.

BOYHOOD HOME OF MAJOR GENERAL FREDERICK FUNSTON

207 N. Jefferson, Iola, 620-365-3051

This house, built in 1860, was the home of Fred Funston, a decorated soldier noted for directing the recovery efforts following the San Francisco earthquake of 1906. Originally located on a homestead about five miles north of Iola, the house has been restored according to the Victorian décor of the 1880s and 1890s. Many original family items are on display.
Admission: free. May-October, Wednesday-Saturday 12:30-4:30 p.m.; November-April, Tuesday-Saturday 2-4 p.m.

WHERE TO STAY
★★BEST WESTERN INN

1315 N. State St., Iola, 620-365-5161, 800-769-0007; www.bestwestern.com

Do not be deceived by this old school motel. The updated rooms are clean and comfortable and parking directly in front of your door makes for a convenient stay.
58 rooms. Restaurant. Pool. Pets accepted. $61-150

LAWRENCE

See also Kansas City, Leavenworth, Ottawa, Topeka

Lawrence had a stormy history in the territorial years. It was founded by the New England Emigrant Aid Company, which aimed to populate the area with antislavery proponents transplanted from New England and other "free states" as a means of warding off slavery. The center of Free State activities, the town was close to a state of war from 1855 until the Free Staters triumphed in 1859. The Confederate guerrilla leader, William Quantrill, made one of his most spectacular raids on Lawrence in 1863, burning the town and killing 150 citizens. After the Civil War, the town experienced a gradual and peaceful growth. It is the site of the University of Kansas.

WHAT TO SEE
HASKELL INDIAN NATIONS UNIVERSITY

155 Indian Ave., Lawrence, 785-749-8404; www.haskell.edu

This school was founded in 1884 to provide education for Native Americans. More than 120 tribes are represented among the students. The campus is a registered historic landmark. The American Indian Athletic Hall of Fame is located here.

LAWRENCE ARTS CENTER

940 New Hampshire St., Lawrence, 785-843-2787; www.lawrenceartscenter.com

Galleries featuring the work of local artists and craftspeople; performance hall for theater, dance, and music; art classes and workshops for all ages. Monday-Saturday 9 a.m.-5 p.m.

OLD WEST LAWRENCE HISTORIC DISTRICT

402 N. Second St., Lawrence, 785-865-4499

Take a self-guided tour through this area of notable 19th-century homes.

UNIVERSITY OF KANSAS

Corner of 15th and Iowa streets, Lawrence, 785-864-2700; www.ku.edu

With 26,000 students, this university stretches over a 1,000-acre campus. Kansas Jayhawks athletics (especially basketball) are a prime attraction in Lawrence. Some campus attractions include the Campanile Bell Tower, Museum of Natural History, Museum of Anthropology and Spencer Museum of Art.

WHERE TO STAY
★★★ELDRIDGE HOTEL

701 Massachusetts St., Lawrence, 785-749-5011, 800-527-0909;
www.eldridgehotel.com

This hotel, with a history dating to the Civil War, is located in the heart of quaint downtown Lawrence, near the University of Kansas. The setting is charming, but the décor is crisp and contemporary. The original ceilings and woodwork have been nicely maintained.

48 rooms. Restaurant. Bar. $151-250

★★HOLIDAY INN LAWRENCE

200 McDonald Drive, Lawrence, 785-841-7077; www.holiday-inn.com/lawrenceks

Consistent and reliable hotel with recently renovated rooms. The new Paddy O'Quigleys sports bar is a good place to wind down after your day of travel.

192 rooms. Restaurant. Bar. Business center. Pool. Pets accepted. $61-150

★★HALCYON HOUSE BED AND BREAKFAST

1000 Ohio St., Lawrence, 785-841-0314, 888-441-0314; www.thehalcyonhouse.com

This Victorian inn was built in 1885 but has been updated with modern touches like high-speed Internet access and a full breakfast is served each morning.

9 rooms. Complimentary breakfast. No children under 12. $61-150

LEAVENWORTH

See also Kansas City, Lawrence

Leavenworth was the first incorporated town in Kansas Territory. At first strongly proslavery, Leavenworth had many border conflicts, but during the Civil War it was loyal to the Union. In the years just before the war, the town was the headquarters for a huge overland transportation and supply operation sending wagons and stagecoaches northwest on the Oregon Trail and southwest on the Santa Fe Trail. Fort Leavenworth, adjoining the city, is the oldest military post west of the Mississippi River that has been in continuous operation (since 1827). A federal penitentiary is on the grounds adjacent to the fort.

WHAT TO SEE
FORT LEAVENWORTH
600 Thomas Ave., Fort Leavenworth, 913-684-5604
Features of interest at this base are the U.S. Army Command and General Staff College, U.S. Disciplinary Barracks, National Cemetery, Buffalo Soldier Monument and branches of the Oregon and Santa Fe trails. The Frontier Army Museum features artifacts of pioneer history and the Army of the West.
Daily.

FRONTIER ARMY MUSEUM
Fort Leavenworth, Reynolds Avenue, Leavenworth, 913-684-3767
Discover the history of Fort Leavenworth and the United States Regular Army on the Frontier. See historic army uniforms, weapons and equipment, including a 1917 JN4D Jenny biplane and the carriage that Abraham Lincoln traveled in when he visited in 1859.
Monday-Friday 9 a.m.-4 p.m., Saturday 10 a.m.-4 p.m.

PARKER CAROUSEL
320 S. Esplanade, Leavenworth, 913-682-1331; www.firstcitymuseums.org
This restored 1913 carousel features hand-carved, one-of-a-kind horses. Admission: adults $5, children $3. Thursday-Saturday 11 a.m.-5 p.m., Sunday 1-5 p.m. Closed January.

LEAWOOD

A Kansas City suburb was established after World War II and grew after the building of several housing developments. It's now one of the fastest growing cities in Kansas.

WHERE TO EAT
★GATES BAR-B-Q
103 Road, Leawood, 913-383-1752; www.gatesbbq.com
Listen for the signature "Hi, May I help you?" as you enter this classic Kansas City Bar-B-Q restaurant. The ribs are excellent and the sauce is so popular they sell it by the bottle.
American. Lunch, dinner, late-night. $16-35

★★★HEREFORD HOUSE
5001 Town Center Drive, Leawood, 913-327-0800; www.herefordhouse.com
Jack Webb founded the original branch of this steakhouse in Kansas City in 1957. Now, this Town Center Plaza location is one of three, with charcoal-grilled steaks and friendly, no-hassle service.
Steak. Lunch, dinner. Outdoor seating. Children's menu. Bar. $36-85

LIBERAL

Liberal's name comes from the generosity of one of its first settlers, S.S. Rogers. Although water was scarce in southwestern Kansas, Rogers never charged parched and weary travelers for the use of his well—a "liberal" fee.

WHAT TO SEE
CORONADO MUSEUM

567 E. Cedar St., Liberal, 620-624-7624; www.sewardcountymuseum.com
Displays at this museum depict early life of in Liberal. Some exhibits trace Francisco Coronado's route through Kansas. Also included are Dorothy's House from *The Wizard of Oz* and an animated display of the story.
Memorial Day-Labor Day, Monday-Saturday 9 a.m.-6 p.m., Sunday, 1-6 p.m.; Labor Day-Memorial Day, Tuesday-Saturday 9 a.m.-5 p.m., Sunday 1-5 p.m.

MID-AMERICA AIR MUSEUM

2000 W. Second St., Liberal, 620-624-5263; www.kansastravel.org/airmuseum.htm
See an aviation collection of 100 aircraft including civilian aircraft, military aircraft from World War II and planes of the Korean and Vietnam era. Also here is the Liberal Army Airfield exhibit.
Daily.

MANHATTAN

Manhattan is a thriving center for trade, education, government, health care and entertainment. Several early settlements were combined to form Manhattan. Lying in a limestone bowl-shaped depression resulting from glacial action, the town developed as a trading center for farm products. Kansas State University is located in Manhattan.

WHAT TO SEE
KANSAS STATE UNIVERSITY

119 Anderson hall, Manhattan, 785-532-6250, 800-432-8270; www.ksu.edu
With more than 20,000 students, this campus, established around 1863, has buildings constructed of native limestone.

SUNSET ZOO

2333 Oak St., Manhattan, 785-587-2737; www.ci.manhattan.ks.us/sunsetzoo
A zoo with more than 300 animals, residents here include Brownie, thought to be the oldest living grizzly bear in the world. He's kept company by snow leopards, cheetahs, red pandas, bobcats, reptiles, birds and more.
Daily.

TUTTLE CREEK STATE PARK

5800 A River Pond Road, Manhattan, 785-539-7941; www.stateparks.com
This 1,200-acre park is located on a 13,350-acre lake. There is a special observation area with distant views of the Blue River Valley and Randolph Bridge, the largest in Kansas. Beach, bathhouse, fishing, boating, camping.

WHERE TO STAY
★★CLARION HOTEL
530 Richards Drive, Manhattan, 785-539-5311; www.choicehotels.com

Close to Kansas State University, this convenient hotel boasts a three-story atrium with heated indoor pool. Two on-site restaurants offer a choice of dining options.

196 rooms. Restaurant. Business center. Fitness center. Pool. Pets accepted. $61-150

★★HOLIDAY INN MANHATTAN AT THE CAMPUS
1641 Anderson Ave., Manhattan, 785-539-7531, 800-111-000; www.holiday-inn.com

With well-maintained rooms, this hotel directly adjacent to the university offers the convenience of immediate access to the campus.

113 rooms. Restaurant, bar. Business center. Fitness center. Pool. Pets accepted. $61-150

WHERE TO EAT
★★★HARRY'S
418 Poyntz Ave., Manhattan, 785-537-1300; www.harrysmanhattan.com

The historic Wareham hotel is the setting for this restaurant, named in honor of the hotel's first owner, Harry Wareham. Though the restaurant has been restored to look much as it did when it first opened in the 1920s, the menu is decidedly up-to-date, with dishes such as risotto and fried smoked portobellos, or grilled lobster salad with spicy roma tomato chutney.

American. Lunch, dinner. Closed Sunday. Reservations recommended. Children's menu. Bar. $36-85

MCPHERSON

Both the city and the county bear the name of Civil War hero General James Birdseye McPherson, who was killed in the Battle of Atlanta in 1864. This small town of 14,000 residents has a historic downtown and a restored opera house dating to the 1880s.

WHAT TO SEE
MAXWELL WILDLIFE REFUGE
101 N. Main St., Canton, 620-628-4455, 800-324-8022; www.mcphersonks.org

This 2,800-acre prairie provides a natural environment for elk, deer and buffalo. The refuge has an observation tower, a 46-acre fishing lake, boat ramp and nature trail.

Daily.

WHERE TO STAY
★★BEST WESTERN HOLIDAY MANOR
2211 E. Kansas Ave., McPherson, 620-241-5343, 888-841-0038;
www.bestwestern.com

109 rooms. Restaurant. Pool. Pets accepted. $61-150

OVERLAND PARK

The suburb Overland Park, which wasn't incorporated until 1960, is located directly south of Kansas City and has a historic downtown.

WHAT TO SEE
DEANNA ROSE CHILDREN'S FARMSTEAD
138th Street and Switzer Road, Overland Park, 913-897-2360; www.opkansas.org
Feed and pet farm animals, hop on a horse-drawn wagon or walk through a replica of an early 1900s Kansas farmhouse at this farmstead.
April-October, daily. Closed November-March.

OVERLAND PARK ARBORETUM AND BOTANICAL GARDENS
8909 W. 179th St., Overland Park, 913-685-3604; www.opkansas.org
This park features 300 acres of land, including three miles of hiking trails (some wheelchair accessible) through gardens. Naturalized areas feature a Meadow Garden, Butterfly Garden and Woodland Garden.
Guided tours by appointment. Daily.

WHERE TO STAY
★★COURTYARD KANSAS CITY OVERLAND PARK/CONVENTION CENTER
11001 Woodson Ave., Overland Park, 913-317-8500, 800-321-2211; www.courtyard.com
168 rooms. Restaurant. Business center. Fitness center. Pool. $61-150

★★DOUBLETREE HOTEL OVERLAND PARK-CORPORATE WOODS
10100 College Blvd., Overland Park, 913-451-6100, 800-222-8733; www.doubletree.com
356 rooms. Restaurant, bar. Fitness center. Pool. $61-150

★★EMBASSY SUITES HOTEL KANSAS CITY-OVERLAND PARK
10601 Metcalf Ave., Overland Park, 913-649-7060, 800-362-2779; www.embassysuites.com
200 rooms. Restaurant, bar. Complimentary breakfast. Business center. Fitness center. Pool. $61-150

★★HAMPTON INN KANSAS CITY/OVERLAND PARK
10591 Metcalf Frontage Road, Overland Park, 913-341-1551, 800-426-7866; www.hamptoninn.com
134 rooms. Restaurant, bar. Complimentary breakfast. Business center. Pool. $61-150

★★★OVERLAND PARK MARRIOTT
10800 Metcalf Ave., Overland Park, 913-451-8000, 800-228-9290; www.overlandparkmarriott.com
Located in Overland Park, this well-landscaped suburban hotel can be easily seen from the Interstate (I-435). The Metcalf South Mall is approximately one mile away, and the convention center is within two miles of the hotel.
391 rooms. Restaurant, bar. Business center. Fitness center. Pool. $151-250

WHERE TO EAT
★★FIORELLA'S JACK STACK BARBECUE
9520 Metcalf Ave., Overland Park, 913-385-7427
American, barbecue. Lunch, dinner. Daily. Children's menu. Bar. $16-35

★★IL TRULLO
9056 Metcalf Ave., Overland Park, 913-341-3773; www.iltrullo-kc.com
Italian. Lunch, dinner. Closed Sunday-Monday. Reservations recommended. Children's menu. Bar. $16-35

★★★J. GILBERT'S WOOD FIRED STEAKS AND SEAFOOD
8901 Metcalf Ave., Overland Park, 913-642-8070; www.jgilberts.com
The restaurants in this mini-chain (there are locations in Ohio, Virginia and Connecticut) all have a fireplace as their focal point, a visual reminder of this eatery's dedication to preparing simply delicious wood-fired steaks. The prime Kansas City strip is a favorite, while dishes like pan-seared halibut satisfy those who are less carnivorous.
Steak. Dinner. Reservations recommended. Outdoor seating. Children's menu. Bar. $36-85

★★★NIKKO JAPANESE STEAKHOUSE
10800 Metcalf Road, Overland Park, 913-451-8000; www.marriott.com
A Japanese steakhouse complete with tableside teppanyaki chefs, this restaurant is located inside the Marriott hotel. Entrées, from steak to seafood and more, come with soup, salad, shrimp, steamed rice and vegetables.
Japanese. Dinner. Children's menu. $16-35

★★RAOUL'S VELVET ROOM
7222 W. 119th St., Overland Park, 913-469-0466; www.raoulsvelvetroom.com
American. Dinner, late-night. Reservations recommended. Outdoor seating. Bar. $16-35

★SUSHI GIN
9559 Nall Ave., Overland Park, 913-649-8488; www.sushigin.com
Japanese. Lunch, dinner. Children's menu. Bar. $16-35

★★YIA YIA'S EUROBISTRO
4701 W. 119th St., Overland Park, 913-345-1111; www.kansascitymenus.com/yiayias
Continental, seafood. Lunch, dinner, Sunday brunch. Reservations recommended. Outdoor seating. Children's menu. Bar. $16-35

PRAIRIE VILLAGE
This Kansas City suburb began in the 1940s as a planned community designed by J.C. Nichols, who also created nearby Country Club Plaza, the nation's first suburban shopping center.

WHERE TO EAT
★★★TATSU'S
4603 W. 90th St., Prairie Village, 913-383-9801; www.tatsus.com
This quiet French restaurant grew from a small pastry and lunch shop opened

by chef/owner Tatsu Arai in 1980. Since then, it has become a top Kansas City dining destination. The classic French cuisine includes dishes such as beef bourguignon, poached salmon with champagne sauce or lemon butter sauce and roasted boneless duck breast with peppercorn cream sauce.
French. Lunch, dinner. Bar. $16-35

SALINA
See also Abilene, McPherson
Salina got its start as a trading post for gold hunters stopping through on their way to Pikes Peak. The arrival of the Union Pacific Railroad in 1867 brought new growth, and the wheat crops in the 1870s established a permanent economy. Alfalfa, now one of the state's major crops, was first introduced in Kansas by a Salina resident in 1874. The city was rebuilt in 1903 after the Smoky Hill flood destroyed most of the community. Aviator Steve Fossett made history in 2005 when he launched the first solo, nonstop, round-the-world, nonrefueled flight in the Virgin Atlantic GlobalFlyer from the Salina airport.

WHAT TO SEE
SALINA ART CENTER
242 S. Santa Fe, Salina, 785-827-1431; www.salinaartcenter.org
This center features art exhibits as well as a hands-on art laboratory for children. The cinema shows current art house releases.
Wednesday-Saturday 12-5 p.m., Sunday 1-5 p.m.

SMOKY HILL MUSEUM
211 W. Iron Ave., Salina, 785-309-5776; www.smokyhillmuseum.org
Area history is told through photos and artifacts at this museum. Changing exhibits are featured, as is a general store period room.
Tuesday-Friday 12-5 p.m., Saturday 10 a.m.-5 p.m., Sunday 1-5 p.m.

WHERE TO STAY
★★HOLIDAY INN SALINA
1616 W. Crawford St., Salina, 785-823-1739, 888-465-4329;
www.holiday-inn.com/salinaks
192 rooms. Restaurant, bar. Fitness center. Pool. Pets accepted. $61-150

WHERE TO EAT
★GUTIERREZ
640 Westport Blvd., Salina, 785-825-1649; www.gutzsalina.com
Mexican. Lunch, dinner. Children's menu. Bar. $16-35

SHAWNEE
This Kansas City suburb was founded in the 1850s and features many parks, an outdoor pioneer museum and a historic downtown.

WHERE TO EAT
★★LEONA YARBROUGH'S
10310 Shawnee Mission Parkway, Shawnee, 913-248-0500; www.yarbroughrestaurant.com
American. Lunch, dinner. Children's menu. $16-35

★★PAULO & BILL
16501 Midland Drive, Shawnee, 913-962-9900; www.pauloandbill.com
Italian, American. Lunch, dinner. Outdoor seating. Children's menu. Bar.
$16-35

TOPEKA
See also Kansas City, Lawrence
The capital city of Kansas is located on the Kansas River (locally called the Kaw). World-famous psychiatric clinic and research center, the Menninger Foundation, is located here, and Herbert Hoover's vice president, Charles Curtis, who was part Kaw and a descendant of one of Topeka's earliest settlers, was born here.

WHAT TO SEE
BROWN V. BOARD OF EDUCATION NATIONAL HISTORIC SITE
1515 S.E. Monroe St., Topeka, 785-354-4273; www.nps.gov/brvb
This site commemorates the U.S. Supreme Court's groundbreaking 1954 decision declaring segregation in public schools unconstitutional. Here you'll find Monroe Elementary School, one of Topeka's four formerly segregated elementary schools for African-American children, along with interpretive exhibits and educational programs.
Daily 9 a.m.-5 p.m.

CEDAR CREST GOVERNOR'S MANSION
1 S.W. Cedar Crest Road, Topeka, 785-296-3636; www.governor.ks.gov
This massive house features period architecture with Loire Valley overtones spread out on 244 acres. Built in 1928 and bequeathed to the state in 1955, it became the governor's residence in 1962.
Guided tours: Monday afternoons.

COMBAT AIR MUSEUM
Forbes Field, Hangars 602 and 604, J St., Topeka, 785-862-3303;
www.combatairmuseum.org
Jets, cargo transports, fighters and trainers from 1917-1980 are displayed here, as well as military artifacts. Guided tours, by appointment.
June-September, Monday-Saturday 9 a.m.-4:30 p.m.; October-May, Monday-Saturday noon-4:30 p.m.

GAGE PARK
9635 S.W. Gage Blvd., Topeka, 785-368-9180; www.topeka.org
Tennis, swimming, softball and volleyball facilities are available here, along with playground equipment for different ages and abilities. The newly restored carousel was built in 1908 and operates from 10 a.m.-8 p.m. during the summer and on weekends only in September and October. This park is also home to the Topeka Zoo.

KANSAS STATE HISTORICAL SOCIETY
6425 S.W. Sixth Ave., Topeka, 785-272-8681; www.kshs.org
The Kansas Museum of History includes the Library of Kansas and informa-

---

WILDLIFE ON THE PRAIRIE

East central Kansas boasts beautiful tallgrass prairies, some of the few remaining in the United States. Take this drive in early spring, when the old grass is burned to make way for spring growth, or in early summer, when wildflowers are abundant. Head west from Topeka on I-70 to Manhattan. Nearby, the Konza Prairie is a major site for prairie research, with hiking and wildlife-watching. Continue south on Highway 177 to the Tallgrass Prairie National Preserve near Strong Falls. Covered-wagon train trips are offered at El Dorado, northeast of Wichita on Highway 177. From Wichita, take I-135 north to McPherson and visit the McPherson-Maxwell Game Preserve, with one of the states' largest bison herds, as well as elk, deer and buffalo. Return to I-70 at Salina, then head back east to your starting point.

---

tion on Native American and Western history and genealogy.
Tuesday-Saturday.

STATE CAPITOL

300 W. 10th St., Topeka, 785-296-3966; www.governor.ks.gov

The design of this building was based on the U.S. Capitol. On the grounds are statues of Lincoln and Pioneer Woman, both by Topeka-born sculptor Merrell Gage. Murals on the second floor are by John Steuart Curry; those on the first floor are by David H. Overmyer.
Monday-Friday.

TOPEKA ZOO

635 S.W. Gage Blvd., Topeka, 785-368-9180; www.topeka.org/zoo

An orangutan and gorilla exhibit, black bear exhibit, lion display, tropical rain forest and more are featured at this museum.
Daily 10 a.m.-5 p.m.

SPECIAL EVENTS
HUFF 'N PUFF HOT AIR BALLOON RALLY

Lake Shawnee, Topeka, 785-554-2003; www.huff-n-puff.org

Dozens of hot air balloons take to the skies in this annual event.
September.

WASHBURN SUNFLOWER MUSIC FESTIVAL

1700 S.W. College Ave., Topeka, 785-670-1511; www.sunflowermusicfestival.org

This annual festival features international symphonic musicians performing nightly.
First two weeks in June.

WHERE TO STAY
★★CLUBHOUSE INN & SUITES TOPEKA

924 S.W. Henderson Road, Topeka, 785-273-8888, 800-258-2466;
www.clubhouseinn.com

121 rooms. Complimentary breakfast. Restaurant, bar. Pool. Business center. Pets accepted. $61-150

ACROSS THE PRAIRIE LANDSCAPE

This loop trail passes through prairie landscapes and across the Kansas of past, present and future. Begin in Wichita, the state's largest city. The city's historic role as a cow capital along the Chisholm Trail is preserved at the Old Cowtown Museum, a historic village with 40 buildings from the city's early boom years in the 1870s. Nearby is the Wichita Art Museum, with a fine collection of American Impressionists and a grand outdoor sculpture garden. Gardeners will enjoy Botanica, The Wichita Garden, which has a number of theme gardens.

Drive northeast on I-35 to Cassoday, home to several good antique stores, and join Highway 177 northbound. Known as the Flint Hills Scenic Byway, this route passes through a rugged landscape of rolling hills, mesas and virgin prairie. Stop in Cottonwood Falls to visit the Chase County Courthouse, which is the oldest in Kansas. The building was constructed from local limestone in a striking French Renaissance style.

Just north is the Tallgrass Prairie National Preserve, which protects 11,000 acres of native prairie grassland that is home to 40 species of grasses, 200 species of birds, 30 species of mammals and up to 10-million insects per acre. A number of trails lead across the plains, which in spring are carpeted with wildflowers. The preserves headquarters are located at the Z Bar Ranch, an imposing stone ranch house cum mansion from the 1880s.

Council Grove is one of Kansas's most historic towns. In fact, the entire settlement has been designated a National Historic Landmark. Council Grove was the last provisioning stop on the old Santa Fe Trail between the Missouri River and Santa Fe, and the town is filled with landmarks of the frontier West.

Continue north on Highway 57 to Junction City, located at the confluence of the Republican and Smoky Hill rivers. The town owes its existence to Fort Riley, founded in 1853 to protect pioneers traveling along the Santa Fe and Oregon trails. The fort, just north of town along Highway 57, contains a number of historic sites, including the state's first territorial capital, an early home of General George Custer and the U.S. Cavalry Museum, which chronicles the history of the mounted horse soldier from the Revolutionary War to 1950.

Continue east on I-70 to Abilene, famous as an Old West cow town and as the boyhood home of President Dwight D. Eisenhower. In addition to the frontier and presidential museums you would expect, Abilene offers a couple of unusual attractions, including dinner excursions on an antique train and the American Indian Art Center, which represents 90 artists from 30 Native American nations.

★★DAYS INN TOPEKA

1510 S.W. Wanamaker Road, Topeka, 785-272-8538, 800-329-7466; www.daysinn.com
62 rooms. Restaurant, bar. Complimentary breakfast. Pool. Business center. Pets accepted. $61-150

★★RAMADA DOWNTOWN TOPEKA

420 S.E. Sixth Ave., Topeka, 785-234-5400, 800-272-6232; www.ramada.com
214 rooms. Restaurant, bar. Complimentary breakfast. Business center. Fitness center. Pool. Pets accepted. $61-150

WHERE TO EAT
★CARLOS O'KELLY'S

3425 S. Kansas Ave., Topeka, 785-266-3457; www.carlosokellys.com
Mexican. Lunch, dinner. Children's menu. Bar. $16-35

★★MCFARLAND'S
4133 S.W. Gage Center Drive, Topeka, 785-272-6909
American. Lunch, dinner. Closed Monday. Children's menu. Bar. $16-35

WICHITA
See also El Dorado, Newton
The largest city in Kansas has a metropolitan flavor, with its tall buildings and wide streets. Still a major marketing point for agricultural products, the city is now best known as an aircraft production center. McConnell Air Force Base is here.

The town's first settlers were the Wichita, who built a village of grass lodges on the site. The following year James R. Mead set up a trading post and in 1865 sent his assistant, Jesse Chisholm, on a trading expedition to the Southwest. His route became famous as the Chisholm Trail, over which longhorn cattle were driven through Wichita to the Union Pacific at Abilene. As the railroad advanced to the southwest, Wichita had its turn as a "cow capital" in the early 1870s. By 1880, farmers drawn by the land boom had run fences across the trail and the cattle drives were shifted west to Dodge City. Wheat production and the discovery of oil after World War I revived the city.

WHAT TO SEE
ALLEN-LAMBE HOUSE MUSEUM AND STUDY CENTER
255 N. Roosevelt St., Wichita, 316-687-1027; www.allenlambe.org
Designed in 1915 by Frank Lloyd Wright as a private residence, this structure is considered the last of Wright's prairie houses. The house features furniture designed by Wright in collaboration with interior designer George M. Niedecken.
Guided tours: by appointment only, minimum of five people.

BOTANICA, THE WICHITA GARDENS
701 Amidon, Wichita, 316-264-0448; www.botanica.org

Displays of exotic flowers and plants native to Kansas fill this botanical garden.
April-December, daily; January-March, Monday-Friday.

CHENEY STATE PARK
16000 N.E. 50 St., Cheney, 316-542-3664
A 1,913-acre park on a 9,537-acre lake, this area is popular with sailboat and windsurfing enthusiasts. Large-scale regattas are a featured part of the many lake activities.

CORBIN EDUCATION CENTER
1845 Fairmount, Wichita
This Prairie-style structure, located on the campus of Wichita State University, was designed by Frank Lloyd Wright.

LAKE AFTON PUBLIC OBSERVATORY
25000 W. 39th St. South, Wichita, 316-978-7827; www.webs.wichita.edu/lapo
Public programs offer the opportunity to view a variety of celestial objects

through a 16-inch reflecting telescope. Programs begin 30 minutes after sunset. September-May, Friday-Saturday; June-August, Friday-Sunday. Closed December 23-January 1.

MID-AMERICA ALL-INDIAN CENTER MUSEUM

650 N. Seneca, Wichita, 316-262-5221; www.theindiancenter.org
This museum features changing exhibits of past and present Native American art.
Tuesday-Saturday 10 a.m.-4 p.m.

OLD COWTOWN MUSEUM

1865 Museum Blvd., Wichita, 316-660-1871; www.oldcowtown.org
This 40-building historic village museum depicts Wichita life in the 1870s. The Diamond W. Chuckwagon Supper features all-you-can-eat barbecue and a performance by the Prairie Wranglers, a country-western band.
April 25-October, Wednesday-Saturday 9:30 a.m.-4:30 p.m., Sunday, noon-4:30 p.m.; November-April 24, Tuesday-Saturday 10 a.m.-4 p.m. Closed Sunday-Monday.

SEDGWICK COUNTY ZOO

5555 Zoo Blvd., Wichita, 316-660-9453; www.scz.org
See animals in their natural habitats at this Wichita zoo. A new Asian tiger exhibit is being constructed and is expected to open in 2009.
Daily.

WICHITA ART MUSEUM

1400 W. Museum Blvd., Wichita, 316-268-4921; www.wichitaartmuseum.org
This museum features traveling exhibits, a collection of American art, paintings and sculpture by Charles M. Russell, pre-Columbian art and works by contemporary and historic Kansas artists.
Tuesday-Sunday.

WICHITA CENTER FOR THE ARTS

9112 E. Central Ave., Wichita, 316-634-2787; www.wcfta.com
With changing and permanent exhibits, this center features a gallery, theater and art school. Tuesday-Sunday.

WICHITA-SEDGWICK COUNTY HISTORICAL MUSEUM

204 S. Main St., Wichita, 316-265-9314; www.wichitahistory.org
Local history, Native American artifacts, period rooms, a costume collection and more on are display at this museum.
Tuesday-Friday 11 a.m.-4 p.m., Saturday-Sunday 1-5 p.m.

SPECIAL EVENT
WICHITA RIVER FESTIVAL

1820 E. Douglas Ave., Wichita, 316-267-2817; www.wichitariverfestival.com
This annual festival includes a twilight pop concert and fireworks, antique bathtub races, a hot air balloon launch, athletic events and entertainment. Mid-May.

WHERE TO STAY
★★HOLIDAY INN WICHITA

549 S. Rock Road, Wichita, 316-686-7131, 888-465-4329; www.holiday-inn.com

250 rooms. Restaurant, bar. Business center. Fitness center. Pool. Pets accepted. $61-150

★★★HYATT REGENCY WICHITA

400 W. Waterman, Wichita, 316-293-1234, 800-633-7313; www.ichita.hyatt.com

Perched on the Arkansas River, this contemporary hotel has updated rooms with duvet-topped beds. The Southwinds Bar and Grill serves red meat of every kind (the grilled spicy cowboy rib-eye steak is a standout) in an upscale setting.

303 rooms. Restaurant, bar. Business center. Fitness center. Pool. $61-150

★★★MARRIOTT WICHITA

9100 E. Corporate Hills Drive, Wichita, 316-651-0333, 800-610-0673;
www.marriott.com

After a complete renovation in 2007, this hotel is now a smoke-free environment with updated guest rooms that feature luxury beds, flat-screen TVs and wireless Internet access. The Black Angus Grille serves steakhouse classics, while Corrigan's Sports Bar is a prime place for catching up on the latest scores and noshing on pub fare.

294 rooms. Restaurant, bar. Business center. Fitness center. Pool. $61-150

WHERE TO EAT
★★★OLIVE TREE

2949 N. Rock Road, Wichita, 316-636-1100; www.olivetree-bistro.com

This family-owned, European-style bistro has an extensive wine list and a menu with both small and large plates of Mediterranean-inspired dishes. Entrées are eclectic and include everything from Thai green curry made with eggplant to fennel pollen roasted chicken.

American. Dinner, late-night, Sunday brunch. $16-35

★★★★★ KANSAS

MISSOURI

in 1803, Missouri, with its strategic waterways and the already-thriving town of St. Louis, became a gateway to the West and remained one throughout the entire westward expansion. Its two largest cities, St. Louis and Kansas City, sit on its eastern and western edges like bookends. St. Louis was the Midwest's first great city, the center of commerce and transportation thanks to its location on two major rivers. Kansas City was once the quintessential cow town and, the Gateway Arch notwithstanding, was the true way station to the West—to cattle trails and to the frontier.

Today, Missouri offers a diverse array of sights. St. Louis and Kansas City have fine dining (and great barbecue), nightlife and music (especially blues and jazz). St. Louis has a world famous zoo and one of the largest city parks in the nation. It has a significant art museum as well as the International Bowling Hall of Fame. St. Louis, home to the Cardinals and a legion of knowledgeable fans, is often hailed as the nation's best baseball town. Kansas City has the world's first planned shopping center (Country Club Plaza), a 60-acre water park, and did we mention barbecue?

For outdoor recreation, Missouri could vie for the title of Land of Awesome Lakes. Its largest one, Lake of the Ozarks, is 92 miles end to end and has 1,150 miles of shoreline. There's also the 55,000-acre Truman Lake, part of the Harry S. Truman State Park, southeast of Kansas City, and Pomme de Terre Lake, 78 acres of water near Springfield.

Then there are the rivers, and we don't just mean the Mississippi and Missouri. Four state parks dot the Meramec River, which runs for nearly 100 miles. Nearly 90 percent of the river is shallow, which makes it a perfect waterway for float trips. Another of Missouri's river gems is the Black, running through Poplar Bluff and north into the Arcadia Valley. It too promises great floating.

Wherever you are in the state, there's something to explore. Around Hannibal by the Mississippi, you can recapture Mark Twain's riverboat days. Along the Missouri River in St. Joseph, the flavor is more Lewis and Clark and pioneers. Southwest is Springfield, a gateway to both the Ozarks and to Branson, that one-of-a-kind capital of cornpone, country and crooning. In the middle is Jefferson City, a prototypical sleepy capital town with a beautiful capitol standing astride the Missouri River.

BRANSON

See also Springfield

The resort town of Branson has become a mecca for fans of country music and old-fashioned acts. Variety shows, comedy acts and performers of all ages hit the stages of the many theaters in town nightly.

WHAT TO SEE
ANDY WILLIAMS MOON RIVER THEATER
2500 W. Highway 76, Branson, 417-334-4500; www.andywilliams.com
This theater is the domain of 1960s singer Andy Williams, who is sometimes joined on stage by guest performers, which in the past have included Charo and Glen Campbell.
April-December.

BALDKNOBBERS JAMBOREE
2835 W. 76 Country Blvd., Branson, 417-334-4528, 800-998-8908;
www.baldknobbers.com
This country music variety show features comedy, music and skits.
March-mid-April, Friday-Saturday; mid-April-mid-December, Monday-Saturday.

BRANSON SCENIC RAILWAY
206 E. Main St., Branson, 417-334-6110, 800-287-2462; www.bransontrain.com
Forty-mile roundtrip through Ozark Foothills.
Mid-March-mid-December, schedule varies.

COLLEGE OF THE OZARKS
100 Opportunity Ave., Point Lookout, 417-334-6411, 800-222-0525; www.cofo.edu
Established in 1906, this is a small liberal arts college of 1,500 where students work, rather than pay, for their education.

DUTTON FAMILY THEATER
3454 W. Highway 76, Branson, 417-332-2772; www.theduttons.com
A musical variety show featuring all seven members of the Dutton family and their spouses playing a variety of instruments.
April-December.

★★★★★ MISSOURI

65

ELVIS AND THE SUPERSTARS SHOW
205 S. Commercial, Branson, 417-336-2112, 800-358-4795; www.elvisinbranson.com
A musical tribute to Elvis Presley, this show features an impersonator belting out tunes by the King from his early days to Vegas years.
Year-round.

GRAND COUNTRY MUSIC HALL
1945 W. Highway 76, Branson, 417-335-2484, 1-888-514-1088;
www.grandcountry.com
Shows at this performance space include everything from Amazing Pets to the Ozarks Mountain Jamboree.

HUGHES BROTHERS CELEBRITY THEATRE
3425 W. Highway 76, Branson, 417-334-0076; www.hughes-brothers.com
The five Utah-born Hughes brothers, along with their wives and children, entertain six days a week in this musical variety show.

WIDE OPEN COUNTRY

The beautiful Ozark hills drew people to southwest Missouri long before Branson became famous for its country music theaters. From Springfield, drive 41 miles south on Highway 65 to Branson. Touring options here include a railroad that travels through the Ozarks to Arkansas, and the Ducks, amphibious vehicles that roll around town and onto Table Rock Lake. Other area attractions beyond the music theaters packing Highway 76 (Country Boulevard) include the Shepherd of the Hills homestead and outdoor theater and Silver Dollar City theme park. Once you've had your fill of Branson, head east out of town on Highway 76, a scenic stretch through part of the Mark Twain National Forest, then take Highway 5 north. Stop at Mansfield to see the Laura Ingalls Wilder farm, where the author wrote the Little House books. Return to Springfield via Highway 60 west.

Approximately 150 miles.

JIMMY OSMOND'S AMERICAN JUKEBOX SHOW

3600 W. Highway 76, Branson, 417-336-6100; www.osmondfamilytheater.com
The youngest Osmond performs hit songs from the '40s to the present. April-December.

JIM STAFFORD THEATRE

3440 W. Highway 76, Branson, 417-335-8080; www.jimstafford.com
Novelty singer Jim Stafford, who had several hits in the '70s, performs at this theater.

PRESLEY'S COUNTRY JUBILEE

2920 W. Highway 76, Branson, 417-334-4874, 800-335-4847; www.presleys.com
Four generations of a family perform country music and more. March-mid-December.

RIPLEY'S BELIEVE IT OR NOT! MUSEUM

3326 W. Highway 76, Branson, 417-337-5300; www.ripleys.com
This outpost of the curiosities museum has hundreds of exhibits in eight galleries.
Daily 9:30 a.m.-11 p.m.

SHEPHERD OF THE HILLS

5586 W. Highway 76, Branson, 417-334-4191; www.oldmatt.com
Jeep-drawn conveyance tours include authentically furnished Old Matt's Cabin, home of the prominent characters in Harold Bell Wright's Ozark novel The Shepherd of the Hills.
Late April-late October, daily.

SHOWBOAT BRANSON BELLE

4800 State Highway 165, Branson, 417-336-7171, 800-475-9370;
Lunch and dinner cruises depart from Highway 165 near Table Rock Dam. April-December, daily.

STONE HILL WINERY

601 Highway 165, Branson, 417-334-1897; www.stonehillwinery.com

Guided tours and bottling demonstrations.
Daily.

TABLE ROCK DAM AND LAKE

4600 Highway 165, Branson, 417-334-4101; www.swl.usace.army.mil/parks/tablerock

This 43,100-acre reservoir, formed by impounding waters of White River, offers swimming, waterskiing, scuba diving; fishing for bass, crappie, and walleye; boating; hunting for deer, turkey, rabbit and waterfowl; picnicking; playgrounds and camping.
Daily.

WHERE TO STAY

★★★BIG CEDAR LODGE

612 Devils Pool Road, Ridgedale, 417-335-2777; www.bigcedarlodge.com

Guests can stay in one of three lodges, a cabin or a cottage. The resort offers boating and swimming on the lake, tennis, golf, horseback riding, a 10,000-acre nature park with hiking trails and more.
224 rooms. Restaurant, bar. Fitness center. Pool. Tennis. $61-150

★★★CHATEAU ON THE LAKE

415 N. Highway 265, Branson, 417-334-1161, 888-333-5253;
www.chateauonthelake.com

Chateau on the Lake has a mountaintop location overlooking Table Rock Lake. The resort is located close to town, and features a spa and salon, as well as an old-fashioned soda fountain.
300 rooms. Restaurant, bar. Business center. Fitness center. Pool. Spa. Tennis. Pets accepted. $151-250

★★THE BRANSON CLARION HOTEL & CONFERENCE CENTER

2820 W. Highway 76, Branson, 417-334-7666, 800-725-2236

166 rooms. Restaurant, bar. Complimentary breakfast. Fitness center. Pool. $61-150

★★★LODGE OF THE OZARKS

3431 W. Highway 76, Branson, 417-334-7535, 877-866-2219;
www.lodgeoftheozarks.com

This hotel offers large rooms and is walking distance from theaters, shopping and other attractions.
190 rooms. Restaurant, bar. Complimentary breakfast. Pool. $61-150

★★RADISSON HOTEL BRANSON

120 S. Wildwood Drive, Branson, 417-335-5767, 800-333-3333; www.radisson.com/bransonmo

472 rooms. Restaurant, bar. Fitness center. Pool. $61-150

★★★THOUSAND HILLS GOLF AND CONFERENCE RESORT
245 S. Wildwood Drive, Branson, 417-336-5873, 877-262-0430;
www.thousandhills.com
This sprawling resort has both cabins and condominiums available for rent alongside the Thousand Hills Golf Course. Most have jacuzzi tubs, fireplaces and fully stocked kitchens. The resort also has a fitness center, indoor and outdoor pools and tennis courts. Fitness center. Golf. $251-350

WHERE TO EAT
★★CANDLESTICK INN
127 Taney St., Branson, 417-334-3633; www.candlestickinn.com
Seafood, steak. Lunch, dinner. Children's menu. Bar. $36-85

★MR G'S CHICAGO-STYLE PIZZA
202 1/2 N. Commercial, Marvel Cave Park, 417-335-8156
Italian. Lunch, dinner. Bar. $16-35

CAPE GIRARDEAU
See also Sikeston, Ste. Genevieve
On early maps, a rocky promontory on the Mississippi River, 125 miles below St. Louis, was labeled Cape Girardot (or Girardeau), named for a French ensign believed to have settled there about 1720. In 1792, an agent for the Spanish government, Louis Lorimier, set up a trading post at the site of the present city and encouraged -settlement.

Cape Girardeau's location assured flourishing river traffic before the Civil War. The war, however, ended river trade and the earliest railroads bypassed the town, triggering further decline. In the late 1880s, the arrival of new railroads and the 1928 completion of a bridge across the Mississippi contributed to the city's growth. Southeast Missouri State University, which has a mural in its library depicting the history of the area, is located in the town.

WHAT TO SEE
BOLLINGER MILL STATE HISTORIC SITE
113 Bollinger Mill Road, Cape Girardeau, 573-243-4591; www.mostateparks.com
This day-use park features a historic 19th-century gristmill and the oldest covered bridge in the state. Guided tours are available.
Daily.

CAPE RIVER HERITAGE MUSEUM
538 Independence, Cape Girardeau, 573-334-0405
Exhibits on Cape Girardeau's early heritage, 19th-century industry, education and culture.
March-December, Friday-Saturday; also by appointment.

COURT OF COMMON PLEAS BUILDING
Spanish and Themis streets, Cape Girardeau
The central portion of this building was built around 1854 to replace previous log structure. During the Civil War, cells in the basement housed prisoners. There is an outstanding view of the Mississippi River from the park.

GLENN HOUSE

325 S. Spanish St., Cape Girardeau, 573-334-1177; www.glennhouse.org

A Victorian house with period furnishings, memorabilia of the Mississippi River and the steamboat era is displayed here.

April-December, Friday-Sunday.

OLD ST. VINCENT'S CHURCH

131 S. Main St., Cape Girardeau, 573-335-1631; www.oldstvincents.com

English Gothic Revival church showing Roman influences. More than 100 medieval-design plaster masks. Hand-carved doors.

Tours by appointment.

ST. LOUIS IRON MOUNTAIN AND SOUTHERN RAILWAY

Intersection of Highways 61 and 25, Jackson, 573-243-1688, 800-455-7245;
www.slimrr.com

A 1946 steam locomotive pulls vintage 1920s cars through scenic woodlands. Trips range from 80 minutes to five hours.

April-October, Saturday-Sunday.

TRAIL OF TEARS STATE PARK

429 Moccasin Spring, Cape Girardeau, 573-334-1711; www.mostateparks.com

A more than 3,000-acre park on limestone bluffs overlooking the Mississippi River, this park commemorates the forced migration of the Cherokee Nation over the Trail of Tears to Oklahoma.

Daily.

WHERE TO STAY
★★DRURY INN

104 S. Vantage Drive, Cape Girardeau, 573-334-7151, 800-378-7946;
www.druryhotels.com

139 rooms. Restaurant, bar. Complimentary breakfast. Fitness center. Pool. Pets accepted. $61-150

★★HOLIDAY INN

3253 William St., Cape Girardeau, 573-334-4491, 888-465-4329; www.holidayinn.com

102 rooms. Restaurant, bar. Fitness center. Pool. $61-150

WHERE TO EAT
★BG'S OLDE TYME DELI & SALOON

205 S. Plaza Way, Cape Girardeau, 573-335-8860

American. Lunch, dinner. Children's menu. Bar. $15 and under

★BROUSSARD'S CAJUN CUISINE

120 N. Main St., Cape Girardeau, 573-334-7235; www.broussardscajuncuisine.com

Cajun, Creole. Lunch, dinner. Bar. $16-35

CHESTERFIELD

This is suburb was under water during the Great Flood of 1993 due to parts being located in the Chesterfield Valley. It is the largest city west of St. Louis.

WHERE TO EAT
★★ANNIE GUNN'S
16806 Chesterfield Airport Road, Chesterfield, 636-532-7684;
www.smokehousemarket.com
American. Lunch, dinner, late-night. Outdoor seating. Bar. $36-85

★★PAUL MANNO'S
75 Forum Center, Chesterfield, 314-878-1274
Italian. Dinner. Closed Sunday; also late June-early July. Reservations recommended. Bar. $16-35

CHILLICOTHE

Chillicothe, seat of Livingston County, is a Shawnee word meaning "our big town." It was named for Chillicothe, Ohio. Sloan's Liniment was developed here about 1870 by Earl Sloan. An Amish community located approximately 25 miles northwest of town, near Jamesport, has many interesting shops.

WHAT TO SEE
GENERAL JOHN J. PERSHING BOYHOOD HOME STATE HISTORIC SITE
1000 Pershing Drive, Laclede, 660-963-2525; www.mostateparks.com/pershingsite.htm
This 11-room house, built in 1858, was the childhood home of the World War I hero. Also here is a statue of "Black Jack" Pershing, a Wall of Honor and the relocated Prairie Mound School, the one-room schoolhouse where Pershing taught before entering West Point.
Daily.

PERSHING STATE PARK
29277 Highway 130, Chillicothe, 660-963-2299; www.stateparks.com
This 3,527-acre memorial to General John J. Pershing offers fishing, canoeing, hiking trails, picnicking, camping. North of the park is the Locust Creek covered bridge, the longest of four remaining covered bridges in the state.
Daily.

WHERE TO STAY
★★GRAND RIVER INN
606 W. Business 36, Chillicothe, 660-646-6590, 888-317-8290; www.grandriverinn.com
60 rooms. Restaurant, bar. Complimentary breakfast. Fitness center. Pool. Pets accepted. $61-150

COLUMBIA
See also Hermann, Jefferson City

An educational center from its earliest years, Columbia is the home of Columbia College, Stephens College and the University of Missouri, the oldest state university west of the Mississippi. Established as Smithton, the town was moved a short distance to ensure a better water supply and renamed Columbia. In 1822, the Boone's Lick Trail was rerouted to pass through the town. Classes began at the University of Missouri in 1841, and the town has revolved around the institution ever since. The School of Journalism, founded in 1908, was the first degree-granting journalism school in the world.

WHAT TO SEE
EDISON ELECTRIC DYNAMO
Lobby of University of Missouri Engineering Building, E. Sixth Street and Stewart Road, Columbia
The recently restored dynamo, given to the university in 1882 by its inventor, Thomas Alva Edison, was used on campus in 1883 for the first demonstration of incandescent lighting west of the Mississippi.
Monday-Friday.

ELLIS LIBRARY
Lowry Mall between Memorial Union and Jesse Hall, Ninth Street and Conley Avenue, Columbia, 573-882-4391; www.mulibraries.missouri.edu/containing
One of the largest libraries in the Midwest, it features a rare-book room containing a page from a Gutenberg Bible. The State Historical Society of Missouri, located on the east ground wing, has early newspapers and works by Missouri artists.

MUSEUM OF ANTHROPOLOGY
100 Swallow Hall, Columbia, 573-882-3764; www.anthromuseum.missouri.edu
Artifacts from 9000 B.C. to the present.
Monday-Friday.

MUSEUM OF ART AND ARCHAEOLOGY
1 Pickard Hall, Columbia, 573-882-3591

Comprehensive collection including more than 13,000 objects from around the world; from the Paleolithic period to the present. Cast gallery has items made from original Greek and Roman sculptures.
Tuesday-Sunday.

NIFONG PARK
3700 Ponderosa St., Columbia, 573-443-8936; www.gocolumbiamo.com
The park includes a visitor center, restored 1877 Maplewood house (April-October, Sunday, limited hours), Maplewood Barn Theater (summer), Boone County Historical Society Museum, petting zoo, lake and picnicking.
Daily.

SHELTER GARDENS
1817 W. Broadway, Columbia, 573-445-8441
Miniature mid-American environment with a pool and stream, domestic and wild flowers, more than 300 varieties of trees and shrubs, rose garden. There are concerts here in the summertime.
Daily, weather permitting.

STEPHENS COLLEGE
1200 E. Broadway, Columbia, 573-442-2211; www.stephens.edu
On this 240-acre campus is the Firestone Baars Chapel on Walnut Street, designed in 1956 by Eero Saarinen.
Monday-Friday.

UNIVERSITY OF MISSOURI-COLUMBIA
311 Jesse Hall, Columbia, 573-882-6333; www.missouri.edu
This 1,334-acre campus with more than 22,000 students contains numerous collections, exhibits, galleries and attractions.

WHERE TO STAY
★★HOLIDAY INN
2200 I-70 Drive S.E., Columbia, 573-445-8531, 800-465-4329; www.holiday-inn.com
311 rooms. Restaurant, bar. Fitness center. Pool. Pets accepted. $61-150

★★QUALITY INN
1612 N. Providence Road, Columbia, 573-449-2491, 800-228-5751;
www.qualityinn.com
142 rooms. Restaurant, bar. Fitness center. Pool. Pets accepted. $61-150

WHERE TO EAT
★★BOONE TAVERN
811 E. Walnut St., Columbia, 573-442-5123; www.boonetavern.com
American. Lunch, dinner. Outdoor seating. Children's menu. Bar. $16-35

★FLAT BRANCH PUB & BREWING
115 S. Fifth St., Columbia, 573-499-0400; www.flatbranch.com
American. Lunch, dinner. Outdoor seating. Children's menu. Bar. $16-35

EXCELSIOR SPRINGS
See also Independence, Kansas City
Excelsior Springs was established in 1880 when two settlers, Anthony W. Wyman and J. V. D. Flack, discovered various natural springs on Wyman's property. Today the city is a health resort offering visitors bottled water from the springs and medicinal baths in the city-operated bathhouse.

WHAT TO SEE
EXCELSIOR SPRINGS HISTORICAL MUSEUM
101 E. Broadway, Excelsior Springs, 816-630-0101
This museum includes murals, a bank, antiques, antique bedroom, doctor's office, dental equipment.
Tuesday-Saturday.

JESSE JAMES'S FARM
Jesse James Farm Road, Excelsior Springs, 816-736-8500
On this farm, you can see the house where outlaw Jesse James was born and raised with his brother Frank.
Daily.

WATKINS WOOLEN MILL STATE PARK AND STATE HISTORIC SITE

26600 Park Road N. Lawson, 816-580-3387; www.mostateparks.com

This woolen factory and gristmill, built and equipped in 1860, still contains original machinery along with the original owner's house, summer kitchen, ice house, smokehouse and school.

Daily.

WHERE TO STAY
★★★THE INN ON CRESCENT LAKE

1261 St. Louis Ave., Excelsior Springs, 816-630-6745, 866-630-5253;
www.crescentinn.com

This inn was built in 1915 on 22 acres of landscaped yard, surrounded by two crescent-shaped ponds. The rooms are individually decorated and have private baths.

10 rooms. Restaurant. Complimentary breakfast. Fitness center. Pool. No children under 12. $61-150

GEORGE WASHINGTON CARVER NATIONAL MONUMENT

Born a slave on the farm of Moses Carver, George Washington Carver (1864-1943) rose to become an eminent teacher, humanitarian, botanist, agronomist and pioneer conservationist. Carver was the first African American to graduate from Iowa State University. He received both a Bachelor's and a Master's degree in science. He then headed the Department of Agriculture at Booker T. Washington's Tuskegee Institute in Alabama.

Authorized as a national monument in 1943, this memorial to Carver honors a vital part of the American historical heritage. The visitor center contains a museum and audio/visual presentation depicting Carver's life and work. A self-guided trail passes the birthplace site, the statue of Carver by Robert Amendola, the restored 1881 Moses Carver house, the family cemetery and the woods and streams where Carver spent his boyhood. Daily.

★★★★★ **MISSOURI**

HANNIBAL

Hannibal is world-famous as the hometown of the great novelist Samuel Clemens (Mark Twain) as well as the setting of *The Adventures of Tom Sawyer*, which records many actual events of Clemens' boyhood. He served his printer's apprenticeship here and gained a fascination with steamboats in the days when the river was the source of the town's prosperity.

WHAT TO SEE
BECKY THATCHER HOUSE

209-211 Hill St., Hannibal

House where Laura Hawkins (Becky Thatcher) lived during Samuel Clemens' boyhood; upstairs rooms have authentic furnishings.

Daily.

JOHN M. CLEMENS JUSTICE OF THE PEACE OFFICE

205 Hill St., Hannibal

Restored courtroom where Twain's father presided as justice of the peace.

MARK TWAIN CAVE

7097 Country Road 453, Hannibal, 573-221-1656; www.marktwaincave.com

This is the cave in *The Adventures of Tom Sawyer* in which Tom and Becky Thatcher were lost and where Injun Joe died.

Tours: daily.

MARK TWAIN MUSEUM AND BOYHOOD HOME

208 Hill St., Hannibal, 573-221-9010

Museum houses Mark Twain memorabilia, including books, letters, photographs and family items.

Daily.

MARK TWAIN RIVERBOAT EXCURSIONS

Center St., Hannibal, 573-221-3222, 800-621-2322; www.marktwainriverboat.com

One-hour cruises on the Mississippi River; also two-hour dinner cruises.

Early May-October, daily.

MOLLY BROWN BIRTHPLACE AND MUSEUM

600 Butler St., Hannibal, 573-221-2100; www.visitmollybrown.com

Antique-filled home has memorabilia of the "unsinkable" Molly Brown, who survived the *Titanic* disaster.

Monday 10 a.m.-3 p.m., Thursday-Saturday 10 a.m.-4 p.m., Sunday 11 a.m.-4 p.m. Closed Tuesday and Wednesday.

PILASTER HOUSE AND GRANT'S DRUGSTORE

Hill and Main streets, Hannibal

The Clemens family lived in this Greek Revival house, which contains a restored old-time drugstore, pioneer kitchen, doctor's office and quarters where John Clemens, Twain's father, died.

ROCKCLIFFE MANSION

Hill Street, Hannibal, 573-221-4140; www.rockcliffemansion.com

Restored Beaux Arts mansion overlooking the river; 30 rooms, many original furnishings. Samuel Clemens addressed a gathering here in 1902.

Guided tours: daily.

WHERE TO STAY

★★★GARTH WOODSIDE MANSION BED AND BREAKFAST

11069 New London Road, Hannibal, 573-221-2789, 888-427-8409;
www.garthmansion.com

With eight guest rooms, each with its own private bath, this Second Empire/Victorian mansion where Mark Twain was often a guest is located on 33 acres of grass, woodland, gardens and ponds.

8 rooms. Complimentary breakfast. $61-150

★HOTEL CLEMENS

401 N. Third St., Hannibal, 573-248-1150; www.hotelclemens.us

78 rooms. Complimentary breakfast. Pool. $61-150

MARK TWAIN'S HANNIBAL

Start a tour of Hannibal, an old Mississippi riverboat town and hometown to Samuel Longhorn Clemens—better known as Mark Twain—at the Hannibal Convention and Visitors Bureau (505 N. Third St.). Towering above the visitor center is the Mark Twain Lighthouse, located at the crest of Cardiff Hill. This is the largest inland lighthouse in the United States, offering great views of Hannibal and the Mississippi from the top.

A block south of the Visitors Bureau is the Mark Twain Boyhood Home and Museum (208 Hill St.), which features the original 1843 Clemens home, restored to look as it did when Twain lived here in the 1840s. Next door (211 Hill St.) is the period home of Laura Hawkins, Mark Twain's childhood sweetheart and the inspiration for the character Becky Thatcher in Twain's novels. On the corner of Hill and Main streets is the Clemens Law office, where Twain's father, J. M. Clemens, presided as Hannibal's justice of the peace. Attached to the building is a historic courtroom, which served as the model for scenes from *The Adventures of Tom Sawyer*. At the base of Cardiff Hill at Main Street is the Tom and Huck Statue, which commemorates Twains most famous characters, Huck Finn and Tom Sawyer. Frederick Hibbard sculpted this bronze statue in 1926.

Stretching along Main Street are a number of historic buildings and shops. Follow Main Street south, passing boutiques in historic storefronts. A worthy stop is Mrs. Clemens' Antique Mall (305 N. Main), which features two floors of antiques and an ice cream parlor. At Bird and Main streets stands the handsome Pilaster House/ Grant's Drug Store, dating from the 1830s. The Clemens family lived here briefly in the 1940s, and Judge Clemens died here in 1847. Today, the building is preserved as an 1890s apothecary.

At Main and Center streets is the Mark Twain Museum, a restored structure that contains a collection of original Norman Rockwell paintings used for illustrated editions of *Adventures of Huckleberry Finn*. The museum also serves as a memento of Hannibal's riverboat past.

WHERE TO EAT
★LOGUE'S
121 Huckleberry Heights Drive, Hannibal, 573-248-1854

American. Breakfast, lunch, dinner. Children's menu. $15 and under

HERMANN
See also Columbia

German immigrants, unhappy with the English atmosphere of Philadelphia, bought this land and founded the town with the purpose of maintaining their German culture. Grape cultivation and winemaking started early and thrived until Prohibition. Today, the town has several working wineries and plenty of German-influenced buildings, restaurants and shops.

WHAT TO SEE
DEUTSCHHEIM STATE HISTORIC SITE
109 W. Second St., Hermann, 573-486-2200; www.mostateparks.com

This site includes the authentically furnished Pommer-Gentner House on Market Street and Strehly House and Winery (circa 1840-1867) on West Second Street.

Tours: daily.

GRAHAM CAVE STATE PARK
217 Highway TT, Montgomery, 573-564-3476; www.mostateparks.com
Native Americans occupied this cave approximately 10,000 years ago. About
350 acres with fishing, nature trails, playground, camping.
Daily.

HERMANNHOF WINERY
330 E. First St., Hermann, 573-486-5959
This 150-year-old winery includes 10 wine cellars. Stop in for a tasting.
Daily.

HISTORIC HERMANN MUSEUM
312 Schiller St., Hermann, 573-486-2017; www.historichermann.com
This Heritage Museum is lcoated in an 1871 building, with artifacts of early
settlers. The River Room depicts the history of early river men; the children's
museum has toys and furniture from the 1890s; a handmade German bedroom set; and an 1886 pump organ. A mechanism of the town clock may be
seen here as well.
April-October, Tuesday-Sunday.

SPECIAL EVENT
GREAT STONE HILL GRAPE STOMP
Stone Hill Winery and Restaurant, 1110 Stone Hill Highway, Hermann, 800-909-9463;
www.stonehillwinery.com
Jump into in a barrel full of juicy grapes to celebrate the beginning of grape
harvest.
Second Saturday in August.

WHERE TO STAY
★HERMANN MOTEL
112 E. 10th St., Hermann, 573-486-3131; www.hermannmotel.com
24 rooms. $61-150

WHERE TO EAT
★★VINTAGE
1110 Stone Hill Highway, Hermann, 573-486-3479, 800-909-9463;
www.stonehillwinery.com
American, German. Lunch, dinner. Closed mid-December-mid-February.
Reservations recommended. Children's menu. $16-35

INDEPENDENCE
See also Excelsior Springs, Kansas City, Lexington
Independence was an outfitting point for westbound wagon trains from 1830-
1850. The scene of much of the Mormon Wars in the early 1830s, it was
ravaged by raiders and occupied by Union and Confederate troops during
the Civil War. Today, it's best known as the hometown of President Harry S.
Truman.

WHAT TO SEE
1859 MARSHAL'S HOME AND JAIL MUSEUM
217 N. Main St., Independence, 816-252-1892; www.jchs.org
Restored building contains dungeon-like cells, marshal's living quarters, regional history museum. One-room schoolhouse.
April-October, daily; November-December, March, Tuesday-Sunday.

BINGHAM-WAGGONER ESTATE
313 W. Pacific, Independence, 816-461-3491; www.bwestate.org
Famous Missouri artist George Caleb Bingham lived here from 1864-1870; also the homestead of the Waggoner family, millers of "Queen of the Pantry" flour.
April-October, daily.

FORT OSAGE
105 Osage, Sibley, 816-795-8200
Restoration of one of the first U.S. outposts in the Louisiana Territory following the purchase from France. Built in 1808 by William Clark of the Lewis and Clark expedition, the fort includes officers' quarters, soldiers' barracks, trading post, factor's house, museum; costumed guides.
Mid-April-mid-November, Wednesday-Sunday; mid-November-mid-April, Saturday-Sunday.

HARRY S. TRUMAN COURTROOM AND OFFICE MUSEUM
Jackson County Courthouse, 112 W. Lexington, Independence, 816-795-8200
Restored office and courtroom where Truman began his political career as presiding county judge. Tours.
Sunday-Thursday, by appointment.

NATIONAL FRONTIER TRAILS CENTER
318 W. Pacific, Independence, 816-325-7575; www.ci.independence.mo.us
Partially restored flour mill at the site of the Santa Fe, California and Oregon trails serves as a museum, interpretive center, library and archive of westward pioneer expansion.
Daily.

TRUMAN FARM HOME
12301 Blue Ridge Blvd., Grandview, 816-254-2720
Harry Truman lived in this two-story, white frame house in the decade preceding World War I. During these years—"the best years," according to Truman, he farmed the surrounding 600 acres, worked as a mason and postmaster, served as a soldier and courted Bess Wallace. Interior features period furnishings, including original family pieces.
Mid-May-late August, Friday-Sunday.

TRUMAN PRESIDENTIAL MUSEUM AND LIBRARY
500 W. Highway 24, Independence, 816-268-8200; www.trumanlibrary.org
Includes presidential papers, mementos of public life and a reproduction of President Truman's White House office. Graves of President and Mrs. Truman in courtyard.
Museum: daily. Library: Monday-Friday.

WHERE TO STAY
★COMFORT INN EAST
4200 S. Noland Road, Independence, 816-373-8856; www.choicehotels.com
170 rooms. Complimentary breakfast. Pool. Pets accepted. $61-150

WHERE TO EAT
★★RHEINLAND
208 N. Main St., Independence, 816-461-5383
German. Breakfast, lunch, dinner, brunch. Children's menu. $16-35

★★SALVATORE'S
12801 Highway 40 E. Independence, 816-737-2400; www.salvatores.us
Italian. Lunch, dinner. Outdoor seating. Children's menu. Bar. $16-35

★★★V'S ITALIANO
10819 Highway 40 E., Independence, 816-353-1241; www.vsrestaurant.com
This family-style Italian restaurant serves up heaping portions of classic dishes like veal parmigiana and osso bucco. Entrées come with fresh slices of Italian rum cake.
American, Italian. Lunch, dinner, Sunday brunch. Children's menu. Bar. $16-35

JEFFERSON CITY
See also Columbia, Sedalia
Jefferson City was chosen for the state capital in 1826. Near a river landing, it consisted of a foundry, a shop and a mission. Government business drives this small historic town. Named for Thomas Jefferson, it is known locally as "Jeff City."

WHAT TO SEE
COLE COUNTY HISTORICAL SOCIETY MUSEUM
109 Madison St., Jefferson City, 573-635-1850; www.colecohistsoc.org
One of three four-story row houses built in the Federal style, this museum features Victorian furnishings and household items, plus inaugural gowns from Missouri's first ladies dating from 1877.
Tuesday-Saturday.

GOVERNOR'S MANSION
100 Madison St., Jefferson City, 573-751-7929; www.missourimansion.org
This Renaissance Revival house was designed by George Ingham Barnett and features period furnishings, stenciled ceilings, period wall coverings and late 19th-century chandeliers.
Tours Tuesday and Thursday. Closed August and December.

JEFFERSON LANDING STATE HISTORIC SITE
Jefferson and Water streets, Jefferson City, 573-751-3475
Restored mid-1800s riverboat landing. Lohman Building features exhibits and audiovisual presentation on the history of Jefferson City and the Missouri Capitol. Union Hotel contains a gallery of exhibits by local artisans.
Tuesday-Saturday.

STATE CAPITOL

High Street and Broadway, Jefferson City, 573-751-4127

On a bluff overlooking the Missouri River, this building of Carthage stone is the third state capitol in Jefferson City; both predecessors burned. A Thomas Hart Benton mural is in the House Lounge, on the third floor west wing. Also here are paintings by N. C. Wyeth and Frank Brangwyn. Daily.

WHERE TO STAY

★★★CAPITOL PLAZA HOTEL

451 W. McCarty St., Jefferson City, 573-635-1234, 800-338-8088;
www.capitolplazajeffersoncity.com

This full-service hotel offers renovated guest rooms, a pool, whirlpool and cascading waterfall in the atrium, a restaurant, café and lounge and more. It is located across from the Truman building and near attractions.

200 rooms. Restaurant, bar. Fitness center. Pool. Pets accepted. $61-150

★★HOTEL DEVILLE

319 W. Miller St., Jefferson City, 573-636-5231, 800-392-3366; www.devillehotel.com

97 rooms. Restaurant, bar. Pool. $61-150

WHERE TO EAT

★★MADISON'S CAFÉ

216 Madison St., Jefferson City, 573-634-2988; www.madisonscafe.com

Italian. Lunch, dinner. Children's menu. $16-35

JOPLIN

See also George Washington Carver National Monument

The discovery of lead here convinced an early settler to establish a town. As the mining boom continued, another community, Murphysburg, grew up on the west side of Joplin Creek. The two towns were rivals until 1873 when both agreed to merge. Today Joplin, one of Missouri's larger cities, is home to many manufacturing industries.

WHAT TO SEE

DOROTHEA B. HOOVER HISTORICAL MUSEUM

W. Seventh Street and Schifferdecker Avenue, Joplin, 417-623-1180;
www.joplinmuseum.org

This museum features period rooms with late 19th-century furnishing; miniatures, including a circus, photographs, musical instruments, Victorian doll house and playhouse; antique toys; dolls; and Native American artifacts.

THOMAS HART BENTON EXHIBIT

303 E. Third St., Joplin

Includes the mural, Joplin at the Turn of the Century, 1896-1906, as well as photographs, clay models, personal letters and other paintings by Benton. Monday-Friday.

WHERE TO STAY
★DRURY INN

3601 S. Range Line Road, Joplin, 417-781-8000, 800-378-7946; www.druryhotels.com
109 rooms. Complimentary breakfast. Fitness center. Pool. Pets accepted.
$61-150

★★HOLIDAY INN

3615 Range Line Road, Joplin, 417-782-1000, 800-465-4329; www.holiday-inn.com
262 rooms. Restaurant, bar. Fitness center. Pool. Pets accepted. $61-150

WHERE TO EAT
★KITCHEN PASS

1212 S. Main St., Joplin, 417-624-9095; www.kitchenpass.net
Seafood, steak. Lunch, dinner. Closed Sunday. Children's menu. Bar. $16-35

★WILDER'S STEAKHOUSE

1216 Main St., Joplin, 417-623-7230
Seafood, steak. Dinner. Sunday closed. Bar. $36-85

KANSAS CITY

See also Excelsior Springs, Independence, Lexington, St. Joseph

Kansas City was developed as a steamboat landing for the town of Westport, four miles south on the Santa Fe Trail, and a competitor with Independence as the trail's eastern terminus and outfitting point. The buildings that sprang up along this landing eclipsed Westport, which was eventually incorporated into the new city. Kansas City's roaring overland trade was disturbed by the border warfare of the 1850s and the Civil War, but peace and the railroads brought new prosperity. A network of railway lines following the natural water-level routes that converge at the mouth of the Kansas River made Kansas City a great terminus.

Famous for their "booster" spirit, its citizens were aroused to the need for civic improvement in the 1890s by the crusade of William Rockhill Nelson, the Kansas City Star publisher. As a result, today's Kansas City boasts 52 boulevards totaling 155 miles and more fountains than any city except Rome. It's also known around the world for its superb barbecue and its rhythm and blues scene.

WHAT TO SEE
ARABIA STEAMBOAT MUSEUM

400 Grand Blvd., Kansas City, 816-471-4030; www.1856.com
Excavated pioneer artifacts from the steamboat *Arabia*, which went down in 1856. The boat, discovered in 1988, carried 200 tons of cargo. Replica of main deck; hands-on displays.
Daily.

ART AND DESIGN CENTER

4510 State Line Road, Kansas City
More than 20 shops and galleries are located in this historic area.

CITY MARKET

Main to Grand streets, Third-Fifth streets, Kansas City
Outdoor farmers market since early 1800s.
April-September, daily. Indoor farmers market: daily.

COUNTRY CLUB PLAZA

4745 Central St., Kansas City, 816-753-0100
The nation's first planned shopping center (built in 1922) consists of 55 acres encompassing more than 180 shops and 25 restaurants in and around Spanish/Moorish-style arcaded buildings. The plaza features tree-lined walks, statues, fountains and murals; recreations of Spain's Seville light and Giralda tower; horse-drawn carriage rides; free entertainment.
Daily.

CROWN CENTER

2450 Grand, Kansas City, 816-274-8444; www.crowncenter.com
This entertainment complex offers shopping, theaters, restaurants and hotels around a landscaped central square; exhibits and ice skating (mid-November-March).
Shops: daily.

JESSE JAMES BANK MUSEUM

103 N. Water St., Liberty, 816-781-4458
Restored site of the first daylight bank robbery by the James gang in 1866. You can view Jesse James memorabilia; a hand-scribed bank ledger, books and other relics of early banking.
Monday-Saturday.

JOHN WORNALL HOUSE MUSEUM

6115 Wornall Road, Kansas City, 816-444-1858; www.wornallhouse.org
This restored farmhouse interprets the lives of prosperous Missouri farm families from 1830-1865 and includes a herb garden.
Tuesday-Sunday. Closed January.

KALEIDOSCOPE

2450 Grand Blvd., Kansas City, 816-274-8300; www.hallmarkkaleidoscope.com
Kaleidoscope is a participatory creative art exhibit for children ages 5-12. A Discovery Room features a hands-on creative area.
Mid-June-August, Monday-Saturday; September-mid-June, Saturday or by appointment.

KANSAS CITY CHIEFS (NFL)

Arrowhead Stadium, 1 Arrowhead Drive, Kansas City, 816-920-9300, z800-676-5488; www.kcchiefs.com
Professional football team.

KANSAS CITY MUSEUM

Union Station, 3218 Gladstone Blvd., Kansas City, 816-483-8300; www.kcmuseum.com
Science, history and technology exhibits are housed in the former estate of

lumber millionaire Robert A. Long. There is a re-creation of 1821 trading post with an 1860 storefront and functioning 1910 drugstore; a planetarium; and gift shop.
Tuesday-Sunday.

KANSAS CITY ROYALS (MLB)

Kauffman Stadium, 1 Royal Way, Kansas City, 816-921-8000; www.kcroyals.com
Professional baseball team.

KANSAS CITY WIZARDS (MLS)

Arrowhead Stadium, 1 Arrowhead Drive, Kansas City, 816-920-9300;
www.kcwizards.com
Professional soccer team.

KANSAS CITY ZOO

Swope Park, 6800 Zoo Drive, Kansas City, 816-513-5700; www.kansascityzoo.org
Explore 200 acres landscaped to resemble natural animal habitats. There are sea lion and wild bird shows; an IMAX theater; and miniature train, pony and camel rides.
Daily.

NELSON-ATKINS MUSEUM OF ART

4525 Oak St., Kansas City, 816-751-1278; www.nelson-atkins.org
Collections range from Sumerian art of 3000 BC to contemporary paintings and sculpture; period rooms; decorative arts; Kansas City Sculpture Park featuring Henry Moore sculpture garden.
Tuesday-Sunday.

UNION CEMETERY

227 E. 28th St., Kansas City
Some notables are buried here including artist George Caleb Bingham and Alexander Majors, the founder of the Pony Express. There are also graves of more than 1,000 Civil War soldiers.

WESTPORT

Broadway and Westport Road, Kansas City
Renovated 1830s historic district includes specialty shops, galleries and restaurants; Pioneer Park traces Westport's role in the founding of Kansas City.
Daily.

WORLDS OF FUN

4545 N.E. Worlds of Fun Ave., Kansas City, 816-454-4545; www.worldsoffun.com
A 170-acre entertainment complex with amusement rides, live entertainment, children's area, special events, restaurants; includes looping steel and wooden roller coasters.
Late May-August, daily; April and September-October, Saturday-Sunday.

SPECIAL EVENTS
KANSAS CITY PRO RODEO
Benjamin Ranch, 6401 E. 87th St., Kansas City, 816-761-1234

Saddle bronco riding, steer wrestling, bareback riding, barrel racing, calf roping and bull riding are some of the events held at the Benjamin Ranch. Fourth of July week.

KANSAS CITY SYMPHONY
1020 Central St., Kansas City, 816-471-0400; www.kcsymphony.org

Concert series of symphonic and pop music.
Friday-Sunday, some Wednesdays.

LYRIC OPERA
1029 Central St., Kansas City, 816-471-4933

This Lyric opera shows productions in English.
April-May and mid-September-mid-October, Monday, Wednesday, Friday-Saturday; holiday production in December.

MISSOURI REPERTORY THEATRE
Center for the Performing Arts, 4949 Cherry St., Kansas City, 816-235-2700; www.kcrep.org

This professional equity theater company presents classic and contemporary productions along with an annual performance of *A Christmas Carol.*
September-May, Tuesday-Sunday.

STARLIGHT THEATER
Swope Park, 4600 Starlight Road, Kansas City, 816-363-7827

This outdoor amphitheater features Broadway musicals and concerts.
Early June-August.

ST. PATRICK'S DAY PARADE
Pershing and Grand streets, Kansas City, 816-931-7373, 816-373-5405; www.kcirishparade.com

One of the nation's largest, this St. Patrick's Day parade is approximately one mile long and features a variety of themed floats, bands and performers. March.

WHERE TO STAY
★★CROWN PLAZA HOTEL
1301 Wyandotte St., Kansas City, 816-474-6664, 800-222-8733; www.crownplaza.com

388 rooms. Restaurant, bar. Business center. Fitness center. Pool. Pets accepted. $151-250

★★★HOTEL PHILLIPS
106 W. 12th St., Kansas City, 816-221-7000, 800-433-1426; www.hotelphillips.com

Located downtown, this boutique hotel is a convenient base. While the historic Art Deco integrity of this 1931 landmark has been preserved, modern amenities have been added to the rooms and suites. Phillips Chophouse has a 1930s feel. Live music can be heard at 12 Baltimore Café and Bar.
217 rooms. Restaurant, bar. Business center. Fitness center. $151-250

★★★HOTEL SAVOY

219 W. Ninth St., Kansas City, 816-842-3575, 800-728-6922; www.savoyhotel.com

This restored 1888 landmark building features original architectural details such as stained and leaded glass, tile floors and tin ceilings. The Savoy Grille is located on the property, and many attractions are nearby.

22 rooms. Restaurant, bar. Complimentary breakfast. $61-150

★★★HYATT REGENCY CROWN CENTER

2345 McGee St., Kansas City, 816-421-1234, 888-591-1234;
www.crowncenter.hyatt.com

Connected to the Crown Center by an elevated walkway and located near the Truman Sports Complex, an amusement park and the international airport, this hotel is convenient and comfortable.

733 rooms. Restaurant, bar. Business center. Fitness center. Pool. Tennis. $151-250

★★★★INTERCONTINENTAL KANSAS CITY AT THE PLAZA

401 Ward Parkway, Kansas City, 816-756-1500, 888-424-6835; www.ichotelsgroup.com

This elegant and contemporary hotel is located within the Plaza shopping and dining area. It has a 24-hour business center and a fitness center with outdoor pool and spa treatments. The Oak Room restaurant serves steaks and chops.

366 rooms. Restaurant, bar. Business center. Fitness center. Pool. Pets accepted. $151-250

★★★MARRIOTT KANSAS CITY AIRPORT

775 Brasilia Ave., Kansas City, 816-464-2200, 800-810-2771; www.marriott.com

Located on the Kansas City International Airport's grounds, this hotel has been updated with luxury bedding and High-speed Internet access.

378 rooms. Restaurant, bar. Business center. Fitness center. Pool. $151-250

★★★KANSAS CITY MARRIOT COUNTRY CLUB PLAZA

4445 Main St., Kansas City, 816-531-3000, 800-228-9290; www.marriott.com/mcipl

Situated 10 minutes from downtown, this hotel is within walking distance of the city's top shopping and restaurants. A non-smoking hotel, this location has updated rooms with luxury bedding.

295 rooms. Restaurant, bar. Business center. Fitness center. Pool. $61-150

★★★MARRIOTT KANSAS CITY DOWNTOWN

200 W. 12th St., Kansas City, 816-421-6800, 800-228-9290; www.marriott.com

This large hotel is located downtown near the city market, casinos and family attractions.

983 rooms. Restaurant, bar. Business center. Fitness center. Pool. Pets accepted. $151-250

★★★THE RAPHAEL HOTEL

325 Ward Parkway, Kansas City, 816-756-3800, 800-821-5343; www.raphaelkc.com

This hotel is located in the midtown area near shops, restaurants and other attractions.

123 rooms. Restaurant, bar. Business center. $151-250

★★★SHERATON SUITES COUNTRY CLUB PLAZA

770 W. 47th St., Kansas City, 816-931-4400, 800-325-3535; www.sheraton.com

This is an all-suite hotel offering many facilities, including a restaurant, lounge, indoor and outdoor heated pools, whirlpool and weight room. The hotel is located near sports, cultural and family attractions.

257 rooms. Restaurant, bar. Business center. Fitness center. Pool. Pets accepted. $61-150

★★★THE WESTIN CROWN CENTER

1 Pershing Road, Kansas City, 816-474-4400, 800-228-3000; www.westin.com/crowncenter

Located in the downtown area within Hallmark's Crown Center, where visitors will find shops, restaurants and theaters, this hotel is also near the Liberty Memorial and the Bartle Convention Center.

729 rooms. Restaurant, bar. Business center. Fitness center. Pool. Tennis. Pets accepted. $151-250

WHERE TO EAT

★★★★THE AMERICAN RESTAURANT

200 E. 25th St., Kansas City, 816-545-8001; www.theamericankc.com

The flagship restaurant of the Crown Center, the American has attracted Kansas City diners for 40 years. With a concept designed by the legendary James Beard, the father of American cooking, and Joe Baum, the restaurateur of the former Windows on the World in New York City, the restaurant is as elegant as ever, with downtown views, polished service, and one of the city's best wine lists. The kitchen staff, led by executive chef Celina Tio, prepares American fare using local seasonal produce.

American. Lunch, dinner. Closed Sunday. Reservations recommended. Children's menu. Bar. $36-85

★★★★

MISSOURI

★★★ANDRE'S TEAROOM

5018 Main St., Kansas City, 816-561-6484, 800-892-1234; www.andreschocolates.com

An offshoot of legendary Swiss chocolate maker Andres Bollier's candy shop, this tearoom serves continental favorites such as leek and gruyere pie or vol au vent in a quaint setting. After lunch, stock up on truffles or a linzer torte to take home.

Continental. Lunch. Closed Sunday-Monday. $16-35

★ARTHUR BRYANT'S BARBEQUE

1727 Brooklyn Ave., Kansas City, 816-231-1123; www.arthurbryantsbbq.com

American. Lunch, dinner. Closed holidays. $15 and under

★★★BLUESTEM

900 Westport Road, Kansas City, 816-561-1101; www.bluestemkc.com

Bluestem is the product of two acclaimed chefs, Colby and Megan Garrelts, who worked at such restaurants as Aureole in Las Vegas and Tru in Chicago. The space is divided into a 40-seat restaurant, clad in cobalt blue walls and warm candlelight, and an adjacent wine bar that offers more casual fare. A three-, five- or seven-course prix menu is available, as well as a twelve-course tasting menu. Entrées might include a torchon of foie gras, wild Tasmanian salmon with oxtail or LaBelle duck with sweet potato gnocchi and apple emulsion. Desserts are outstanding, simplistic in their approach but full of intense flavors.

American. Dinner, brunch. Bar. Reservations recommended. $36-85

★★CALIFORNOS
4124 Pennsylvania, Kansas City, 816-531-1097; www.californos.com
American. Lunch, dinner. Closed Sunday. Reservations recommended. Outdoor seating. Bar. $16-35

★★CASCONE'S ITALIAN RESTAURANT
3733 N. Oak, Kansas City, 816-454-7977; www.cascones.com
Italian. Lunch, dinner. Reservations recommended. Outdoor seating. Children's menu. Bar. $16-35

★★CHAPPELL'S
323 Armour Road, North Kansas City, 816-421-0002; www.chappellsrestaurant.com
Steak. Lunch, dinner. Closed Sunday. Children's menu. Bar. $16-35

★★CLASSIC CUP CAFÉ
301 W. 47th St., Kansas City, 816-753-1840; www.classiccup.com
American. Breakfast, lunch, dinner, Sunday brunch. Outdoor seating. Bar. $16-35

★★★EBT
1310 Carondelet Drive, Kansas City, 816-942-8870; www.ebtrestaurant.com
Mid-1900s sandstone columns and two ornate brass elevators provide the setting for this restaurant, with dishes such as pistachio-encrusted salmon and pepper steak. Tableside presentations are offered, and there is an extensive wine list.
American. Lunch, dinner. Closed Sunday-Monday. Reservations recommended. Children's menu. Bar. $36-85

★★FIGLIO
209 W. 46th Terrace, Kansas City, 816-561-0505; www.dineoutinkc.com
Italian. Lunch, dinner, brunch. Reservations recommended. Outdoor seating. Children's menu. Bar. $16-35

★★FIORELLA'S JACK STACK BARBECUE
13441 Holmes St., Kansas City, 816-942-9141, 877-419-7427; www.jackstackbbq.com
American. Lunch, dinner. Reservations recommended. Outdoor seating. Children's menu. Bar. $16-35

★★GAROZZO'S RISTORANTE
526 Harrison, Kansas City, 816-221-2455; www.garozzos.com
Italian. Lunch, dinner. Reservations recommended. Children's menu. Bar. $16-35

★★GOLDEN OX
1600 Genessee St., Kansas City, 816-842-2866; www.goldenox.com
Steak. Lunch, dinner. Children's menu. Bar. $36-85

★★★GRAND STREET CAFÉ
4740 Grand St., Kansas City, 816-561-8000; www.eatpbj.com

A stylish and modern botanical theme is found throughout this dining room. Double cut pork chops with cinnamon apples and brown sugar jus, caramelized sea scallops with Maine lobster butter and a crispy potato pancake, and grilled filet mignon with a veal demi-cabernet sauce and French green beans are among the menu items. Brunch is popular. A small, cozy patio with eight tables offers al fresco dining.

American. Lunch, dinner, Sunday brunch. Reservations recommended. Outdoor seating. Children's menu. Bar. $36-85

★★HARDWARE CAFÉ
5 E. Kansas Ave., Liberty, 816-792-3500

American. Breakfast, lunch, dinner. Closed Sunday. Children's menu. $16-35

★★JESS & JIM'S STEAK HOUSE
517 E. 135th St., Kansas City, 816-941-9499, 816-942-2959; www.jessandjims.com

Steak. Lunch, dinner. Children's menu. Bar. $36-85

★★★JJ'S
910 W. 48th St., Kansas City, 816-561-7136; www.jjs-restaurant.com

Upscale European fare is served at this friendly bistro. Entrées spotlight fresh, local ingredients and might include Kansas City strip steak with smoked gouda mashed potatoes.

American. Lunch, dinner. Reservations recommended. Bar. $36-85

★L.C.'S BAR-B-Q
5800 Blue Parkway, Kansas City, 816-923-4484

American. Lunch, dinner. Closed Sunday. $16-35

★★★LE FOU FROG
400 E. Fifth St., Kansas City, 816-474-6060; www.lefoufrog.com

This French bistro is a good place to dine when seeing a show at the convention center. Sauces are light and presentation is excellent. Portions are big, from the escargot to the steak au poivre.

French. Lunch, dinner. Closed Monday. Reservations recommended. Outdoor seating. Bar. $36-85

★★★LIDIA'S KANSAS CITY
101 W. 22nd St., Kansas City, 816-221-3722; www.lidiasitaly.com

Created by the acclaimed New York restaurateur Lidia Bastianich, this trendy restaurant offers a rustic atmosphere, with rough brick walls and exposed wooden beams. The menu is classic, with dishes such as salmon alla griglia.

Italian. Lunch, dinner. Reservations recommended. Outdoor seating. Children's menu. Bar. $16-35

★★MACALUSO'S ON 39TH
1403 W. 39th St., Kansas City, 816-561-0100; www.macalusoson39th.com

Italian. Dinner. Closed Sunday. Reservations recommended. Bar. $36-85

★★★THE MAJESTIC STEAKHOUSE
931 Broadway, Kansas City, 816-471-8484; www.majesticsteakhouse.com
The historic Fitzpatrick Saloon building in downtown Kansas City is home to one of the best, most entertaining steakhouses in town. It's also a great place to indulge in a cigar. The restaurant features turn-of-the-century décor with stained-glass windows, ceiling fans and an ornate tin ceiling.
Steak. Lunch, dinner. Reservations recommended. Bar. $36-85

★★★MARINA GROG & GALLEY
22 A St., Lees Summit, 816-578-5511; www.marinagrogandgalley.com
Take in beautiful lake views from the elegant dining room. Seafood menu. Dinner. Outdoor seating. Children's menu. Bar. $36-85

★★★O'DOWD'S LITTLE DUBLIN
4742 Pennsylvania Ave., Kansas City, 816-561-2700; www.odowdslittledublin.com
This authentic Irish pub, with much of its interior built in Ireland then shipped here, serves the best fish and chips in town.
Irish. Lunch, dinner, late-night. Closed Memorial Day. Reservations recommended. Outdoor seating. Children's menu. Bar. $16-35

★PHOENIX PIANO BAR & GRILL
302 W. Eighth St., Kansas City, 816-472-0001; www.phoenixjazz.net
American. Lunch, dinner, late-night. Closed Sunday. $16-35

★★★PLAZA III STEAKHOUSE
4749 Pennsylvania Ave., Kansas City, 816-753-0000; www.plazaiiisteakhouse.com
The epitome of the Kansas City steakhouse, this restaurant serves USDA prime aged cuts of Midwestern beef, chops, fresh fish and lobster. Lunch includes the famous steak soup.
Steak. Lunch, dinner. Reservations recommended. Children's menu. Bar. $36-85

★★★RAPHAEL DINING ROOM
325 Ward Parkway, Kansas City, 816-756-3800, 800-821-5343; www.raphaelkc.com
Housed in the Raphael Hotel, this restaurant has an elegant dining room and refined service. The Kansas City strip steak with port wine sauce and melted gorgonzola is a menu standout.
International. Breakfast, lunch, dinner. Reservations recommended. Bar. $36-85

★SMUGGLER'S INN
1650 Universal Plaza Drive, Kansas City, 816-483-0400
American. Lunch, dinner. Bar. $16-35

LAKE OZARK
See also Osage Beach
This resort community rests on the huge, man-made reservoir called Lake of the Ozarks. In summer the area is packed with tourists who come to boat and float on the lake or stay in its many resorts.

WHAT TO SEE
JACOB'S CAVE

23114 Highway TT, Versailles, 573-378-4374; www.jacobscave.com

Famous for its depth illusion, reflective pools, prehistoric bones and the world's largest geode.

Memorial Day-Labor Day, daily 9 a.m.-5 p.m.; Labor Day-Memorial Day, daily 9 a.m.-4 p.m.

LAKE OF THE OZARKS

Highway 54, Lake Ozark; www.funlake.com

Completed in 1931, the 2,543-foot-long Bagnell Dam impounds the Osage River to form this 54,000-acre recreational lake, which has an irregular 1,150-mile shoreline. Fishing, boating and swimming are excellent here.

LAKE OF THE OZARKS STATE PARK

403 Highway 134, Kaiser, 573-348-2694

This more than 17,000-acre park, the largest in the state, has 89 miles of shoreline with two public swimming and boat launching areas. On the grounds is a large cave with streams of water that continuously pour from stalactites.

WHERE TO STAY
★★★THE LODGE OF FOUR SEASONS

Horseshoe Bend Parkway, Lake Ozark, 573-365-3000; www.4seasonsresort.com

Located in the Ozark Hills, the property overlooks the winding shoreline. Many of the rooms and two- and three-bedroom condominiums have views of the lake or Japanese garden and pool. A golf course and health spa are on the premises.

350 rooms. Restaurant, bar. Fitness center. Pool. Spa. Golf. $151-250

WHERE TO EAT
★★BENTLEY'S

Highway 54 Business, Lake Ozark, 573-365-5301; www.bentleysrestaurantmo.com

Seafood, steak. Dinner. Closed Sunday. Children's menu. Bar. $16-35

★★J.B. HOOK'S GREAT OCEAN FISH & STEAKS

2260 Bagnell Dam Blvd., Lake Ozark, 573-365-3255; www.jbhooks.com

Seafood, steak. Lunch, dinner. Outdoor seating. Bar. $16-35

LEBANON

Lebanon was founded in the mid-1800s beside an Indian trail that today is Interstate 44 (I-44). As the seat of the newly created Laclede County, the town was originally called Wyota. The name was changed when a respected minister asked that it be renamed after his hometown of Lebanon, Tennessee.

WHAT TO SEE
BENNETT SPRING STATE PARK
26248 Highway 64A, Lebanon, 417-532-4307, 800-334-6946;
www.bennettspringstatepark.com
Nearly 3,100 acres. Swimming pool, trout fishing (March-October); picnicking, store, dining lodge, camping, cabins. Restaurant. Nature center. Daily.

SPECIAL EVENT
HILLBILLY DAYS
Bennett Springs State Park, Lebanon, 417-588-3256
Arts and crafts, contests, country music, antique cars.
Father's Day weekend.

OSAGE BEACH
See also Lake Ozark
A major resort community on the Lake of the Ozarks, the town came into existence with the 1931 completion of the lake.

WHERE TO STAY
★★DOGWOOD HILLS RESORT INN
1252 Highway KK, Osage Beach, 573-348-1735, 800-220-6571;
www.dogwoodhillsresort.com
47 rooms. Restaurant (March-October), bar. Pool. Golf. Pets accepted. $61-150

★★INN AT GRAND GLAIZE
5142 Highway 54, Osage Beach, 573-348-4731, 800-348-4731;
www.innatgrandglaize.com
1,591 rooms. Restaurant, bar. Fitness center. Pool. $61-150

★★★TAN-TAR-A RESORT
Highway KK, Osage Beach, 573-348-3131, 1-800-826-8272; www.tan-tar-a.com
This property is on the scenic Lake of the Ozarks and offers more than 30 recreational activities, including indoor and outdoor pools, waterskiing, a full spa, jogging, golf and more. The hotel is near many area restaurants and attractions.
365 rooms. Restaurant, bar. Fitness center. Pool. Golf. Tennis. $61-150

WHERE TO EAT
★★THE BRASS DOOR
5167 Highway 54, Osage Beach, 573-348-9229; www.the-brass-door.com
Steak, seafood. Dinner. Children's menu. $36-85

★★DOMENICO'S CARRY-OUT PIZZA
4737 Highway 54, Osage Beach, 573-348-2844
Italian, American. Dinner. Children's menu. Bar. $16-35

★★HAPPY FISHERMAN
4676 Highway 54, Osage Beach, 573-348-3311
American. Dinner. Closed mid-December-January. Children's menu. Bar.
$16-35

★★POTTED STEER
5085 Highway 54, Osage Beach, 573-348-5053; www.blueheronpottedsteer.com
Dinner. Closed Sunday-Monday. Bar. $16-35

★★VISTA GRANDE
4579 Highway 54, Osage Beach, 573-348-1231;
www.vistagrandemexicanrestaurant.com
American, Mexican. Lunch, dinner. Children's menu. Bar. $16-35

PILOT KNOB
This village of less than 700 people was the site of the Civil War Battle of
Pilot Knob. Union and Confederate forces clashed over control of nearby
Fort Davidson in 1864.

WHAT TO SEE
JOHNSON'S SHUT-INS STATE PARK
Highway North, Middle Brook, 573-546-2450; www.mostateparks.com
This nearly 8,500-acre area, left in its wilderness state, has a spectacular can-
yon-like defile along the river. The park is at the southern end of the 20-mile-
long Ozark backpacking trail, which traverses Missouri's highest mountain,
Taum Sauk. Enjoy swimming, fishing, hiking, picnicking, a playground, and
improved camping sites.
Daily.

WHERE TO STAY
★★WILDERNESS LODGE
Peola Road, Lesterville, 573-637-2295, 888-969-9129; www.wildernesslodgeresort.com
27 rooms. Restaurant, bar. Business center. Pool. $61-150

ROLLA
According to legend, this town was named by a homesick settler from Ra-
leigh, North Carolina, who spelled the name as he pronounced it. Called "the
child of the railroad" because it began with the building of the St. Louis-San
Francisco Railroad, the town is located in a scenic area with several streams
nearby. Mark Twain National Forest maintains its headquarters in Rolla.

WHAT TO SEE
MARAMEC SPRING PARK AND REMAINS OF OLD IRONWORKS
21880 Maramec Spring Drive, Rolla, 573-265-7387
The spring discharges an average of 96-million gallons per day. The iron-
works was first established in 1826; the present furnace was built in 1857.
Daily.

MARK TWAIN NATIONAL FORESTS

401 Fairgrounds Road, Rolla, 573-364-4621; www.fs.fed.us

More than 192,000 acres; cradles the headwaters of the Gasconade, Little Piney and Big Piney rivers. Paddy Creek Wilderness Area covers about 6,800 acres with 30 miles of hiking and riding trails.

ST. JAMES WINERY

540 Sidney St., 573-265-7912, 800-280-9463; www.stjameswinery.com

Dry and semidry wines, sparkling wines, concord, catawba and berry wines are all produced here.

Daily 8 a.m.-10 p.m.

WHERE TO STAY
★★ZENO'S MOTEL AND STEAK HOUSE

1621 Martin Springs Drive, Rolla, 573-364-1301; www.zenos.biz.

51 rooms. Restaurant, bar. Fitness center. Pool. $61-150

WHERE TO EAT
★JOHNNY'S SMOKE STAK

201 Highway 72, Rolla, 573-364-4838

American. Lunch, dinner. Children's menu. $15 and under

SEDALIA

See also Clinton, Jefferson City

Known as the "queen city of the prairies," Sedalia was a prosperous railhead town in the 1800s with great cattle herds arriving for shipment to eastern markets. During the Civil War, the settlement functioned as a military post. A monument at Lamine and Main Streets marks the site of the Maple Leaf Club, one of the city's many saloons that catered to railroad men. The monument is dedicated to Scott Joplin, who composed and performed the *Maple Leaf Rag* here, triggering the ragtime craze at the turn of the 20th century. Whiteman Air Force Base is 21 miles west of Sedalia.

WHAT TO SEE
BOTHWELL LODGE STATE HISTORIC SITE

19349 Bothwell State Park, Sedalia, 660-827-0510; www.mostateparks.com

An Arts and Crafts house built between 1897 and 1928 for a local businessman, the lodge is open for tours. The park includes approximately 180 acres, with hiking trails and picnic areas.

Daily.

PETTIS COUNTY COURTHOUSE

415 S. Ohio, Sedalia, 660-826-4892; www.pettiscomo.com

Historic courthouse contains local artifacts and exhibits.

Monday-Friday.

MISSOURI ★★★★★

92

SEDALIA RAGTIME ARCHIVES

State Fair Community College Library, Maple Leaf Room, 3201 W. 16th St., Sedalia, 660-530-5800

These archives include original sheet music, piano rolls, tapes of interviews with Eubie Blake.
Monday-Friday.

SPECIAL EVENTS
MISSOURI STATE FAIR

2503 W. 16th St., Sedalia, 660-530-5600, 660-827-8150; www.mostatefair.com

One of the country's leading state fairs, this event has been held here since 1901. Stage shows, rodeo, competitive exhibits, livestock, auto races.
August.

SCOTT JOPLIN RAGTIME FESTIVAL

321 S. Ohio, Sedalia, 660-826-2271, 866-218-6258; www.scottjoplin.org

This festival features entertainment by ragtime greats.
Early June.

WHERE TO STAY
★★BEST WESTERN STATE FAIR MOTOR INN

3120 S. Limit Ave., Sedalia, 660-826-6100, 1-800-780-7234; www.bestwestern.com

117 rooms. Restaurant, bar. Complimentary breakfast. Fitness center. Pool. Pets accepted. $61-150

SIKESTON

Although settlers were in this region before the Louisiana Purchase, John Sikes established the town of Sikeston in 1860 on El Camino Real, the overland route from St. Louis to New Orleans, at the terminus of the Cairo and Fulton Railway (now the Union Pacific).

SPECIAL EVENTS
BOOTHEEL RODEO

1220 N. Ingram Road, Sikeston, 573-471-7196, 800-455-2855; www.sikestonrodeo.com

Enjoy ountry music and rodeo events along with a parade.
First full week in August.

WHERE TO STAY
★★BEST WESTERN COACH HOUSE INN

220 S. Interstate Drive, Sikeston, 573-471-9700, 877-471-9700; www.bestwestern.com

61 rooms. Restaurant, bar. Complimentary breakfast. Pool. Pets accepted. $61-150

★DRURY INN

2602 E. Malone Ave., Sikeston, 573-471-4100, 800-378-7946; www.druryhotels.com

80 rooms. Complimentary breakfast. Business center. Pool. Pets accepted. $61-150

WHERE TO EAT
★FISHERMAN'S NET
915 S. Kings Highway, Sikeston, 573-471-8102; www.fishermansnet.net
Seafood. Lunch, dinner. Closed Sunday-Monday. Children's menu. $15 and under

★LAMBERT'S
2305 E. Malone Ave., Sikeston, 573-471-4261; www.throwedrolls.com
American. Lunch, dinner. Children's menu. $16-35

SPRINGFIELD
See also Branson
In the southwest corner of the state and at the northern edge of the Ozark highlands, Springfield, known as Ozark Mountain Country's Big City, is near some of Missouri's most picturesque areas. A few settlers came here as early as 1821, but settlement was temporarily discouraged when the government made Southwestern Missouri a reservation. Later, the tribes were moved west and the town developed. Its strategic location made it a military objective in the Civil War. Confederates took the town in the Battle of Wilson's Creek, August 10, 1861; Union forces recaptured it in 1862. "Wild Bill" Hickok, later one of the famous frontier marshals, was a scout and spy for Union forces headquartered in Springfield. Perhaps the city's most famous native son is actor Brad Pitt, who grew up here and later attended the University of Missouri in Columbia.

WHAT TO SEE
BASS PRO SHOPS OUTDOOR WORLD SHOWROOM AND FISH AND WILDLIFE MUSEUM
1935 S. Campbell Ave., Springfield, 417-887-7334; www.outdoor-world.com
This 300,000-square-foot sporting goods store features a four-story water-fall, indoor boat and RV showroom, art gallery and indoor firing range. The restaurant has a 30,000-gallon saltwater aquarium.
Monday-Saturday 7 a.m.-10 p.m., Sunday 9 a.m.-7 p.m.

DICKERSON PARK ZOO
3043 N. Fort, Springfield, 417-864-1800, 417-833-1570; www.dickersonparkzoo.org
Animals are housed at this zoo in naturalistic settings. It also features an elephant herd and train rides.
April-September, daily 9 a.m.-5 p.m.; October-March, daily 10 a.m.-4 p.m.

DISCOVERY CENTER
438 St. Louis St., Springfield, 417-862-9910; www.discoverycenter.org
This interactive hands-on museum includes its "Discovery Town Theatre" where kids can be a star on stage, create a newspaper, run a make-believe TV station or dig for dinosaur bones.
Tuesday-Sunday.

LAURA INGALLS WILDER-ROSE WILDER LANE MUSEUM AND HOME

3068 Highway A, Mansfield, 417-924-3626, 877-924-7126;
www.lauraingallswilderhome.com

The house where Laura Ingalls Wilder wrote the *Little House* books houses artifacts and memorabilia of the author, her husband Almanzo and daughter Rose Wilder Lane. Included are four handwritten manuscripts and many items mentioned in Wilder's books, including Pa's fiddle.

March-mid-November, daily 9 a.m.-5 p.m.; June-August, daily 9 a.m.-5.30 p.m.

WHERE TO STAY
★★CLARION HOTEL

3333 S. Glenstone Ave., Springfield, 417-883-6550, 800-756-7318;
www.clarionhotel.com

192 rooms.. Restaurant, bar. Fitness center. Pool. Pets accepted. $61-150

★HAMPTON INN

222 N. Ingram Mill Road, Springfield, 417-863-1440, 800-426-7866;
www.hamptoninn.com

99 rooms. Restaurant. Complimentary breakfast. Fitness center. Pool. $61-150

★★★SHERATON HAWTHORN PARK HOTEL

2431 N. Glenstone Ave., Springfield, 417-831-3131, 800-223-0092; www.sheraton.com
201 rooms. Restaurant, bar. Fitness center. Pool. $61-150

WHERE TO EAT
★★GEE'S EAST WIND

2951 E. Sunshine, Springfield, 417-883-4567; www.blueheronpottedsteer.com
Chinese, American. Lunch, dinner. Closed Sunday; last week in June, first week in July. Children's menu. Bar. $16-35

★J. PARRIONO'S PASTA HOUSE

1550 E. Battlefield, Springfield, 417-882-1808
Italian. Lunch, dinner. Children's menu. Bar. $16-35

ST. CHARLES

See also St. Louis

St. Charles, one of the early settlements on the Missouri River, was the first capital of the state from 1821-1826. Between 1832 and 1870, a wave of German immigrants settled here and developed the town, but St. Louis, by virtue of its location on the Mississippi, became the state's most important city. Frenchtown, a northern ward of old St. Charles, is home to many antiques shops.

WHAT TO SEE
FIRST MISSOURI STATE CAPITOL STATE HISTORIC SITE
200-216 S. Main St., St. Charles, 636-940-3322; www.mostateparks.com
Eleven rooms of the capitol have been restored to their original state; nine rooms have 1820 period furnishings; also restoration of the Peck Brothers General Store and house.
Daily.

KATY TRAIL STATE PARK
St. Charles, 660-882-8196, 800-334-6946; www.mostateparks.com
A 236-mile bicycling and hiking trail across Missouri, this is among the longest of its kind in the United States.

LEWIS AND CLARK CENTER
Bishop's Landing, 1050 Riverside, St. Charles, 636-947-3199;
www.lewisandclarkcenter.org
Museum depicts the 1804-1806 expedition from St. Charles to the Pacific Ocean. Hands-on exhibits, life-size models of Sacagawea and the men of the expedition; Mandan and Sioux villages.
Monday-Saturday 10 a.m.-5 p.m., Sunday noon-5 p.m.

SPECIAL EVENT
LEWIS AND CLARK HERITAGE DAYS
Frontier Park, Riverside Drive, St. Charles, 800-366-2427;
www.lewisandclarkheritagedays.com
Reenactment of the explorers' encampment in 1804 prior to embarking on their exploration of the Louisiana Purchase; parade, fife and drum corps. authentic period clothing, children's activities, military encampment, grand parade, music and demonstrations.
Mid-May.

WHERE TO STAY
★★HOLIDAY INN
4341 Veteran's Memorial Parkway, St. Peters, 636-928-1500, 800-972-3145;
www.holiday-inn.com
195 rooms. Restaurant, bar. Business center. Fitness center. Pool. Pets accepted. $61-150

WHERE TO EAT
★★ST. CHARLES VINTAGE HOUSE
1219 S. Main St., St. Charles, 636-946-7155; www.stcharlesvintagehouse.com
American, German, seafood. Dinner. Closed Monday. Outdoor seating. Children's menu. Bar. $16-35

ST. JOSEPH
See also Kansas City, Weston
A historic city with beautiful parks, St. Joseph retains traces of the frontier settlement of the 1840s in its "original town" near the Missouri River. It was founded and named by Joseph Robidoux III, a French fur trader from St.

Louis, who established his post in 1826. St. Joseph, the western terminus of the first railroad to cross the state, became the eastern terminus of the Pony Express, whose riders carried mail to and from Sacramento, California, from 1860-1861 using relays of fast ponies. The record trip, which carried copies of President Lincoln's inaugural address, was made in seven days and 17 hours. The telegraph ended the need for the Pony Express.

WHAT TO SEE
ALBRECHT-KEMPER MUSEUM OF ART
2818 Frederick Blvd., St. Joseph, 816-233-7003, 888-254-2787;
www.albrecht-kemper.org
Exhibits of 18th-, 19th- and 20th-century American paintings, sculpture, graphic art.
Friday 10 a.m.-4 p.m., Saturday and Sunday 1-4 p.m.

GLORE PSYCHIATRIC MUSEUM
3408 Frederick Ave., St. Joseph, 816-364-1209, 800-530-8866; www.gloremuseum.org
Housed in a ward of the original 1874 administration building, the museum displays the evolution of treatment philosophy and techniques over a 400-year period.
Daily.

JESSE JAMES HOME
1202 Penn St., St. Joseph, 816-232-8206; www.stjoseph.net/ponyexpress
This is the one-story frame cottage where the outlaw had been living quietly as "Mr. Howard" until he was killed here on, April 3, 1882, by an associate, Robert Ford.
Some original furnishings.
Daily.

PATEE HOUSE MUSEUM
1202 Penn St., St. Joseph, 816-232-8206; www.stjoseph.net/ponyexpress
Built in 1858 as a hotel, this building once served as headquarters of the Pony Express. Contains pioneer exhibits related to transportation and communication and includes restored an 1860 Buffalo Saloon, wood-burning engine and the original last mail car from the Hannibal and St. Joseph railroad.
April-October, daily; January-March and November, Saturday-Sunday.

PONY EXPRESS MUSEUM
914 Penn St., St. Joseph, 816-279-5059, 800-530-5930; www.ponyexpress.org
This museum is located in the old Pikes Peak (Pony Express) Stables, the starting point of the service's first westward ride. Original stables; displays illustrate the creation, operation, management and termination of the famed mail service.
Monday-Saturday 9 a.m.-5 p.m., Sunday 1-5 p.m.

PONY EXPRESS REGION TOURIST INFORMATION CENTERS
502 N. Woodvine Road, St. Joseph, 816-232-1839; www.stjomo.com
Housed in historic railroad cabooses, centers provide brochures and informa-

tion on St. Joseph, Northwest Missouri and Northeast Kansas; free maps.
Daily.

ROBIDOUX ROW MUSEUM

219-227, E. Poulin St., St. Joseph, 816-232-5861
Built by the city's founder, French fur trader Joseph Robidoux, as temporary
housing for newly arrived settlers who had purchased land from him. Authentically restored; some original furnishings.
Tours. Tuesday-Sunday.

WHERE TO STAY
★★HOLIDAY INN

102 S. Third St., St. Joseph, 816-279-8000, 800-824-7402; www.holiday-inn.com
170 rooms. Restaurant, bar. Fitness center. Pool. Pets accepted. $61-150

WHERE TO EAT
★★36TH STREET FOOD & DRINK COMPANY

501 N. Belt Highway, St. Joseph, 816-364-1565; www.36thstreet.com
American, Italian. Lunch, dinner. Closed Sunday. Bar. $16-35

★BARBOSA'S CASTILLO

906 Sylvanie St., St. Joseph, 816-233-4970; www.barbosasrestaurant.com
Mexican. Lunch, dinner. Closed Sunday. Children's menu. Bar. $16-35

ST. LOUIS

See also Clayton, St. Charles, Ste. Genevieve
One of the oldest settlements in the Mississippi Valley, St. Louis was founded by Pierre Laclede as a fur trading post and was named for Louis IX of
France. Early French settlers, a large German immigration in the mid-1800s
and a happy mix of other national strains contribute to the city's cosmopolitan flavor. In 1804, it was the scene of the transfer of Louisiana to the United
States, which opened the way to westward expansion. During the Civil War,
though divided in sympathy, the city was a base of Union operations. In
1904, the Louisiana Purchase Exposition, known as the St. Louis World's
Fair, brought international fame to the city.

For more than 200 years, St. Louis has been the dominant city in the state.
It's the home of St. Louis University, the University of Missouri-St. Louis
and Washington University. After the steamboat era, St. Louis grew westward
away from the riverfront, which deteriorated into slums. This original center
of the city has now been developed as the Jefferson National Expansion Memorial. Recent redevelopment of downtown and the riverfront is revitalizing
the city. Busch Stadium brings St. Louis Cardinals fans into the downtown
area and the rehabilitated Union Station offers visitors a vast shopping experience within a restored turn-of-the-century railroad station that was one of
the nation's most magnificent.

WHAT TO SEE
ANHEUSER-BUSCH BREWERY
12th and Lynch streets, St. Louis, 314-577-2626; www.budweisertours.com
Trace the making of Budweiser beer from farm fields to finished product in a tour of the nation's largest brewery. Inside the 150-year-old plant, you'll also experience a historic brewhouse, beechwood aging cellars, a packing facility and Clydesdale stables. Adults can sample Budweiser products. Daily.

BUTTERFLY HOUSE AND EDUCATION CENTER
Faust Park, 15193 Olive Blvd., Chesterfield, 636-530-0076; www.butterflyhouse.org
A three-story crystal palace conservatory with more than 2,000 butterflies in free flight. Educational programs, films, miracle of metamorphosis display. Memorial Day-Labor Day, daily; Labor Day-Memorial Day, Tuesday-Sunday.

CAMPBELL HOUSE MUSEUM
1508 Locust St., St. Louis, 314-421-0325
Mansion with original 1840-1880 furnishings. March-December, Wednesday-Sunday.

CATHEDRAL OF ST. LOUIS
4431 Lindell Blvd., St. Louis, 314-373-8242; www.cathedralstl.org
The city's cathedral, built in 1907, is a fine example of Romanesque architecture with Byzantine details. The interior mosaic work is among the most extensive in the world.

CHRIST CHURCH CATHEDRAL
1210 Locust St., St. Louis, 314-231-3454
Founded in 1919, this was the first Episcopal parish west of the Mississippi River. English Gothic sandstone building; altar carved in England from stone taken from a quarry in Caen, France; Tiffany windows on north wall. Sunday-Friday. Tours: by appointment.

CLIMATRON
4344 Shaw Blvd., St. Louis, 314-577-5141; www.mobot.org
Seventy-foot high, prize-winning geodesic dome—first of its kind to be used as a conservatory—houses a two-level, half-acre tropical rain forest with canopies, rocky outcrops, waterfalls and mature tree collection; exhibits explain the many facets of a rain forest. Entrance to Climatron through series of sacred lotus and lily pools.

DELTA QUEEN AND MISSISSIPPI QUEEN
St. Louis, 800-543-1949; www.deltaqueen.com
Paddle wheelers offer three- to eight-night cruises on the Ohio, Cumberland, Mississippi and Tennessee rivers.

EADS BRIDGE

St. Louis Riverfront area

Designed in 1874 by engineer James B. Eads, the Eads was the first bridge to span the wide southern section of the Mississippi and the first bridge in which steel and the cantilever were used extensively. The approach ramps are carried on enormous Romanesque stone arches.

EUGENE FIELD HOUSE AND TOY MUSEUM

634 S. Broadway, St. Louis, 314-421-4689; www.eugenefieldhouse.org

This was the birthplace of the famous children's poet. The museum includes mementos, manuscripts, antique toys and many original furnishings.
Wednesday-Saturday, Sunday; also by appointment.

GATEWAY ARCH

The Gateway Arch Riverfront, St. Louis, 877-982-1410; www.gatewayarch.com

Eero Saarinen's Gateway Arch is a 630-foot stainless steel arch that symbolizes the starting point of the westward expansion of the United States. Visitor center includes capsule transporter to observation deck.
Memorial Day-Labor Day, daily 8 a.m.-10 p.m.; Labor Day-Memorial Day, daily 9 a.m.-6 p.m.

GRANT'S FARM

10501 Gravois Road, St. Louis, 314-843-1700; www.grantsfarm.com

This 281-acre wooded tract contains a log cabin and land once owned by Ulysses S. Grant. On property there is a barn, carriage house, trophy room; deer, buffalo, longhorn steer and other animals roam freely in their natural habitat.
May-September, Tuesday-Sunday; mid-April-May and September-mid-October, Wednesday-Sunday.

INTERNATIONAL BOWLING MUSEUM AND HALL OF FAME

111 Stadium Plaza, St. Louis, 314-231-6340; www.bowlingmuseum.com

View wacky bowling shirts and the sublime Hall of Fame, or bowl a few frames. The museum shares the building with the St. Louis Cardinals Museum, which boasts an outstanding collection of Redbirds memorabilia.
April-September, daily 9 a.m.-5 p.m.; October-March, Tuesday-Saturday 11 a.m.-4 p.m.

JAPANESE GARDEN

4344 Shaw Blvd., St. Louis, 314-577-5100, 800-642-8842; www.mobot.org

Largest traditional Japanese garden in North America, with lake landscaped with many varieties of water irises, waterfalls, bridges and a teahouse.

JEFFERSON BARRACKS HISTORICAL PARK

533 Grant Road, St. Louis, 314-544-5714; www.nps.gov

This army post was established in 1826 and used through 1946. St. Louis County now maintains 424 acres of the original tract. Restored buildings include a stable, a laborer's house, two powder magazines, an ordnance room and a visitor center.
Wednesday-Sunday.

JEFFERSON NATIONAL EXPANSION MEMORIAL

11 N. Fourth St., St. Louis, 314-655-1700; www.nps.gov/jeff

The Jefferson National Expansion Memorial, located along the Mississippi River, pays tribute to Thomas Jefferson and his influence on freedom and democracy.

OLD COURTHOUSE

11 N. Fourth St., St. Louis, 314-655-1600; www.nps.gov

With it's construction beginning in 1837 and completed in 1862, this building houses five museum galleries on St. Louis history, including various displays, dioramas and films. The first two trials of the Dred Scott case were held in this building.
Daily.

LACLEDE'S LANDING

720 N. Second St., St. Louis, 314-241-1155; www.lacledeslanding.com

Early St. Louis commercial district (mid-1800s) includes a nine-block area of renovated pre-Civil War and Victorian buildings that house specialty shops, restaurants and nightclubs.

MISSOURI BOTANICAL GARDEN

4344 Shaw Blvd., St. Louis, 314-577-9400, 800-642-8842; www.mobot.org

This 79-acre park includes rose, woodland and herb gardens; scented garden for the blind; electric tram rides; and a butterfly house. Sections of the botanical garden are more than a century old.
Daily 9 a.m.-5 p.m.

MISSOURI HISTORY MUSEUM-MISSOURI HISTORICAL SOCIETY

5700 Lindel Blvd., St. Louis, 314-746-4599; www.mohistory.org

Exhibits on St. Louis and the American West; artwork, costumes and decorative arts; toys, firearms; 19th-century firefighting equipment; St. Louis history slide show; ragtime-rock 'n' roll music exhibit; 1904 World's Fair and Charles A. Lindbergh collections.
Daily.

MUSEUM OF TRANSPORTATION

3015 Barrett Station Road, Kirkwood, 314-965-7998;
www.transportmuseumassociation.org

The Museum of Transportation houses an extensive collection of passenger and freight train equipment (ranging from elevated cars from Chicago to the last steam locomotive to operate in Missouri), as well as the riverboats and airplanes.
Daily.

MUSEUM OF WESTWARD EXPANSION

11 N. Fourth St., St. Louis, 314-655-1700; www.nps.gov

The Museum of Westward Expansion offers exhibits on the people and events of 19th-century Western America, special exhibits and films on St. Louis, construction of the arch and the westward movement.
Daily.

NASCAR SPEEDPARK

5555 St. Louis Mills Blvd., Hazelwood, 314-227-5600; www.nascarspeedpark.com

This mini amusement park is northwest of downtown, and is now one of five now open across North America. The park features everything from an arcade to a rock-climbing wall to a NASCAR merchandise store. But its main draw is its multitude of racetracks. You can climb into a mock stock car and experience centrifugal forces, turns and crash impacts as you "drive" a full-motion NASCAR Silicon Motor Speedway simulator.

Daily.

OLD CATHEDRAL

209 Walnut St., St. Louis, 314-231-3250; www.catholic-forum.com

The 1831 basilica of St. Louis, King of France, is located on the site of the first church built in St. Louis in 1770. The museum on the west side contains the original church bell and other religious artifacts.

Daily.

POWELL SYMPHONY HALL

718 N. Grand Blvd., St. Louis, 314-534-1700; www.slso.org

Decorated in ivory and 24-karat gold leaf, the hall, built in 1925 as a movie and vaudeville house, is now home of the St. Louis Symphony Orchestra.

Mid-September-mid-May.

SIX FLAGS ST. LOUIS

I-44 and Six Flags Road, Eureka, 636-938-4800; www.sixflags.com

This edition of the theme park franchise has rides and attractions for kids and grownups, plus live shows throughout summer. Among the two-dozen or so rides here are several roller coasters.

Mid-May-late August, daily; early April-mid-May and late August-October, Saturday-Sunday. Hours vary.

ST. LOUIS ART MUSEUM

1 Fine Arts Drive, St. Louis, 314-721-0072; www.stlouis.art.museum

Built for the 1904 World's Fair as the Palace of Fine Arts, this museum has collections of American and European paintings, prints, drawings and decorative arts.

Tuesday-Sunday.

ST. LOUIS BLUES (NHL)

Scottrade Center, 1401 Clark Ave., St. Louis, 314-241-2500; www.blues.nhl.com

Professional hockey team.

ST. LOUIS CARDINALS (MLB)

Busch Stadium, 250 Stadium Plaza, St. Louis, 314-421-3060; www.cardinals.mlb.com

Professional baseball team.

ST. LOUIS RAMS (NFL)

Edward Jones Dome, 901 N. Broadway, St. Louis, 314-425-8830; www.stlouisrams.com

Professional football team.

ST. LOUIS SCIENCE CENTER

5050 Oakland Ave., St. Louis, 314-289-4444, 800-456-7572; www.slsc.org
Features three buildings with more than 700 exhibits. Also Omnimax theater, planetarium, children's discovery room.
Daily.

ST. LOUIS UNION STATION

1820 Market St., St. Louis, 314-421-6655; www.stlouisunionstation.com
This block-long stone chateauesque railroad station was the world's busiest passenger terminal from 1905 to the late 1940s. After the last train pulled out on October 31, 1978, the station and train shed were restored and redeveloped as a marketplace with more than 100 specialty shops and restaurants, nightclubs and a hotel.

ST. LOUIS UNIVERSITY

221 N. Grand, St. Louis, 314-977-8886, 800-758-3678; www.slu.edu
The oldest university west of the Mississippi River, the campus was opened in 1818 and includes the Pius XII Memorial Library with its Vatican Microfilm Library (the only depository for copies of Vatican documents in the Western Hemisphere).
Daily.

ST. LOUIS ZOO

1 Government Drive, St. Louis, 314-781-0900, 800-966-8877; www.stlzoo.org
The St. Louis Zoo is considered one of the best in the country. Lions, cheetahs and giraffes roam in natural African settings while other areas showcase exotic species from the poles to the tropics.
Memorial Day-Labor Day, daily 8 a.m.-7 p.m.; Labor Day-Memorial Day, daily 9 a.m.-5 p.m.

ULYSSES S. GRANT NATIONAL HISTORIC SITE

7400 Grant Road, St. Louis, 314-842-3298; www.nps.gov/ulsg
The White Haven property was a focal point in Ulysses's and his wife Julia's lives for four decades. Grounds feature more than 50 species of trees and are a haven for a variety of wildlife. Visitors center includes exhibits and information on the Grants and White Haven.
Guided tours: daily.

WASHINGTON UNIVERSITY

1 Brookings Drive, St. Louis, 314-935-5959; www.wustl.edu
Founded in 1853, this prestigious liberal arts institution is home to 11,000 students. The campus of this university includes the Graham Chapel, Edison Theatre and Francis Field, site of the first Olympic Games in the United States.

SPECIAL EVENTS
FAIR ST. LOUIS
Jefferson National Expansion Memorial Park, St. Louis, 314-434-3434;
www.celebratestlouis.org
This three-day festival features a parade, food, air and water shows, and entertainment.
July Fourth weekend.

THE MUNY
Forest Park, St. Louis, 314-361-1900; www.muny.org
This 12,000-seat outdoor theater hosts light opera and musical comedy.
Mid-June-August.

ST. LOUIS SYMPHONY ORCHESTRA
Powell Symphony Hall, 718 N. Grand Blvd., St. Louis, 314-534-1700, 314-533-2500;
www.slso.org
Classical music performances take place at this Symphony Hall.
September-May.

WHERE TO STAY
★★★CHASE PARK PLAZA
212-232 N. Kingshighway Blvd., St. Louis, 314-633-3000; 877-587-2427;
www.chaseparkplaza.com
This historic hotel in St. Louis's Central West End has guest rooms decorated with period furnishings. A resort-like feel pervades the hotel, which has a five-screen movie theater, spa and salon, courtyard with outdoor pool and 24-hour concierge.
250 rooms. Restaurant, bar. Business center. Fitness center. Pool. Spa. $151-250

★★CHESHIRE LODGE
6300 Clayton Road, St. Louis, 314-647-7300, 800-325-7378; www.cheshirelodge.com
Bar. Fitness center. Pool. $61-150

★★COURTYARD ST. LOUIS DOWNTOWN
2340 Market St., St. Louis, 314-241-9111, 800-321-2211; www.courtyard.com
151 rooms. Fitness center. Pool. $61-150

★★DRURY INN
201 S. 20th St., St. Louis, 314-231-3900; www.druryinn.com
This is a restored 1907 railroad hotel featuring amenities such as a complimentary breakfast and a pool to relax in.
176 rooms. Restaurant, bar. Complimentary breakfast. Fitness center. Pool. Pets accepted. $61-150

★★★★FOUR SEASONS ST. LOUIS
999 N. Second St., St. Louis, 314-881-5800; www.fourseasons.com
St. Louis has not been this exciting since the Cardinals won the World Series in 2006. The arrival of the Four Seasons brings new levels of both energy

and luxury to the city's downtown. The airy guest rooms have contemporary furnishings and a light wood color palette, plus amenities such as a LCD television and an iPod docking station. Just be sure to request a room facing south to get a view of the Gateway Arch. If you venture out, head for the Vegas-style casino Lumiere Place just at your doorstep. Or if you feel like staying in, retreat to the outdoor pool with hot tub overlooking downtown St. Louis, or make for the spa and indulge in the signature Caviar Serum Facial. Grab a drink or dinner at Italian restaurant Cielo at sunset to capture the striking urban view from the terrace.

186 rooms. Restaurant, bar. Business center. Fitness center. Pool. Spa. $251-350

★★★HILTON ST. LOUIS AT THE BALLPARK

1 S. Broadway, St. Louis, 314-421-1776, 800-228-9290; www.hilton.com

As its name suggests, this hotel is located across the street from the home of the Cardinals, Busch Stadium. The entire space has been recently renovated in a contemporary style, with rooms outfitted with granite bathrooms and duvet-topped beds.

675 rooms. Restaurant, bar. Business center. Fitness center. Pool. Pets accepted. $151-250

★★★HILTON ST. LOUIS DOWNTOWN

400 Olive St., St. Louis, 314-436-0002, 800-445-8667; www.hilton.com

A historic landmark, the Hilton St. Louis occupies the original Merchant Laclede building. All of St. Louis' attractions are within walking distance of this hotel, including the Gateway Arch, Busch Stadium and America's Center. 195 rooms. Restaurant, bar. Fitness room. Business center. Pets accepted. $61-150

★★★HILTON ST. LOUIS FRONTENAC

1335 S. Lindbergh Blvd., St. Louis, 314-993-1100, 800-325-7800; www.hilton.com

Located between downtown St. Louis and Lambert International Airport, this hotel is near the St. Louis Zoo, the Science Center, Six Flags Amusement Park and adjacent to the upscale Plaza Frontenac shopping mall.

263 rooms. Restaurant, bar. Fitness center. Pool. Pets accepted. $151-250

★★HOLIDAY INN

811 N. Ninth St., St. Louis, 314-421-4000, 800-289-8338; www.holiday-inn.com

295 rooms. Restaurant, bar. Fitness center. Pool. Pets accepted. $61-150

★★★HYATT REGENCY ST. LOUIS

1 St. Louis Union Station, St. Louis, 314-231-1234, 800-633-7313;
www.stlouis.hyatt.com

Located in the renovated Union Station railroad terminal, the main lobby and lounge of this hotel occupy the Grand Hall. The mall in the station has many stores and restaurants. Décor here is traditional, but contemporary details include an updated fitness center and luxury linens on the beds.

539 rooms. Restaurant, bar. Business center. Fitness center. Pool. $151-250

★★★MARRIOTT ST. LOUIS AIRPORT

10700 Pear Tree Lane, St. Louis, 314-423-9700, 877-264-8771; www.marriott.com

This airport hotel provides complimentary shuttle service and updated business and fitness centers. The Rock River Grill and Rock River Tavern serve a variety of classic American fare.

601 rooms. Restaurant, bar. Business center. Fitness center. Pool. $151-250

★★★OMNI MAJESTIC HOTEL

1019 Pine St., St. Louis, 314-436-2355, 800-843-6664; www.omnihotels.com

This European-style hotel is located in downtown St. Louis and is listed in the National Register of Historic Buildings.

91 rooms. Restaurant, bar. Business center. Fitness center. Pets accepted. $151-250

★★PARKWAY HOTEL

4550 Forest Park Blvd., St. Louis, 314-256-7777, 866-314-7700;
www.theparkwayhotel.com

220 rooms. Restaurant, bar. Business center. Fitness center. $61-150

★★RADISSON HOTEL AND SUITES

200 N. Fourth St., St. Louis, 314-621-8200, 800-333-3333;
www.radisson.com/stlouismo

440 rooms. Restaurant, bar. Fitness center. Pool. $151-250

★★★RENAISSANCE ST. LOUIS GRANDSUITES AND HOTEL

800 Washington Ave., St. Louis, 314-621-9600, 800-468-3571;
www.renaissancehotels.com

This historic downtown hotel is close to St. Louis' top attractions. There are five onsite restaurants and a full fitness center, as well as an indoor pool.

1083 rooms. Restaurant, bar. Business center. Fitness center. Pool. Pets accepted. $61-150

★★★RENAISSANCE ST. LOUIS HOTEL AIRPORT

9801 Natural Bridge Road, St. Louis, 314-429-1100, 800-340-2594;
www.renaissancehotels.com

This hotel is adjacent to the Lambert International Airport and has been recently updated with pillow-top mattresses and an onsite Starbucks.

393 rooms. Restaurant, bar. Business center. Fitness center. Pool. $151-250

★★★★THE RITZ-CARLTON, ST. LOUIS

100 Carondelet Plaza, Clayton, 314-863-6300, 800-241-3333; www.ritzcarlton.com

This sophisticated hotel features spacious and plush guest rooms, all with private balconies with views of the city skyline. A comprehensive fitness center includes lap and hydrotherapy pools. The Wine Room is a unique spot for sampling one of the hotel's more than 7,000 bottles of wine while the restaurant offers a fine dining experience.

301 rooms. Restaurant, bar. Business center. Fitness center. Pool. Pets accepted. $351 and up

★★★SEVEN GABLES INN

26 N. Meramec Ave., Clayton, 314-863-8400, 800-433-6590; www.sevengablesinn.com
Surrounded by upscale shops, galleries and restaurants, this inn offers a blend of old world charm and modern conveniences. The inn was inspired by sketches in Nathaniel Hawthorne's novel *The House of Seven Gables*. 32 rooms. Restaurant, bar. Complimentary breakfast. $61-150

★★★SHERATON CLAYTON PLAZA

7730 Bonhomme Ave., Clayton, 314-863-0400, 800-325-3535;
www.sheraton.com/clayton
This hotel, located in Clayton just outside St. Louis, is loaded with amenities from an indoor pool to an onsite Enterprise car rental desk, a sundeck and a fitness center.
259 rooms. Restaurant, bar. Business center. Fitness center. Pool. Pets accepted. $151-250

★★★SHERATON ST. LOUIS CITY CENTER HOTEL AND SUITES

400 S. 14th St., St. Louis, 314-231-5007, 800-325-3535; www.sheraton.com
This downtown hotel has oversized rooms with queen-size sleeper sofas for extra guests. Other amenities include a fitness center, an indoor pool and an on-site sports bar.
288 rooms. Restaurant, bar. Business center. Fitness center. Pool. Pets accepted. $151-250

★★★THE WESTIN ST. LOUIS

811 Spruce St., St. Louis, 314-621-2000, 800-228-3000; www.westin.com/stlouis
Adjacent to Busch Stadium and convenient to shopping and restaurants, this contemporary hotel has a spa, a health club and an acclaimed restaurant and bar.
255 rooms. Restaurant, bar. Business center. Fitness center. Spa. Pets accepted. $151-250

WHERE TO EAT
★★BIG SKY CAFÉ

47 S. Old Orchard, Webster Groves, 314-962-5757; www.bigskycafe.net
American. Dinner. Bar. Outdoor seating. $16-35

★BLUEBERRY HILL

6504 Delmar Blvd., St. Louis, 314-727-4444; www.blueberryhill.com
American. Lunch, dinner, late-night. Outdoor seating. Bar. $15 and under

★★BRISTOL SEAFOOD GRILL

11801 Olive Blvd., Creve Coeur, 314-567-0272; www.bristolseafoodgrill.com
Seafood. Lunch, dinner, Sunday brunch. Children's menu. Bar. $36-85

★BROADWAY OYSTER BAR

736 S. Broadway, St. Louis, 314-621-8811; www.broadwayoysterbar.com
Cajun, Creole. Lunch, dinner, late-night. Outdoor seating. Bar. $16-35

★★CAFÉ NAPOLI

7754 Forsyth Blvd., Clayton, 314-863-5731; www.cafenapoli.com

Italian. Lunch, dinner. Bar. $36-85

★★★CARDWELL'S AT THE PLAZA

94 Plaza Frontenac, St. Louis, 314-997-8885; www.cardwellsattheplaza.com

International. Lunch, dinner. Reservations recommended. Outdoor seating. Children's menu. Bar. $16-35

★★★CARDWELL'S IN CLAYTON

8100 Maryland, Clayton, 314-726-5055; www.cardwellsinclayton.com

This restaurant's celebrity chefs dish up an innovative American-style menu in a modern dining room.

Seafood. Lunch, dinner. Closed Sunday. Outdoor seating. Children's menu. Bar. $16-35

★★CHARLIE GITTO'S

207 N. Sixth St., St. Louis, 314-436-2828; www.charliegittos.com

American, Italian. Lunch, dinner. Closed Sunday. Children's menu. Bar. $16-35

★CROWN CANDY KITCHEN

1401 St. Louis Ave., St. Louis, 314-621-9650; www.crowncandykitchen.net

American. Lunch, dinner. $15 and under

★★CUNETTO HOUSE OF PASTA

5453 Magnolia Ave., St. Louis, 314-781-1135; www.cunetto.com

Italian. Lunch, dinner. Closed Sunday. Outdoor seating. Bar. $16-35

★★DIERDORF & HART'S STEAK HOUSE

701 E. Market St., St. Louis, 314-878-1801; www.dierdorfharts.com

Steak. Dinner. Reservations recommended. Bar. $36-85

★★★DOMINIC'S RESTAURANT

5101 Wilson Ave., St. Louis, 314-771-1632; www.dominicsrestaurant.com

Friendly service and a menu of well-crafted, traditional Italian cuisine have earned this restaurant a loyal following since it opened in 1971. Entrées include breast of chicken alla Romano, lobster picante and veal T-bone chop with truffle sauce. Pasta dishes range from pappardelle with mushrooms to risotto with lobster. The wine list is Italian-focused with many exceptional vintages.

Italian. Dinner. Closed Sunday. Reservations recommended. Children's menu. Bar. $$$

★★FRANK PAPA'S RISTORANTE

2241 S. Brentwood Blvd., Brentwood, 314-961-3344; www.frankpapas.com

Italian. Dinner. Closed Sunday. Bar. $36-85

★★FRAZER'S RESTAURANT AND LOUNGE

1811 Pestalozzi St., St. Louis, 314-773-8646; www.frazergoodeats.com

International. Dinner. Closed Sunday. Outdoor seating. Bar. $16-35

★★★THE GARDENS AT MALMAISON

3519 St. Albans Road, St. Albans, 636-458-0131; www.gardensmalmaison.com

A rustic replica of a French inn tucked away in the countryside outside of St. Louis, this restaurant offers a small, fresh seasonal menu.

French. Dinner. Closed Tuesday-Wednesday. Outdoor seating. Jacket required. Bar. $36-85

★GINO'S RESTAURANT

4502 Hampton Ave., St. Louis, 314-351-4187

Italian. Dinner. Closed Monday. Reservations recommended. Outdoor seating. Children's menu. Bar. $16-35

★★★GIOVANNI'S

5201 Shaw Ave., St. Louis, 314-772-5958; www.giovannisonthehill.com

This restaurant is best described as timeless Italian. The highlight is its focus on fresh seafood, which is flown in daily. The veal and beef dishes are also superlative.

Italian. Dinner. Closed Sunday. Reservations recommended. Bar. $36-85

★★GIUSEPPE'S

4141 S. Grand Blvd., St. Louis, 314-832-3779; www.giuseppesongrand.com

Italian. Lunch, dinner. Closed Monday. Bar. $16-35

★★★THE GRILL

The Ritz-Carlton, St. Louis, 100 Carondelet Plaza, Clayton, 314-863-6300, 800-241-3333; www.ritzcarlton.com

Located in the Ritz-Carlton, St. Louis hotel, this upscale dining room serves up contemporary interpretations of American classics. The décor includes extensive mahogany paneling and woodwork, overstuffed leather banquettes, dramatic lighting and a marble fireplace. Nightly entertainment is featured (piano or acoustic guitar), and on weekends, there's live music (jazz, blues, or swing) in the hotel lounge.

American. Dinner. Reservations recommended. Bar. $36-85

★★★HACIENDA

9748 Manchester Road, Rock Hill, 314-962-7100; www.hacienda-stl.com

Built as a residence for a steamboat captain in 1861, this rambling, casual restaurant consistently delivers in its preparation of the Mexican favorites.

Mexican. Lunch, dinner. Outdoor seating. Bar. $16-35

★HAMMERSTONE'S

2028 S. Ninth, St. Louis, 314-773-5565; www.hammerstones.net

American. Breakfast, lunch, dinner. Outdoor seating. Children's menu. Bar. $16-35

★★HARRY'S

2144 Market St., St. Louis, 314-421-6969; www.harrysrestaurantandbar.com

American. Lunch, dinner, late-night. Reservations recommended. Outdoor seating. Bar. $36-85

WARM AND TOASTY

Ravioli: Classic Italian dish consisting of pasta squared around a filling of meat or cheese, boiled and topped with a sauce. In most places, yes, but in St. Louis, the near-mandatory appetizer in classic Italian joints takes a twist on the recipe. In the Hill District that is home to many old-time Italian dining spots—as well in just about any of the many excellent strip-mall Italian restaurants in the suburbs—the ravioli takes a detour into some breading and then to the deep-fryer before it reaches the plate.

Many establishments claim to have invented the dish. Among the more legitimate contenders is Charlie Gitto's (originally called Angelo's). The story goes that a chef accidentally dropped some raviolis into bread crumbs and decided to deep-fry them for the heck of it. A tradition was born.

Whatever the truth is, toasted ravioli—which is generally a concoction encasing savory beef or veal, topped with marina sauce and sprinkled with Parmesan cheese—is a St. Louis original and a comforting opener to any dinner.

★★HARVEST
1059 S. Big Bend Road, St. Louis, 314-645-3522; www.harveststlouis.com
International. Dinner. Closed Monday. Reservations recommended. Bar. $36-85

★★J. F. SANFILIPPO'S
705 N. Broadway, St. Louis, 314-621-7213; www.jfsanfilippos.com
Italian. Lunch, dinner. Closed Sunday (except during football season). Children's menu. Bar. $16-35

★JOHN D. MCGURK'S
1200 Russell Blvd., St. Louis, 314-776-8309; www.mcgurks.com
American, Irish. Lunch, dinner. Bar. $16-35

★★★JOHN MINEO'S
13490 Clayton Road, Town and Country, 314-434-5244; www.johnmineos.com
For decades, this Italian-continental restaurant has lured diners with dishes such as Dover sole and veal chop, as well as daily fresh fish specials and housemade pasta.
Italian. Dinner. Jacket required. Bar. $36-85

★★JOSEPH'S ITALIAN CAFÉ
107 N. Sixth St., St. Louis, 314-421-6366; www.josephsofstlouis.com
Italian. Lunch, dinner. Closed Sunday. Outdoor seating. Children's menu. Bar. $16-35

★★★KEMOLL'S
1 Metropolitan Square, St. Louis, 314-421-0555; www.kemolls.com
Since 1927, this downtown landmark restaurant has served classic specialties in an elegant atmosphere. The name was originally shortened from the Sicilian name Camuglia, and the restaurant is run by fourth-generation family members.
Italian. Dinner. Closed Sunday. Reservations recommended. $36-85

★★★KREIS'S
535 S. Lindbergh Blvd., St. Louis, 314-993-0735; www.kreisrestaurant.com

This German-influenced steakhouse (think meat and potatoes) has been at the same location more than 50 years. It's housed in a renovated 1930s brick house with beamed ceilings.

Steak. Dinner. Bar. $16-35

★★LOMBARDO'S
10488 Natural Bridge Road, St. Louis, 314-429-5151; www.lombardosrestaurants.com

Italian. Lunch, dinner. Closed Sunday. Reservations recommended. Bar. $16-35

★★★LOMBARDO'S TRATTORIA
201 S. 20th St., St. Louis, 314-621-0666; www.lombardosrestaurants.com

Family-owned and operated for three generations, this restaurant is located in a converted hotel. The menu lists family classics as well as creative seasonal entrées.

Italian. Lunch, dinner. Closed Sunday. Reservations recommended. Bar. $16-35

★★LORUSSO'S CUCINA
3121 Watson Road, St. Louis, 314-647-6222; www.lorussos.com

Italian. Lunch, dinner. Closed Monday. Reservations recommended. Children's menu. Bar. $16-35

★MAGGIE O'BRIEN'S
2000 Market St., St. Louis, 314-421-1388; www.maggieobriens.com

American, Irish. Lunch, dinner. Outdoor seating. Children's menu. Bar. $16-35

★★MIKE SHANNON'S
100 N. Seventh St., St. Louis, 314-421-1540; www.shannonsteak.com

Steak. Lunch, dinner. Reservations recommended. Outdoor seating. Children's menu. Bar. $16-35

★★PORTABELLA
15 N. Central Ave., Clayton, 314-725-6588; www.portabellarestaurant.com

Mediterranean. Lunch, dinner. Bar. $36-85

★★REMY'S
222 S. Bemiston, Clayton, 314-726-5757; www.allgreatrestaurants.com

Mediterranean. Lunch, dinner, late-night. Outdoor seating. Bar. $16-35

★RIDDLE PENULTIMATE
6307 Delmar Blvd., University City, 314-725-6985; www.riddlescafe.com

International. Dinner, late-night. Closed Monday. Outdoor seating. Bar. $16-35

★★SALEEM'S LEBANESE CUISINE
6501 Delmar Blvd., St. Louis, 314-721-7947

Middle Eastern. Lunch, dinner. Closed Sunday. Outdoor seating. Bar. $16-35

★★SCHLAFLY TAP ROOM

2100 Locust St., St. Louis, 314-241-2337; www.schlafly.com

American. Lunch, dinner. Outdoor seating. Bar. $16-35

★★★SCHNEITHORST'S HOFAMBERG INN

1600 S. Lindbergh Blvd., Ladue, 314-993-4100; www.schneithorst.com

Unusual ethnic influences give traditional German cuisine an unexpected new face on this menu. Atlantic salmon with rain forest fruit relish and seafood strudel are a few examples. In true German fashion, 33 specialty beers are also available on tap.

German, American. Breakfast, lunch, dinner. Outdoor seating. Children's menu. Bar. $16-35

★★SIDNEY STREET CAFÉ

2000 Sidney St., St. Louis, 314-771-5777; www.sidneystreetcafe.com

American. Dinner. Closed Sunday-Monday. Reservations recommended. Children's menu. Bar. $16-35

★SPIRO'S

3122 Watson Road, St. Louis, 314-645-8383; www.spiros-restaurant.com

American. Lunch, dinner. Closed Monday. Reservations recommended. Children's menu. $16-35

★THAI CAFÉ

6170 Delmar Blvd., St. Louis, 314-862-6868; www.thaicuisine.com

Thai menu. Lunch, dinner. $16-35

★★★★TONY'S

410 Market St., St.Louis, 314-231-7007; www.tonysstlouis.com

Italian food may bring to mind images of pasta with red sauce, but at Tony's you'll find a menu of authentic Italian fare prepared with a measured and sophisticated hand. Expect appetizers like smoked salmon with mascarpone cheese and entrées like tenderloin of beef with foie gras in a port wine demiglaze. The room has an urban, postmodern style, with sleek low lighting, linen-topped tables and glossy, wood-paneled walls. The chef's tasting menu is a nice choice for gourmands with healthy appetites.

Italian. Dinner. Closed Sunday; also first week of January and first week of July. Reservations recommended. Jacket required. Bar. $36-85

★★TRATTORIA MARCELLA

3600 Watson Road, St. Louis, 314-352-7706; www.trattoriamarcella.com

Italian. Dinner. Closed Sunday-Monday. Reservations recommended. Bar. $16-35

★★YEMANJA BRASIL

2900 Missouri Ave., St. Louis, 314-771-7457; www.brazildining.com

Brazilian. Dinner. Outdoor seating. Bar. $16-35

★ZIA'S

5256 Wilson Ave., St. Louis, 314-776-0020; www.zias.com

Italian. Lunch, dinner. Closed Sunday. Outdoor seating. Bar. $16-35

STE. GENEVIEVE

See also Bonne Terre, Cape Girardeau, St. Louis

Sainte Genevieve, the first permanent settlement in Missouri, developed on the banks of the Mississippi River early in the 18th century when Frenchmen began mining lead in the region. After a flood in 1785, the village was moved to higher ground. Once St. Louis's chief rival, Sainte Genevieve preserves its French heritage in its festivals, old houses and massive redbrick church.

WHAT TO SEE
BOLDUC HOUSE MUSEUM

125 S. Main St., Ste. Genevieve, 573-883-3105; www.bolduchouse.com

This restored French house with walls of upright heavy oak logs features period furnishings, orchard and an herb garden.
April-November, daily.

FELIX VALLE HOME STATE HISTORIC SITE

198 Merchant St., Ste. Genevieve, 573-883-7102;
www.mostateparks.com/felixvalle.htm

A restored and furnished Federal-style stone house of an early fur trader. Guided tours are available.
Daily.

GUIBOURD-VALLE HOUSE

1 N. Fourth St., Ste. Genevieve, 573-883-7544

Late 18th-century restored vertical log house on a stone foundation; French heirlooms. Attic with Norman truss and hand-hewn oak beams secured by wooden pegs. Courtyard; rose garden; stone well; costumed guides.
April-October, daily; March and November, Saturday-Sunday.

SAINTE GENEVIEVE MUSEUM

Merchant Street and DuBourg Place, Ste. Genevieve, 573-883-3461

Display of salt manufacturing, the state's first industry. Scale model of rail car transfer boat, Ste. Genevieve, which carried trains across the Mississippi. Native American artifacts; local mementos.
Daily.

WHERE TO EAT
★ANVIL SALOON

46 S. Third St., Ste. Genevieve, 573-883-7323

Oldest commercially operated building in the city (circa 1850) featuring early Western saloon décor.
German, American. Lunch, dinner. Closed holidays. Bar. $16-35

★OLD BRICK HOUSE

90 S. Market St., Ste. Genevieve, 573-883-2724

True to its name, this is one of the first brick buildings, built in 1785, west of the Mississippi.
American. Breakfast, lunch, dinner. Children's menu. Bar. $16-35

NEBRASKA

IN LITTLE MORE THAN A CENTURY, NEBRASKA—PART OF WHAT WAS ONCE CALLED THE "great American desert"—has evolved from a vast prairie occupied by Native Americans and buffalo to a farming, ranching and manufacturing mainstay of America, with an enticing array of recreational and cultural attractions.

Spaniards visited the region first, but it was on the basis of explorations by Father Marquette and Louis Jolliet in 1673 that French fur traders and missionaries swept over the land, and France claimed it. Nevertheless, it was recognized as Spanish land until 1800, when it became a plaything of European politics and was sold by Napoleon to the United States as part of the Louisiana Purchase in 1803. Famous pathfinders like John C. Fremont, Kit Carson and the men who trapped for John Jacob Astor thought the land was unfit for cultivation.

Today, Nebraska is a "breadbasket" state, with an economy rooted in agriculture. But for the visitor, there is much more than corn, wheat and cows. As with Kansas to the south and South Dakota to the north, to traverse Nebraska from east to west is to trace a transition of terrain, climate and culture—from the tidy farms, sticky summers and small towns, along with the occasional big city, to a more unbridled landscape. Cattle graze on vast tracts of rangeland patrolled by actual cowboys, counties are bigger than some Northeastern states, the air dries out and the wind is almost always blowing as the land gradually slopes upward and becomes the high country stretching to the Rocky Mountains and the West.

At the eastern edge, by the Missouri River, is Omaha, the state's largest city. As one might expect in cattle country, it's a place to find a good steak, but if you're hunting for more adventurous cuisine, you'll find it. Home to a number of Fortune 500 companies as well as a major branch of the state university and the highly regarded Creighton University, Omaha offers its share of big-city sophistication.

Heading west on the interstate, you'll come to Lincoln, the state capital and site of the University of Nebraska main campus and the fabled Cornhuskers football team. A rabid army of red-clad fans chews over the fortunes of their squad year-round.

Farther out, if you are traveling by Kearney on Interstate 80, one attraction you literally can't miss is the Great Platte River Road Archway, a structure that spans 300 feet over the highway and houses a multimedia exhibit that salutes Nebraska's pioneer spirit along with the state's progression into modern times. In the movie *As Good as It Gets*, Jack Nicholson's character pays a visit here.

Wherever you are in Nebraska, the history, whether of the Native population, the settlers from the East, or some of the tragic clashes between the two, is rich The landscape, whether bleak or lush, can be beautiful and is easily explored by car, bike, horse or foot.

FROM CRAZY HORSE TO CARHENGE

Vast, lightly populated and filled with raw beauty, the Sandhills country of western Nebraska takes visitors by surprise. Start in North Platte with a visit to Buffalo Bill Ranch State Historical Park, which preserves the Western icon's home on the range. Head north on Highway 83 to the Nebraska National Forest. At 90,000 acres, it's the largest hand-planted forest in the country. Continue north to Valentine, set along the Niobrara River, a favorite for canoeing. Drive west on Highway 20 to Merriman, site of the Sandhills Ranch State Historical Park (still a working ranch despite its name), then on to Chadron to visit the Museum of the Fur Trade. Continue west to Fort Robinson State Park, where Crazy Horse died. The nearby Pine Ridge and Oglala National Grassland are great spots for horseback riding, mountain biking and hiking. To return to civilization, take Highway 2 south from Crawford to Alliance, home to the famous Carhenge, a variation on England's Stonehenge. From Alliance, head south on Highway 385 to pick up the Oregon Trail route at Bridgeport or return to North Platte on Highway 2 east and Highway 83 south. Approximately 550 miles.

AUBURN

See also Nebraska City

WHAT TO SEE
BROWNVILLE
Highway 136, Auburn
Restored riverboat town of the 1800s. More than 30 buildings, many of which are open to the public.

INDIAN CAVE STATE PARK
RR 1, Shubert, 402-883-2575
On approximately 3,400 acres, this park includes oak-covered Missouri River bluffs and the old St. Deroin town site, which has been partially reconstructed. Also here are ancient petroglyphs in Indian Cave; scenic overlooks of the river. Redbud trees bloom in profusion during spring.

MISSOURI RIVER HISTORY MUSEUM
Highway 136, Auburn, 402-825-3341
Located aboard the Captain Meriwether Lewis, a former Corps of Engineers dredge, this museum contains exhibits on river history.
Memorial Day-Labor Day, daily; Labor Day-Memorial Day, Saturday-Sunday.

NEMAHA VALLEY MUSEUM
1423 19th St., Auburn, 402-274-3203
Exhibits trace history of Nemaha County; period rooms; farm equipment.
Tuesday-Sunday afternoons.

WHERE TO STAY
★AUBURN INN
517 J St., Auburn, 402-274-3143, 800-272-3143
36 rooms. Pets accepted. $61-150

★PALMER HOUSE
1918 J St., Auburn, 402-274-3193, 800-272-3143
22 rooms. Pets accepted. $61-150

WHERE TO EAT
★WHEELER INN
1905 J St., Auburn, 402-274-4931
American. Dinner. Closed Sunday. Bar. $16-35

CHADRON
See also Crawford
The starting point of a sensational 1,000-mile horse race to Chicago in 1893, Chadron saw nine men leave in competition for a $1,000 prize. Doc Middleton, a former outlaw, was one of the starters, but John Berry beat him to the door of Buffalo Bill's Wild West Show in 13 days and 16 hours. The headquarters and a Ranger District office of the Nebraska National Forest and headquarters of the Oglala National Grasslands are located here.

WHAT TO SEE
CHADRON STATE PARK
15951 Highway 385, Chadron, 308-432-6167; www.chadron.com
A park with approximately 950 acres. Paddleboats, hiking, horseback riding, cross-country skiing and camping are available.

MUSEUM OF THE FUR TRADE
6321 Highway 20, Chadron, 308-432-3843; www.furtrade.org
Displays depict the history of the North American fur trade from 1500-1900. Restored trading post and storehouse used by James Bordeaux, a French trader.
Memorial Day-September, daily; rest of year, by appointment.

WHERE TO STAY
★BEST WESTERN WEST HILLS INN
1100 W. 10th St., Chadron, 308-432-3305, 877-432-3305; www.bestwestern.com
67 rooms. Complimentary breakfast. Fitness center. Business center. Pool. Pets accepted. $61-150

★SUPER 8
840 W. Highway 20, Chadron, 308-432-4471; www.super8.com
45 rooms. Complimentary breakfast. Pool. Pets accepted. $61-150

COLUMBUS
Named by its founders for Ohio's capital, Columbus has become a center of industry, agriculture and statewide electrical power.

WHAT TO SEE
PAWNEE PARK
Highway 30, Columbus, 402-564-0914
This park features a swimming pool, ball fields, tennis courts, picnicking

facilities, and a playground on 130 acres along Loup River. A quincentenary bell tower is dedicated to Columbus's voyage to the new world.

PLATTE COUNTY HISTORICAL SOCIETY
2916 16th St., Columbus, 402-564-1856; www.megavision.net/museum
See exhibits on local history, a period schoolroom, barbershop, research library and cultural center.
April-mid-October, Friday-Sunday.

WHERE TO STAY
★★NEW WORLD INN AND CONFERENCE CENTER
265 33rd Ave., Columbus, 402-564-1492, 800-433-1492; www.newworldinn.com
140 rooms. Restaurant, bar. Pool. $61-150

★SUPER 8
3324 20th St., Columbus, 402-563-3456; www.super8.com
63 rooms. Complimentary breakfast. Pets accepted. $61-150

★★★★★ **NEBRASKA**

CRAWFORD
See also Chadron
The area around this community is rich in fossil beds. The Hudson-Meng Bison Kill Site is loaded with animal bones and other artifacts more than 10,000 years old.

WHAT TO SEE
FORT ROBINSON MUSEUM
3200 W. Highway 20, Crawford, 308-665-2919; www.nebraskahistory.org/sites/fortrob
The museum is located in the former fort headquarters building and displays authentic costumes and weapons of Native Americans and soldiers. Other exhibit buildings include guardhouse, a harness repair, blacksmith wheelwright shops, an adobe officer quarters and a veterinary hospital. This is the site of Red Cloud Indian Agency.
Guided tours: Memorial Day-Labor Day. Museum: Memorial Day-Labor Day, daily; Labor Day-Memorial Day, Monday-Friday.

FORT ROBINSON STATE PARK

3200 Highway 20, Crawford, 308-665-2660; www.stateparks.com/fort_robinson.html

This fort was established in 1874 in the midst of Native American fighting (the Sioux leader, Crazy Horse, was killed here). The park displays herds of buffalo. A park entry permit is required.

OGLALA NATIONAL GRASSLAND

16524 Highway 385, Chadron, 308-432-4475

This area includes nearly 95,000 acres of prairie grasses in the badlands of Northwestern Nebraska, popular for hunting (in season), hiking and back-packing.

FORT ROBINSON'S WORLD WAR II HISTORY

Nebraska might seem an unlikely place to encounter World War II history, but out in the northwestern corner of the state you can visit a fort that, having originally stood as an important outpost in the Indian Wars, served as camp for German and Axis prisoners of war in 1943.

The fort compound had already come into wartime use as a K-9 Dogs for Defense training center. But as prisoner capacity in Great Britain became squeezed, Fort Robinson, located far from any city but alongside mainline railways and with opportunities for needed labor, was picked as a spot to hold captured enemy soldiers. The first to arrive in the facility, built to accommodate 3,000 men, were soldiers captured from Rommel's Tenth Panzer Division in North Africa. They traveled by train from Virginia. When they arrived at the camp, the men were searched for contraband; items such as maps, cameras and binoculars were confiscated. Somehow one German soldier had managed to travel with a chihuahua in his coat pocket.

The prisoners worked at a variety of camp-based jobs and were paid 80 cents an hour, as mandated by the Geneva Conventions. But even though the war had caused a labor shortage in agriculture, the Fort Robinson prisoners were not pressed into farm work, whereas at Camp Scottsbluff, approximately 80 miles to the south, German and Italian POWs worked in sugar beet and bean fields.

TRAILSIDE MUSEUM

Main Street, Crawford, 308-665-2929; www.trailside.unl.edu

The newest exhibit at this museum features the fossils of two mammoths discovered in the nearby Little Badlands. The creatures locked tusks in battle and died inter-twined. The museum also features exhibits of natural history from the Fort Robinson area and daily science field trips to Toadstool Park and fossil sites.

Memorial Day-Labor Day, daily; May, Wednesday-Sunday.

WHERE TO STAY
★★FORT ROBINSON LODGE

Crawford, 308-665-2900

53 rooms. Closed late November-mid-April. Restaurant. Pool. Tennis. $61-150

FREMONT

See also Omaha

This town was named for John C. Fremont, a Union general in the Civil War who ran for president of the United States. In the town's early days, the crops were so bad that lots sold for 75 cents each. Finally, travelers on the Overland Trail brought with them enough trade that the town began to prosper and grow. Midland Lutheran College gives a collegiate atmosphere to an otherwise industrial town.

WHAT TO SEE

FREMONT AND ELKHORN VALLEY RAILROAD

1835 N. Somers Ave., Fremont, 402-727-0615, 800-942-7245; www.fremontrailroad.com

Train rides to Nickerson and Hooper aboard vintage rail cars. Reservations are recommended.
Schedule varies.

FREMONT DINNER TRAIN

1835 N. Somers Ave., Fremont, 402-727-8321; www.fremontrailroad.com

Two restored 1940s rail cars make 30-mile round trips through the Elkhorn Valley.
Saturday-Sunday.

LOUIS E. MAY HISTORICAL MUSEUM

1643 N. Nye Ave., Fremont, 402-721-4515

The 25-room house of Fremont's first mayor, built in 1874, features oak and mahogany paneling, art glass windows and rooms furnished in late 19th-century style.
May-August and December, Wednesday-Sunday; April and September-October, Wednesday-Saturday.

WHERE TO STAY

★AMERICA'S BEST VALUE INN

1649 E. 23rd St., Fremont, 402-721-1109; www.bestvalueinn.com

48 rooms. Complimentary breakfast. Pool. Pets accepted. $61-150

★★WILDERNESS LODGE AND COMFORT CENTER

1220 E. 23rd Ave., Fremont, 402-727-1110, 800-743-7666; www.wildernesslodgecc.com

100 rooms. Restaurant, bar. Fitness center. Pool. Pets accepted. $61-150

GRAND ISLAND

See also Hastings, Kearney

Named by French trappers for a large island in the Platte River, the town was moved five miles north in 1869 to its present location on the Union Pacific Railroad, which dominated Grand Island's early existence. Traditionally a trade center for a rich irrigated agriculture and livestock region, the city now has diversified industry, including meat and food processing, agricultural and irrigation equipment and mobile homes.

WHAT TO SEE
CRANE MEADOWS NATURE CENTER
9325 S. Alda Road, Wood River, 308-382-1820
This educational center features exhibits and programs about the Platte River habitat.
Daily.

MORMON ISLAND STATE RECREATION AREA
7425 S. Highway 281, Grand Island, 308-385-6211
Approximately 90 acres with 61 water acres on the Mormon Trail includes swimming, fishing, boating and picknicking.

RAILROAD TOWN ANTIQUE MALL
319 W. Third St., Grand Island, 308-398-2222
Turn-of-the-century outdoor museum contains 60 original buildings, including three houses, the cottage where Henry Fonda was born, schoolhouse, newspaper office, bank, post office, hotel, country church and more.
May-mid-October, daily.

STUHR MUSEUM OF THE PRAIRIE PIONEER
3133 W. Highway 34, Grand Island, 308-385-5316; www.stuhrmuseum.org
This museum situated on an island surrounded by a man-made lake, was designed by Edward Durell Stone.
Daily.

SPECIAL EVENT
HUSKER HARVEST DAYS
Cornhusker Army Ammunition Plant, 309 W. Second St., Grand Island,
www.huskerharvestdays.com
Agricultural exhibits, techniques, and equipment used in irrigation.
Mid-September.

WHERE TO STAY
★DAYS INN
2620 N. Diers Ave., Grand Island, 308-384-8624, 800-329-7466; www.daysinn.com
63 rooms. Complimentary breakfast. Pets accepted. $61-150

★★HOLIDAY INN
2503 S. Locust St., Grand Island, 308-384-1330, 800-548-5542; www.holiday-inn.com
197 rooms. Restaurant, bar. Business center. Pool. $61-150

★★HOWARD JOHNSON
3333 Ramada Road, Grand Island, 308-384-5150, 800-446-4656; www.hojo.com
181 rooms. Restaurant, bar. Complimentary breakfast. Pool. Pets accepted.
$61-150

WHERE TO EAT
★HUNAN
2249 N. Webb Road, Grand Island, 308-384-6964
Chinese. Lunch, dinner. Bar. $16-35

HASTINGS
See also Grand Island
Hastings came into being almost overnight when two railroad lines crossed. Within eight years of its founding, its population swelled to almost 3,000. After 75 years as a depot and supply center, the town turned out large quantities of ammunition during World War II and the Korean War.

WHAT TO SEE
HASTINGS MUSEUM
1330 N. Burlington Ave., Hastings, 402-461-2399; www.hastingsmuseum.org
Includes natural science, pioneer history, Native American lore and historical displays.
Daily.

WILLA CATHER STATE HISTORIC SITE
413 N. Webster St., Red Cloud, 402-746-2653
Author Willa Cather grew up in Red Cloud, and her childhood home has been converted into a museum. Included are her letters, first editions of her books, photos and Cather family memorabilia. Other buildings include the Red Cloud depot, St. Juliana Falconieri Catholic Church, Grace Episcopal Church and *My Ántonia* farmhouse.
Daily.

WHERE TO STAY
★★QUALITY HOTEL AND CONVENTION CENTER
2205 Osborne Drive E., Hastings, 402-463-6721, 888-465-4329;
www.choicehotels.com
101 rooms. Restaurant, bar. Pool. Pets accepted. $61-150

WHERE TO EAT
★BERNARDO'S STEAK HOUSE
1109 S. Baltimore, Hastings, 402-463-4666
Steak. Lunch, dinner. Children's menu. Bar. $16-35

★★TAYLOR'S STEAKHOUSE
1609 N. Kansas, Hastings, 402-462-8000; www.taylorssteakhouseandcatering.com
Steak. Dinner. Closed Sunday. Children's menu. Bar. $36-85

KEARNEY
See also Grand Island, Lexington
Kearney (CAR-nee) is named for the frontier outpost Fort Kearny. It is one of the largest migratory bird flyways in the world, a temporary home for millions of species.

WHAT TO SEE
FORT KEARNY STATE HISTORICAL PARK
1020 V Road, Kearney, 308-865-5305

The first Fort Kearny was erected at Nebraska City in 1846; it was moved here in 1848 to protect the Oregon Trail. In the park are a restored 1864 stockade, a sod blacksmith-carpenter shop, a museum and an interpretive center.
Memorial Day-Labor Day, daily.

GEORGE W. FRANK HOUSE
West Highway 30, Kearney, 308-865-8284; www.unk.edu

This three-story mansion, built in 1889, has a Tiffany window.
June-August, Tuesday-Sunday.

MUSEUM OF NEBRASKA ART
2401 Central Ave., Kearney, 308-865-8559; monet.unk.edu/mona

Collection of paintings, sculptures, drawings and prints created by Nebraskans or with Nebraska as the subject.
Tuesday-Saturday, Sunday afternoons.

TRAILS AND RAILS MUSEUM
710 W. 11th St., Kearney, 308-234-3041; www.bchs.kearney.net/museum.html

Visit a restored 1898 depot, 1880s freighters' hotel and 1871 country schoolhouse. Includes displays of pioneer trails and rails, steam engines and more.
Memorial Day-Labor Day, daily; rest of year by appointment.

UNIVERSITY OF NEBRASKA AT KEARNEY
905 W. 25th St., Kearney, 308-865-8441; www.unk.edu

This branch of the state university offers undergraduate, graduate and specialist degrees. Two art galleries and a planetarium are located on campus.

WHERE TO STAY
★★BEST WESTERN INN OF KEARNEY
1010 Third Ave., Kearney, 308-237-5185, 800-641-5437; www.bestwestern.com

61 rooms. Restaurant. Complimentary breakfast. Fitness center. Pool. Pets accepted. $61-150

★★HOLIDAY INN
110 S. Second Ave., Kearney, 308-237-5971; www.holiday-inn.com

163 rooms. Restaurant, bar. Fitness center. Pool. $61-150

★★RAMADA INN
301 Second Ave., Kearney, 308-237-3141, 800-652-1909; www.ramada.com

209 rooms. Restaurant, bar. Complimentary breakfast. Pool. Pets accepted. $61-150

WHERE TO EAT
★★ALLEY ROSE
2013 Central Ave., Kearney, 308-234-1261; www.alleyrose.com
Lunch, dinner. Closed Sunday. Children's menu. Bar. $16-35

★★GRANDPA'S STEAK HOUSE
13 Central Ave., Kearney, 308-237-2882
Steak. Lunch, dinner. Children's menu. Bar. $16-35

LEXINGTON
See also Kearney
Originally a frontier trading post and settlement along the Oregon Trail, completion of the Union Pacific Railroad brought more settlers to this farmland. Lexington is known as the antiques center of Nebraska.

WHAT TO SEE
DAWSON COUNTY HISTORICAL MUSEUM
805 N. Taft St., Lexington, 308-324-5340; www.dchsmuseum.com
Exhibits include Dawson County history gallery, furnished rural schoolhouse, 1885 Union Pacific depot, 1903 locomotive, farm equipment and 1919 experimental biplane. Collection also includes quilts and prehistoric Native American artifacts.
Monday-Saturday.

SPECIAL EVENT
ANTIQUE AND CRAFT EXTRAVAGANZA
Dawson County Fairgrounds, Lexington, 308-324-5504; www.visitlexington.org
More than 275 antiques, craft and flea market dealers.
Labor Day weekend.

WHERE TO STAY
★FIRST INTERSTATE INN
2503 Plum Creek Parkway, Lexington, 308-324-5601, 800-462-4667; www.1stinns.com
52 rooms. Complimentary breakfast. Pool. Pets accepted. $61-150

★SUPER 8
104 E. River Road, Lexington, 308-324-7434, 800-800-8000; www.super8.com
47 rooms. Complimentary breakfast. Fitness center. $61-150

LINCOLN
See also Nebraska City, Omaha
The second-largest city in Nebraska, Lincoln feuded with Omaha, the territorial seat of government, for the honor of being capital of the new state. When the argument was settled in Lincoln's favor in 1867, books, documents and office furniture were moved in covered wagons late one night to escape the armed band of Omaha boosters. As a young lawyer in the 1890s, William Jennings Bryan went to Congress from Lincoln; in 1896, 1900 and 1908, he ran unsuccessfully for president.

The unicameral (one-house legislature) form of government in Nebraska, which was set up by an amendment to the state constitution in 1934 (mostly by the efforts of Nebraska's famous senator, George W. Norris), is of great interest to students of political science. Supporters say it works efficiently and avoids delays and deadlocks common to two-house legislatures.

WHAT TO SEE
EXECUTIVE MANSION
1135 M St., Lincoln, 402-434-5335; www.lincoln.org
The state governor's mansion features Georgian Colonial architecture.
Tours: Thursday afternoons.

FOLSOM CHILDREN'S ZOO
1222 S. 27th St., Lincoln, 402-475-6741; www.lincolnzoo.org
This zoo features exotic animals, contact areas, botanical gardens and train and pony rides.
April-mid-August, daily.

GREAT PLAINS ART MUSEUM
1155 Q St., Lincoln, 402-472-6220; www.unl.edu
Works by Remington, Russell and other artists are among the nearly 700 pieces in this collection. Also featured are 4,000 volumes of Great Plains and Western Americana.
Tuesday-Sunday; closed between exhibits.

LINCOLN CHILDREN'S MUSEUM
1420 P St., Lincoln, 402-477-4000; www.lincolnchildrensmuseum.org
A variety of cultural and scientific exhibits invite exploration and involve the senses.
Tuesday-Sunday.

LINCOLN MONUMENT
201 N. Seventh St., Lincoln, 402-434-5348
This standing figure of Abraham Lincoln was designed by the sculptor Daniel Chester French, who also produced the seated statue for Henry Bacon's Lincoln Memorial in Washington, D.C.

MUSEUM OF NEBRASKA HISTORY
15th and P streets, Lincoln, 402-471-4754; www.nebraskahistory.org
The history of Nebraska is summarized in exhibits covering events from prehistoric times through the 1950s.
Tuesday-Sunday.

NATIONAL MUSEUM OF ROLLER SKATING
4730 South St., Lincoln, 402-483-7551; www.rollerskatingmuseum.com
Skates, costumes and photographs documenting the sport and industry from 1700 to the present; also archives dealing with world and national competitions since 1910. The only museum in the world devoted solely to roller skating.
Monday-Friday.

PIONEERS PARK

2740 A St., Lincoln, 402-441-7895; www.lincoln.ne.gov

This park features hiking, bike trails, bridle path; a golf course, picnicking areas, and playgrounds. There is also a nature preserve and outdoor amphitheater.

Daily.

STATE CAPITOL

1445 K St., Lincoln, 402-471-0448

Designed by Bertram Goodhue, the most dominant feature of this building is the central tower, which rises 400 feet. Ground was broken in 1922 for this third capitol building at Lincoln and was completed 10 years later. Sculpture by Lee Lawrie includes reliefs and friezes depicting the history of law and justice, great philosophers, symbols of the state and a bronze statue of the Sower (32 feet) atop the tower dome. The great hall, rotunda and legislative chambers are decorated in tile and marble murals, tapestries and wood-inlaid panels. Guided tours.

Daily.

STATEHOOD MEMORIAL—THOMAS P. KENNARD HOUSE

1627 H St., Lincoln, 402-471-4764; www.nebraskahistory.org

This 1869 house is the restored residence of Nebraska's first secretary of state.

Monday-Friday, by appointment.

STRATEGIC AIR & SPACE MUSEUM

28210 W. Park Highway, Ashland, 402-944-3100; www.strategicairandspace.com

Features a permanent collection of 33 aircrafts and six missiles relating to the history of SAC and its importance in the preservation of world peace. Interactive children's gallery, theater, museum store.

Daily.

UNIVERSITY OF NEBRASKA

501 N. 14th St., Lincoln, 402-472-7211; www.unl.edu

This state university of more than 33,000 students has research-extension divisions throughout the state. Following Cornhuskers football is a treasured state pastime.

UNIVERSITY OF NEBRASKA STATE MUSEUM

307 Morrill Hall, 402-472-2642; www.museum.unl.edu

This museum features displays of fossils (dinosaurs and mounted elephants), rocks and minerals, ancient life, Nebraska plants and animals. There are also Native American exhibits as well as changing exhibits.

Daily.

SPECIAL EVENTS
JULY JAMM

12 and N streets, Lincoln, 402-434-6900

This July fest features an art show and musical performances.

Late July.

NEBRASKA STATE FAIR

1800 State Fair Park Drive, Lincoln, 402-474-5371; www.statefair.org
Large fair with livestock, food, contests, games.
Late August.

WHERE TO STAY
★★BEST WESTERN VILLAGER COURTYARD & GARDENS

5200 O St., Lincoln, 402-464-9111; www.bestwestern.com
186 rooms. Restaurant, bar. Complimentary breakfast. Fitness center. Pool.
Pets accepted. $61-150

★CHASE SUITE HOTEL

200 S. 68th Place, Lincoln, 402-483-4900, 888-433-6183; www.chasehotellincoln.com
120 rooms. Complimentary breakfast. Business center. Fitness center. Pool.
Spa. Tennis. Pets accepted. $61-150

THE CORNHUSKER

333 S. 13th St., Lincoln, 402-474-7474, 800-793-7474; www.thecornhusker.com
Continental style meets Midwestern friendliness at Lincoln's luxurious
Cornhusker Hotel. A Nebraska landmark since 1926, today's Cornhusker has
sophisticated décor, fine dining, exceptional amenities and dedicated service.
The tenth-floor Executive Level offers an upgraded experience. Hand-painted murals and fiber-optic starlight help make the Terrace Grille a pleasant
setting for continental cuisine.
297 rooms. Restaurant, bar. Business center. Fitness center. Pool. $61-150

★★HOLIDAY INN

141 N. Ninth St., Lincoln, 402-475-4011, 800-432-0002; www.holiday-inn.com
230 rooms. Restaurant, bar. Pool. $61-150

WHERE TO EAT
★★BILLY'S

1301 H St., Lincoln, 402-474-0084; www.billysrestaurant.com
American. Lunch (Monday-Friday), dinner. Closed Sunday. Bar. $16-35

★YIA YIA

1423 O St., Lincoln, 402-477-9166
Pizza. Lunch, dinner. Closed Sunday. Outdoor seating. Bar. $16-35

NEBRASKA CITY

See also Auburn, Lincoln
Nebraska City began as a trading post but grew larger and wilder as the Missouri River and overland traffic brought bullwhackers, muleskinners and riverboat men with bowie knives and pistols in their belts. Located on the Missouri River, Nebraska City ships grain and agricultural products worldwide.

WHAT TO SEE
ARBOR LODGE STATE HISTORICAL PARK
2300 Second Ave., Nebraska City, 402-873-7222
More than 72 acres of wooded grounds surround the 52-room, neo-Colonial mansion of J. Sterling Morton (the originator of Arbor Day and the secretary of agriculture under Grover Cleveland) and summer residence of his son Joy Morton (the founder of Morton Salt Company).
Mansion: April-December, daily. Park grounds: daily.

MAYHEW CABIN AND HISTORIC VILLAGE FOUNDATION
2012 Fourth Corso, Nebraska City, 402-873-3115; www.johnbrownscave.com
Original log cabin and cave where slaves were hidden before and after the Civil War.
April-November, Wednesday-Sunday.

WILDWOOD HISTORIC HOME
420 S. Steinhart Park Road, Nebraska City, 402-873-6340
A 10-room 1869 house with mid-Victorian-era furnishings, this home has a formal parlor, antique lamps and fixtures. The original brick barn is now an art gallery.
Mid-April-October, Monday-Saturday 10 a.m.-5 p.m., Sunday 1-5 p.m. or by appointment.

SPECIAL EVENTS
APPLEJACK FESTIVAL
Nebraska City, 402-873-3000; www.nebraskacity.com
Celebration of the apple harvest. Parade, antique and craft show, classic car show, football game.
Third weekend in September.

ARBOR DAY CELEBRATION
2300 Second Ave., Nebraska City, 402-873-3000
Tree-planting ceremonies in Arbor Lodge State Historical Park; parade, arts festival, fly-in, breakfast.
Last weekend in April.

WHERE TO EAT
★★EMBERS STEAKHOUSE
1102 Fourth Corso, Nebraska City, 402-873-6416
Steak. Lunch, dinner. Children's menu. Bar. $16-35

NORFOLK
German families from Wisconsin were the first to till the rich soil around Norfolk. The town's livestock business and expanding industries have brought prosperity, making Norfolk the chief marketplace of Northeastern Nebraska.

WHAT TO SEE
COWBOY TRAIL

Highway 81 and Tahazorika Road, Norfolk, 402-371-4862
This 321-mile trail follows the former Chicago and Northwestern railroad line from Norfolk to Chadron. Includes 13,878 feet of hand-railed bridges. Trail is suitable for hiking and mountain biking, with horseback riding allowed alongside the trail.

WHERE TO STAY
★★NORFOLK COUNTRY INN

1201 S. 13th St., Norfolk, 402-371-4430, 800-233-0733; www.norfolkcountryinn.com
127 rooms. Restaurant, bar. Pool. Pets accepted. $61-150

★★RAMADA INN

1227 Omaha Ave., Norfolk, 402-371-7000; www.ramada.com
98 rooms. Restaurant, bar. Pool. Pets accepted. $61-150

★SUPER 8

1223 W. Omaha Ave., Norfolk, 402-379-2220, 800-800-8000; www.super8.com
66 rooms. Complimentary breakfast. Pets accepted. $61-150

WHERE TO EAT
★★BRASS LANTERN

1018 S. Ninth St., Norfolk, 402-371-2500
Steak. Lunch, dinner. Children's menu. Bar. $16-35

★★PRENGER'S

116 E. Norfolk Ave., Norfolk, 402-379-1900; www.prengers.com
American. Lunch, dinner. Children's menu. Bar. $16-35

★★★THE UPTOWN CAFÉ

801 10th St., Stanton, 402-439-5100
Visitors to this restaurant in the middle of the Wild West may be surprised by the refined food and good wine selection. Famed for its support of local artists and musicians, the dining room is filled with paintings and also features live music.
Seafood. Lunch, dinner, late-night. Bar. $16-35

NORTH PLATTE
North Platte, Buffalo Bill Cody's hometown, is the retail, railroad and agricultural hub of West Central Nebraska.

WHAT TO SEE
BUFFALO BILL RANCH STATE HISTORICAL PARK

2921 Scouts Rest Ranch Road, North Platte, 308-535-8035;
The 18-room house, barn and outbuildings of William F. Cody's ranch include an interpretive film and displays of buffalo.
Memorial Day-Labor Day, daily; October-April, Monday-Friday.

FORT MCPHERSON NATIONAL CEMETERY
Interstate 80, exit 190, Maxwell
Soldiers and scouts of Native American and later wars are buried here.

LINCOLN COUNTY HISTORICAL MUSEUM
2403 N. Buffalo Bill Ave., North Platte, 308-534-5640; www.lincolncountymuseum.org
Several authentically furnished rooms and exhibits, including a World War II canteen, depict the life and history of Lincoln County. In back is the re-creation of a railroad village with a restored depot, house, church, schoolhouse, log house and barn.
Memorial Day-Labor Day, daily; Labor Day-Memorial Day, by appointment.

SPECIAL EVENT
NEBRASKALAND DAYS CELEBRATION
509 E. Fourth St., North Platte, 308-532-7939; www.nebraskalanddays.com
Parades, entertainment, food, and the famous PRCA Rodeo are all a part of this fun-filled celebration.
Mid-late June.

WHERE TO STAY
★HAMPTON INN
200 Platte Oasis Parkway, North Platte, 308-534-6000, 800-426-7866;
www.hamptoninn.com
110 rooms. Complimentary breakfast. Business center. Pool. $61-150

★★ROYAL COLONIAL INN
1402 S. Jeffers St., North Platte, 308-534-3630, 800-624-4643;
www.royalcolonialinn.com
140 rooms. Restaurant, bar. Complimentary breakfast. Pool. Pets accepted. $61-150

WHERE TO EAT
★GOLDEN DRAGON
120 W. Leota St., North Platte, 308-532-5588
Chinese. Lunch, dinner. $16-35

OGALLALA
Developed as a shipping point on the Union Pacific Railroad for the great Western cattle herds, Ogallala was the goal of the cattle-driving cowboys who rode day and night with their "eyelids pasted open with tobacco." Many of them are buried in a genuine Boot Hill Cemetery, between 11th and 12th streets on a 100-foot rise above the South Platte River, where there have been no burials since the 1880s.

WHAT TO SEE
ASH HOLLOW STATE HISTORICAL PARK
Highway 26, Ogallala, 308-778-5651
Approximately 1,000 acres on the Oregon Trail. The hills, caves and springs

of Ash Hollow have sustained humans from prehistoric times through the pioneer days. Hiking, picnicking. Interpretive center, restored school.

CRESCENT LAKE NATIONAL WILDLIFE REFUGE
10630 Road 181, Oshkosh, 308-762-4893; www.fws.gov
A nesting and migratory bird refuge comprising more than 45,000 acres with numerous pothole lakes. Birds found in the refuge include Canadian geese, great blue herons, American bitterns, prairie chickens, prairie falcons and long-billed curlews.

FRONT STREET
519 E. First St., Ogallala, 308-284-6000; www.megavision.net/frontstreet
Cowboy museum, general store, saloon, arcade, restaurant. Nightly shows in Crystal Palace during summer.

LAKE MCCONAUGHY STATE RECREATION AREA
1500 Highway 61 N., Ogallala, 308-284-3542
This recreation area covers approximately 5,500 acres on Nebraska's largest lake offering swimming, fishing, boating, picnicking and camping.

LAKE OGALLALA STATE RECREATION AREA
1500 Highway 61 N., Ogallala, 308-284-3542
Located on approximately 300 acres with a 320-acre lake, Ogallala offers fishing, boating, and camping.

MANSION ON THE HILL
1004 N. Spruce St., Ogallala
This 1890s mansion contains period furniture, pioneer household items. Memorial Day-Labor Day, daily.

WHERE TO STAY
★★BEST WESTERN STAGECOACH INN
201 Stagecoach Trail, Ogallala, 308-284-3656, 800-662-2993; www.bestwestern.com
100 rooms. Restaurant, bar. Complimentary breakfast. Fitness center. Pool. Pets accepted. $61-150

★COMFORT INN
110 Pony Express Lane, Ogallala, 308-284-4028, 877-424-6423; www.comfortinn.com
49 rooms. Complimentary breakfast. Pool. $61-150

WHERE TO EAT
★★HILL TOP INN
197 Kingsley Drive, Ogallala, 308-284-4534
Dinner. Closed Monday. Children's menu. Bar. $16-35

OMAHA

See also Fremont, Lincoln

The largest city in Nebraska, Omaha is named for the Native Americans who lived here until they signed a treaty with the federal government on June 24, 1854. Opportunists across the Missouri River in Council Bluffs, Iowa, who had been waiting for the new territory to open, rushed to stake out property, triggering a real estate boom. Omaha also saw the trial of Standing Bear, chief of the Ponca Tribe, which established the precedent that Native Americans were entitled to constitutional rights and protections.

During early boom times, steamboats docked in Omaha daily, bringing gold-seekers and emigrants to be outfitted for the long journey west. Local merchants further prospered when Omaha was named the eastern terminus for the Union Pacific. The first rail was laid in 1865. Public buildings rose on the prairie; schools, plants and stockyards flourished in the 1870s and 1880s. Fighting tornadoes, grasshopper plagues, floods and drought, the people built one of the farm belt's great commercial and industrial cities.

Today, Omaha continues to be a major transportation and agribusiness center but is also a recognized leader in telecommunications, insurance and manufacturing as well as the home of five Fortune 500 companies. Omaha is also the headquarters of STRATCOM, the Strategic Air Command, one of the vital links in the national defense chain.

WHAT TO SEE
AK-SAR-BEN AQUARIUM
21502 W. Highway 31, Gretna, 402-332-3901
This modern facility features more than 50 species of fish native to Nebraska, as well as a terrarium, the World Herald Auditorium, a natural history classroom and orientation and display areas.

DURHAM WESTERN HERITAGE MUSEUM
Omaha Union Station, 801 S. 10th St., Omaha, 402-444-5071;
www.durhammuseum.org
This restored Art Deco railroad depot is now a history museum, featuring exhibits on Omaha history from 1880 to 1954; Byron Reed coin collection; and traveling temporary exhibits.
Tuesday-Sunday.

GENERAL CROOK HOUSE
5730 N. 30th St., Omaha, 402-455-9990; www.omahahistory.org
Built in 1878 to serve as the residence of the commander of the Department of the Platte. Originally called Quarters I, Fort Omaha, the house soon came to be known by the name of its first occupant, General George Crook. The house is of the Italianate architecture with many Victorian antiques and gardens.
Guided tours: by appointment. Daily.

GERALD FORD BIRTH SITE
32nd and Woolworth Avenues, Omaha, 402-444-5955; www.nebraskahistory.org
Model of the original house and White House memorabilia. Betty Ford Memorial Rose Garden.
Daily.

OMAHA'S OLD MARKET

One of the few downtown areas that preserves Omaha's original Victorian-era architecture, the Old Market Area is a five-square-block shopping, dining and gallery district that's the heart and soul of the city center. Window-shop, stop for coffee, pop into art-filled boutiques—this neighborhood is made for strolling. Bounded by Farnam and Jones streets and 10th and 13th streets, the Old Market Area was originally the food-processing center for the region: Swanson Food, Anheuser-Busch and other stalwarts of the food and beverage industry once occupied these buildings. Food is still one of the finest reasons to visit the Old Market Area. Find provisions for a picnic at one of Omaha's best bakeries, Delice European Bakery and Coffee Bar (1206 Howard), and pick up cheese and wine at La Buvette Wine and Grocery (511 S. 11th St.). On Wednesdays and Saturdays in summer and fall, stop for fresh local produce at the farmer's market, held on 11th Street between Jackson and Howard.

Directly south of the Old Market Area on 10th Street is the Durham Western Heritage Museum (801 S. 10th St.), housed in the architecturally stunning Union Station, an Art Deco gem from Omaha's past. The museum has vintage cars and railroad equipment, and a period soda fountain is still in operation.

Walk north on 10th Street five blocks to reach Gene Leahy Mall, a 10-acre park with a lake that serves as a reflecting pond for the modern high-rise architecture of Omaha. Trails wind through the park, linking formal flower gardens, a playground for children, a bandstand and public art displays. To the east, the Leahy Mall connects to Heartland of America Park and Fountain, which is bounded by Eighth Street and the Missouri River. The highlight of the park is its lake, with a fountain that shoots streams of water 300 feet into the air. The General Marion tour boat navigates the lake to take visitors closer to the fountain. At night, the water display is accompanied by pulsing lights.

Return to the Leahy Mall along Douglas Street, which leads into the modern city center. At 24th Street, turn north one block to the Joslyn Art Museum (2200 Dodge St.), Nebraska's premier center for the visual arts. The museum building is itself a work of art, a fanciful Art Deco structure faced with shimmering pink marble. The permanent collection consists of American and European art from the 19th and 20th centuries. A highlight is the cache of works from Karl Bodmer, a German watercolorist who traveled up the Missouri River in the 1830s, capturing the pristine landscapes, Native Americans and wildlife before white pioneer settlement.

GREAT PLAINS BLACK HISTORY MUSEUM

2213 Lake St., Omaha, 402-345-2212

Housed in a building designed in 1907 by prominent Nebraska architect Thomas R. Kimball, the museum preserves the history of African-Americans and their part in the heritage of Omaha and Nebraska since the territorial period of the 1850s. Includes rare photographs, relics, historical displays and films.

Monday-Friday.

HEARTLAND OF AMERICA PARK

Eighth and Douglas streets, Omaha, 402-444-5920

This 31-acre site features picnic facilities, arbors and waterfalls. The park's 15-acre lake has a computer-driven fountain that has a colored light show at night.

HENRY DOORLY ZOO

3701 S. 10th St., Omaha, 402-733-8401; www.omahazoo.org

More than 18,500 animals, many rare, are on display in a 110-acre park. Exhibits include an aquarium, indoor rainforest and walk-through aviary. Daily.

HISTORIC BELLEVUE

112 W. Mission Ave., Bellevue, 402-293-3080, 800-467-2779

Restored buildings include the first church in the Nebraska territory; old depot; settlers' log cabin; and Fontenelle Bank. Sarpy County Historical Museum (2402 SAC Place) has displays concerning the history of the county and changing exhibits.
Tuesday-Sunday.

JOSLYN ART MUSEUM

2200 Dodge St., Omaha, 402-342-3300; www.joslyn.org

This museum's building is of Art Deco design with collections of art, ancient to modern, including European and American paintings, sculpture; art of the Western frontier, Native American art; and traveling exhibitions.
Tuesday-Sunday.

KOUNTZE PLANETARIUM

66th and Dodge streets, Omaha, 402-554-3722; www.physics.unomaha.edu

Planetarium shows display galaxies, stars, planets and other celestial phenomena.

MORMON TRAIL CENTER AT WINTER QUARTERS

3215 State St., Omaha, 402-453-9372; www.lds.org

The winter of 1846-1847 took the lives of more than 600 Mormon emigrants who camped near here. A monument commemorates their hardship. Films and pioneer exhibits are offered in the visitor center.

OLD MARKET

11th and Howard streets, extending to 10th St. and west to 13th, Omaha,
402-341-1877

Art galleries, antique shops and restaurants fill this area revitalizing an old warehouse district. Some of Omaha's oldest commercial buildings line the market's brick-paved streets.

OMAHA CHILDREN'S MUSEUM

500 S. 20th St., Omaha, 402-342-6163; www.ocm.org

Self-directed exploration and play for children and families; constantly changing series of hands-on exhibits in science, the arts and humanities, health and creative play.
Tuesday-Sunday.

PLATTE RIVER STATE PARK

14421 346th St., Louisville, 402-234-2217

These 413 acres are located on rolling bluffs overlooking the Platte River.

There is a swimming pool, paddleboats, hiking and horseback riding trails; tennis courts, an archery range, recreational fields and cross-country skiing.

TWO RIVERS STATE RECREATION AREA

27702 F St., Waterloo, 402-359-5165; www.ngpc.state.ne.us
This recreation area covers more than 600 acres with a water area of 320 acres. You can go swimming; trout fishing, and boating.
Camping: late April-October.

SPECIAL EVENT
RIVER CITY ROUND-UP

Fairgrounds, 302 S. 36th St., Omaha, 402-554-9600; www.rivercityroundup.org
This celebration of agriculture and Western heritage includes parade, barbecues and trail rides.
Late September.

WHERE TO STAY
★★BEST WESTERN REDICK PLAZA HOTEL

1504 Harney St., Omaha, 402-342-1500, 888-342-5339; www.bestwestern.com
89 rooms. Restaurant, bar. Complimentary breakfast. Fitness center. $61-150

★★DOUBLETREE GUEST SUITES OMAHA

7270 Cedar St., Omaha, 402-397-5141, 800-222-8733; www.doubletree.com
187 rooms. Restaurant. Business center. Fitness center. Pool. Pets accepted. $61-150

★★DOUBLETREE HOTEL

1616 Dodge St., Omaha, 402-346-7600, 800-222-8733; www.doubletree.com
414 rooms. Restaurant, bar. Business center. Fitness room. Pool. $61-150

★★EMBASSY SUITES

555 S. 10th St., Omaha, 402-346-9000, 800-362-2779; www.embassysuitesomaha.com
249 rooms. Restaurant, bar. Complimentary breakfast. Fitness center. Pool. Pets accepted. $151-250

★★GREAT ADVENTURE

1811 Hillcrest Drive, Bellevue, 402-292-3800, 800-292-7277
126 rooms. Restaurant, bar. Complimentary breakfast. Pool. Pets accepted. $61-150

★HAMPTON INN

9720 W. Dodge Road, Omaha, 402-391-5300; www.hamptoninn.com
128 rooms. Complimentary breakfast. Business center. Fitness center. $61-150

★★HILTON GARDEN INN

1005 Dodge St., Omaha, 402-341-4400, 800-445-8667; www.hiltongardeninn.com
178 rooms. Restaurant. Business center. Fitness center. Pool. $61-150

★LA QUINTA INN

3330 N. 104th Ave., Omaha, 402-493-1900; www.laquinta.com
133 rooms. Pool. Pets accepted. $61-150

★★★MARRIOTT OMAHA

10220 Regency Circle, Omaha, 402-399-9000; www.marriott.com
This hotel offers two restaurants, a lounge, an indoor and outdoor pool, a health club, and many more amenities. It is located near the Joslyn Art Museum, Old Market, golf courses and tennis facilities.
301 rooms. Restaurant, bar. Fitness center. Pool. $61-150

WHERE TO EAT
★BOHEMIAN CAFÉ

1406 S. 13th St., Omaha, 402-342-9838; www.bohemiancafe.net
American, Eastern European. Lunch, dinner. $16-35

★★BUSTY LE DOUX'S

1014 Howard St., Omaha, 402-346-5100
Cajun. Lunch, dinner. Outdoor seating. Bar. $16-35

★★★CAFÉ DE PARIS

1228 S. Sixth St., Omaha, 402-344-0227
As the name suggests, this is an exceptional French bistro with a menu that does not stray from the classics. A knowledgeable staff and sommelier add to the experience.
French. Dinner. Closed Sunday-Monday. Reservations recommended. Jacket required. Bar. $36-85

★★★FRENCH CAFÉ

1017 Howard St., Omaha, 402-341-3547; www.frenchcafe.com
Elegant French dishes, continually refreshed with contemporary ingredients, have earned this restaurant a good reputation. Pepper steak is a signature dish, and the roasted rack of pork is popular. The wine cellar is substantial.
American, French. Lunch, dinner, Sunday brunch. Closed Monday. Bar. $36-85

★★★GORAT'S STEAK HOUSE

4917 Center St., Omaha, 402-551-3733; www.goratssteakhouse.com
An Omaha landmark for more than 60 years, this steakhouse specializes in classics with thick cuts of filet mignon and more. Enhance the old-school experience with a traditional side dish such as escargot doused in butter or chilled shrimp cocktail.
Steak. Lunch, dinner. Closed Sunday. Reservations recommended. Children's menu. Bar. $36-85

★★INDIAN OVEN

1010 Howard St., Omaha, 402-342-4856

Northern Indian. Lunch, dinner. Closed Sunday. Reservations recommended.
Outdoor seating. Bar. $16-35

★JOHNNY'S CAFÉ

4702 S. 27th St., Omaha, 402-731-4774; www.johnnyscafe.com

Steak. Lunch, dinner. Closed Sunday. Children's menu. Bar. $16-35

★MCFOSTER'S NATURAL KIND CAFÉ

302 S. 38th St., Omaha, 402-345-7477; www.mcfosters.com

American, seafood. Lunch, dinner. Outdoor seating. Children's menu. Bar.
$16-35

★★★SIGNATURES

1616 Dodge St., Omaha, 402-346-7600

Located at the top of the Doubletree Hotel, this restaurant offers a panoramic
view of the city's skyline. A continental concept, the menu draws on influences from all over the world.

Seafood. Breakfast, lunch, dinner, late-night. Bar. $16-35

★★★V. MERTZ

1022 Howard St., Omaha, 402-345-8980; www.vmertz.com

Located just off the brick-walled Old Market Passageway, this cozy restaurant offers a quiet atmosphere. The menu, consisting of continental dishes,
changes weekly and there is an extensive wine list. A jacket and tie are recommended for men.

American. Lunch, dinner. Bar. $16-35

SCOTTSBLUFF

Scottsbluff is the trading center for a large area of western Nebraska and
eastern Wyoming.

WHAT TO SEE
AGATE FOSSIL BEDS NATIONAL MONUMENT

301 River Road, Harrison, 308-668-2211

An approximately 2,700-acre area with two self-guided nature trails, a visitor
center with exhibits of the fossils of animals that roamed the area between 19
and 21 million years ago, and exhibits of Plains Native Americans.
Visitor center, daily.

CHIMNEY ROCK NATIONAL HISTORIC SITE

Highway 26, Bridgeport, 308-586-2581; www.nps.gov/chro

A landmark of the Oregon Trail, Chimney Rock rises almost 500 feet above
the south bank of the North Platte River. Starting as a cone-shaped mound, it
becomes a narrow 150-foot column towering above the landscape. For early
travelers, many of whom sketched and described it in their journals, Chimney Rock marked the end of the prairies. It became a National Historic Site
in 1956.

RIVERSIDE ZOO

1600 S. Beltline W., Scottsbluff, 308-630-6236; www.riversidezoo.org

More than 97 species of both native and exotic animals call this zoo home. The lush park setting features a walk-through aviary, and animals such as the white tiger and moose.

Daily.

SCOTTS BLUFF NATIONAL MONUMENT

190276 Highway 92 W., Gering, 308-436-9700; www.nps.gov/scbl

This 800-foot bluff in western Nebraska was a landmark to pioneers who traveled the California/Oregon Trail by wagon trains. Historians often speak of this natural promontory in the North Platte Valley, which was originally named me-a-pa-te, "hill that is hard to go around," by the Plains Native Americans. Many people, including fur traders, Mormons and gold seekers, came this way. Westward-bound pioneers, Pony Express riders and the first transcontinental telegraph all passed through Mitchell Pass (within Monument boundaries) to skirt this pine-studded bluff. The Oregon Trail Museum at the monument's visitor center depicts the story of westward migration along the trail. A paved road and hiking trail provide access to the summit for a view of the North Platte Valley and other landmarks such as Chimney Rock.

Daily.

WEST NEBRASKA ARTS CENTER

106 E. 18th St., Scottsbluff, 308-632-2226; www.nebraskarts.com

Changing gallery shows in all media throughout the year showcasing the finest artists in the region.

Daily.

WHERE TO STAY
★CANDLELIGHT INN

1822 E. 20th Place, Scottsbluff, 308-635-3751, 800-424-2305;
www.candlelightscottsbluff.com

56 rooms. Complimentary breakfast. Fitness center. $61-150

★COMFORT INN

1902 21st Ave., Scottsbluff, 308-632-7510, 877-424-6423; www.comfortinn.com

49 rooms. Complimentary breakfast. Fitness center. Pool. Pets accepted $61-150

SIDNEY

In 1867, Sidney was established as a division point on the Union Pacific Railroad. Fort Sidney was established shortly thereafter, providing military protection for railroad workers and immigrants. Many relics of the Fort Sidney era remain and have been restored. Sidney, the seat of Cheyenne County, is also a peaceful farm, trading and industrial center.

WHAT TO SEE
CABELA'S

115 Cabela Drive, Sidney, 308-254-5505; www.cabelas.com

Sidney is the corporate headquarters for one of the world's largest outdoor gear outfitters. The 73,000-square-foot building displays more than 60,000 products as well as 500 wildlife mounts. Other attractions in the showroom include an 8,000-gallon aquarium, art gallery, gun library, restaurant and "Royal Challenge," a twice-life-size bronze sculpture of two battling elk. Daily.

FORT SIDNEY POST COMMANDER'S HOME

1108 Sixth Ave., Sidney, 308-254-2150

One of the original buildings of old Fort Sidney, this house was used in the 19th century to protect railroad workers during the Native American wars and has been authentically restored.

Memorial Day-Labor Day, daily.

WHERE TO STAY

★COMFORT INN

730 E. Jennifer Lane, Sidney, 308-254-5011; www.comfortinn.com

55 rooms. Complimentary breakfast. $61-150

★DAYS INN

3042 Silverberg Drive, Sidney, 308-254-2121; www.daysinn.com

47 rooms. Complimentary breakfast. Pool. Pets accepted. $61-150

SOUTH SIOUX CITY

See also Sioux City, IA

This community is an extension of neighboring Sioux City, Iowa.

WHAT TO SEE

PONCA STATE PARK

R.R. 2, Ponca, 402-755-2284; www.ngpc.state.ne.us

Approximately 1,400 acres make up this park, which offers a panoramic view of the Missouri River Valley. There is a swimming pool, fishing, boating, hiking, horseback riding, cross-country skiing, picnicking, and camping.

WHERE TO STAY

★★MARINA INN CONFERENCE CENTER

Fourth and B streets, South Sioux City, 402-494-4000, 800-798-7980; www.marina-inn.com

181 rooms. Restaurant, bar. Pool. Pets accepted. $61-150

NORTH DAKOTA

IN BISMARCK THERE IS A STATUARY GROUP, PIONEER FAMILY, AND BEHIND IT, GLEAMING white against the sky, towers the famous skyscraper capitol. One symbolizes the North Dakota of wagon trains and General Custer. The other symbolizes modern North Dakota: a place where a thousand oil wells have sprouted, dams harness erratic rivers and vast natural resources have been found.

This is a fascinating land of prairies, rich river valleys, small cities, huge ranches and vast stretches of wheat. Bordering Canada for 320 miles to the north, North Dakota shares straight-line borders with Montana to the west and South Dakota to the south. The Red River of the North forms its eastern boundary with Minnesota. The Garrison Dam has changed much of the internal geography of the state's western region, converting the Missouri River, known as "Big Muddy," into a broad waterway with splendid recreation areas bordering the reservoir Lake Sakajawea. To the southwest stretch the Badlands in all their natural grandeur, and the open range about which Theodore Roosevelt wrote so eloquently in his *Ranch Life and the Hunting Trail*.

At various times, Spain, France and England claimed what is now North Dakota as part of their empires. French Canadian fur trappers were the first Europeans to explore the land. After the Louisiana Purchase, explorers Lewis and Clark crossed Dakota, establishing Fort Mandan. The Dakota Territory was organized on March 2, 1861, but major settlement of what later became North Dakota followed after the entry of the Northern Pacific Railroad in the early 1870s.

This is the state in which to trace 19th-century frontier history, to stand at the center of the continent, to see Native American dances and outdoor dramas or to watch the 10 million migratory waterfowl that soar across the sky each spring and fall.

139

BISMARCK

See also Mandan

On the east bank of the Missouri, near the geographic center of the state and within 150 miles of the geographic center of the continent, North Dakota's capitol flourished as a steamboat port called "the Crossing." As the terminus of the Northern Pacific Railway, Bismarck gained new importance and was named for the Chancellor of Germany to attract German capital for building transcontinental railroads. General Custer came to Bismarck to take command of the nearby newly constructed Fort Abraham Lincoln and in 1876 rode out to his fatal rendezvous with Sitting Bull. In 1883, Bismarck became the capital of the Dakota Territory, and in 1889, the seat of the new state.

WHAT TO SEE
NORTH DAKOTA STATE CAPITOL
600 E. Boulevard Ave., Bismarck, 701-328-2480; www.nd.gov/fac/index.html

Constructed in 1933 on a $2 million budget after the original building burned in 1930, this state capitol building stands out from its traditionally domed peers. The 19-story Art Deco limestone tower is one of only four vertically

THE FREE-FLOWING MISSOURI RIVER

There's very little of the free-flowing Missouri River left in North Dakota—only one portion, from Garrison Dam to Bismarck, resembles the broad prairie river as seen by explorers Meriwether Lewis and William Clark. This route explores a section of Missouri River wetlands, allowing modern-day explorers the chance to see the cottonwood forests and wetlands that once stretched along the Missouri, before hydroelectric dams tamed the river.

From Mandan, travel north on Highway 25, which follows the Missouri's western banks. The route passes through farmland and then drops onto a broad, arid basin, with the green, cottonwood-fringed Missouri in the distance. If you don't mind traveling a few miles on gravel roads, turn off Highway 25 east toward the community of Price. Follow the road north along the banks of the river. A number of wildlife refuges string along the river—you may see wild turkeys, deer or bald eagles.

At Hensler, turn west on Highway 200A to visit Fort Clark State Historic Site. Fort Clark was built in 1830 by the American Fur Company as a trading post near a Mandan Indian earthlodge village. A second fort, Primeaus Post, was built on the site in the early 1850s and operated in competition with Fort Clark for most of that decade. Artists Karl Bodmer and George Catlin visited the site, as did German Prince Maximilian, John James Audubon and more than 50 steamboats per year. Many of Bodmer's paintings were of the people and village of Fort Clark.

Continue west along Highway 200A. At Stanton, follow County Highway 37 north to the Knife River Indian Village National Historic Site. One of the largest Hidatsa villages was located at the confluence of the Missouri and the Knife rivers, where this new interpretive center and earthlodge reconstruction are now found. More than 50 earthlodge remains suggest that Native Americans lived in this location for nearly 8,000 years. The circular depressions at the three village sites are up to 40 feet in diameter and are a silent testimony to the people that lived here.

Continue north to join Highway 200 and follow it across the Garrison Dam, the third-largest earth-filled dam in the United States. The dam backs up the Missouri River 175 miles to the west in 378,000-acre Lake Sakajawea. Continue to Highway 83, then head south, zipping past the coal strip mines at Underwood. At Washburn, leave the freeway and follow signs to the Fort Mandan Historic Site, where volunteers have reconstructed Lewis and Clark's log fort. The Lewis and Clark Expedition spent the winter of 1804-1805 here in a cottonwood blockade above the Missouri River. It was here that they met French-Canadian Toussaint Charbonneau, who would serve as their interpreter, and his young Shoshone wife, Sacagawea. This reconstruction of Fort Mandan is downstream from the original site, which has been swallowed by the river. The triangular fort is modest and small, considering that there were 40-odd members of the expedition living here. Also at the park are a visitor center, gift shop and picnic area along the river.

Return to Highway 83 and travel south for seven miles, then exit at Highway 1804 and follow this scenic route south along the free-flowing -Missouri's eastern banks to Bismarck. Approximately 162 miles.

oriented capitols in the United States (along with those in Nebraska, Louisiana and Florida). Beyond its distinctive exterior, the Skyscraper of the Prairies is capped with an observation deck, features lavish interiors fashioned from wood, stone and metal from all over the globe and has a cavernous Great Hall running to the legislative quarters. Tours are available on weekdays in the summer. Also on the grounds are the former Governors' Mansion, now restored and featuring historic displays, and the North Dakota Heritage Center, a regional history museum with an impressive collection of Plains Indian artifacts. Outdoors are two notable sculptures, one of Lewis and Clark guide Sacagawea, and another dubbed The Pioneer Family by Avard Fairbanks.

WARD EARTHLODGE VILLAGE HISTORIC SITE

4480 Fort Lincoln Road, Bismarck, 701-222-6455

Mandan Indians once occupied this bluff above the Missouri River, living in dome-shaped homes built of logs and earth. By the time Lewis and Clark passed through the region, the village was deserted. Depressions remain where the houses once stood, and the site is now part of the city park system. Interpretive signs explain how the village was constructed and elements of Mandan cultural life. Spectacular views from the bluff.

Daily dawn-dusk.

SPECIAL EVENT
UNITED TRIBES POWWOW

3315 University Drive, Bismarck, 701-255-3285; www.unitedtribespowwow.com

Among the most attended powwows in the United States, this annual event is one of the top cultural happenings in North Dakota. Some 1,500 Native American dancers and drummers, representing more than 70 tribes and clothed in traditional garb, perform at the Lone Star Arena at United Tribes Technical College. You'll find singing, dancing and drumming competitions, as well as a softball tournament, a parade, an intertribal summit, a pageant and plenty of food.

Early September.

WHERE TO STAY
★★BEST WESTERN RAMKOTA HOTEL

800 S. Third St., Bismarck, 701-258-7700, 800-780-7234; www.bestwestern.com

306 rooms. Restaurant, bar. Fitness center. Pool. Pets accepted. $61-150

★EXPRESSWAY INN

200 E. Bismarck Expressway, Bismarck, 701-222-2900, 800-456-6388;
www.expresswayinnandsuites.com

163 rooms. Complimentary breakfast. Fitness center. Pool. Pets accepted. $61-150

★FAIRFIELD INN

135 Ivy Ave., Bismarck, 701-223-9293, 800-228-2800; www.fairfieldinn.com

63 rooms. Complimentary breakfast. Pool. $61-150

★★KELLY INN-BISMARCK

1800 N. 12th St., Bismarck, 701-223-8001, 800-635-3559; www.kellyinns.com

101 rooms. Restaurant, bar. Fitness center. Pool. Pets accepted. $61-150

★★RADISSON HOTEL BISMARCK

Sixth Street and Broadway Avenue, Bismarck, 701-255-6000, 800-333-3333;
www.radisson.com

215 rooms. Restaurant, bar. Business center. Fitness center. Pool. Pets accepted. $61-150

★RAMADA LIMITED SUITES

3808 E. Divide Ave., Bismarck, 701-221-3030, 800-295-3895; www.ramada.com
66 rooms.. Complimentary breakfast. Fitness center. Pool. Pets accepted.
$61-150

WHERE TO EAT
★MERIWETHER'S

1700 River Road, Bismarck, 701-258-0666
American. Lunch, dinner, Sunday brunch. Outdoor seating. Children's menu.
Bar. $16-35

★★PEACOCK ALLEY

422 E. Main St., Bismarck, 701-255-7917; www.peacock-alley.com
American, seafood. Lunch, dinner, brunch. Children's menu. Bar. $16-35

DEVILS LAKE

Located near the shore of Devils Lake, this city offers some of the best fishing in North Dakota. The opening of the federal land office here in 1883 sparked the growth of the city.

WHAT TO SEE
DEVILS LAKE

Devils Lake, six miles south of town Highway 2 E., 701-662-4903, 800-233-8048;
www.devilslakend.com
This lake gets its name from the Indian name Miniwaukan, which means "bad water." Bolstered by legends of drowned warriors, the name evolved into Devils Lake. Here, you can enjoy fishing, boating, hunting, golfing, biking, snowmobiling, picknicking and camping.

FORT TOTTEN STATE HISTORIC SITE

Highway 20, Devils Lake, 701-766-4441
Built in 1867 to protect the overland route to Montana, this was the last outpost before 300 miles of wilderness. One of the best-preserved military forts west of the Mississippi; 16 original buildings. Pioneer Daughters Museum; interpretive center, commissary display; videotape program of the site's history. There is a summer dinner theater here also.
Memorial Day-Labor Day, daily; Labor Day-Memorial Day, by appointment.

WHERE TO STAY
★FIRESIDE INN

215 Highway 2 E., Devils Lake, 701-662-6760, 888-266-3948; www.comfortinn.com
87 rooms. Complimentary breakfast. Business center. Pool. Pets accepted.
$61-150

★★TOTTEN TRAIL HISTORIC INN

Fort Totten State Historic Site, 701-766-4874; www.tottentrailinn.com
10 rooms. Closed October-April. Complimentary breakfast. $61-150

FARGO

Fargo, the largest city in North Dakota, was named for William G. Fargo of the Wells-Fargo Express Company. It's the hometown of baseball great Roger Maris, and a museum filled with his personal memorabilia is located in West Acres Mall.

With blackjack legal in North Dakota, Fargo has taken the lead in promoting its gaming tables. There are approximately 30 casinos in the city, making it a major tourist attraction for the three-state region including Minnesota and South Dakota. Charities and nonprofit organizations run the casinos and collect all profits above expenses. The 1996 dark comedy *Fargo* took its name from the city, gently poking fun at the residents' thick northern accents and Scandinavian heritage, but most of the movie actually takes place in Minnesota.

WHERE TO STAY

★AMERICINN
1423 35th St. Southwest, Fargo, 701-234-9946, 800-634-3444;
www.americinnfargo.com
61 rooms. Complimentary breakfast. Business center. Fitness center. Pool. Pets accepted. $61-150

★★BEST WESTERN FARGO DOUBLEWOOD INN
3333 13th Ave. South, Fargo, 701-235-3333, 800-433-3235; www.bestwestern.com
172 rooms. Restaurant, bar. Business center. Pool. Pets accepted. Casino. $61-150

★★BEST WESTERN KELLY INN
1767 S. 44th St., 701-282-2143, 800-580-1234; www.bestwestern.com
83 rooms. Restaurant, bar. Complimentary breakfast. Business center. Fitness center. Pool. Casino. $61-150

★COMFORT SUITES
1415 35th St. South, Fargo, 701-237-5911, 800-228-5150; www.choicehotels.com
66 rooms. Complimentary breakfast. Business center. Pool. Pets accepted. $61-150

★COUNTRY INN & SUITES BY CARLSON
3316 13th Ave., Fargo, 701-234-0565, 888-201-1746; www.countryinns.com
99 rooms. Complimentary breakfast. Business center. Fitness center. Pool. Pets accepted. $61-150

★FAIRFIELD INN
3902 Ninth Ave. Southwest, Fargo, 701-281-0494, 800-228-2800; www.fairfieldinn.com
63 rooms. Complimentary breakfast. Pool. $61-150

★HAMPTON INN
3431 14th Ave. Southwest, Fargo, 701-235-5566, 800-426-7866;
www.hamptoninn.com
75 rooms. Complimentary breakfast. Business center. Pool. $61-150

★★HOLIDAY INN

3803 13th Ave. South, Fargo, 701-282-2700, 877-282-2700; www.holiday-inn.com
315 rooms. Restaurant, bar. Business center. Fitness center. Pool. Pets accepted. $61-150

★HOLIDAY INN EXPRESS

1040 40th St. South, Fargo, 701-282-2000, 800-465-4329; www.hiexpress.com
77 rooms. Complimentary breakfast. Pool. Pets accepted. $61-150

★KELLY INN-FARGO

4207 13th Ave. Southwest, Fargo, 701-277-8821, 800-635-3559;
www.kellyinnfargo.com
59 rooms. Complimentary breakfast. Pool. Business center. Pets accepted.
$61-150

★★RADISSON HOTEL FARGO

201 Fifth St. N., Fargo, 701-232-7363, 800-333-3333; www.radisson.com/fargond
151 rooms. Restaurant, bar. Business center. Fitness center. Pool. Pets accepted. $61-150

★SLEEP INN

1921 44th St. S.W., Fargo, 701-281-8240, 800-424-6423; www.sleepinnfargo.com
61 rooms. Complimentary breakfast. Business center. Fitness center. Pool.
Pets accepted. $61-150

WHERE TO EAT
★★MEXICAN VILLAGE

814 Main Ave., Fargo, 701-293-0120; www.mexicanvillagefm.com
Mexican. Lunch, dinner. Children's menu. $16-35

GRAND FORKS

Grand Forks stands at the point where the Red River of the North and Red
Lake River form a fork. Socially, culturally and commercially the town is
closely allied with its cousin city across the river, East Grand Forks, Minnesota. Originally a French fur trading post, Grand Forks later developed
as a frontier river town. The arrival of the railroad and cultivation of nearby
farmland brought about another change in its personality. The University of
North Dakota plays a dominant role in the city's culture and economy. Grand
Forks Air Force Base is 14 miles west on Highway 2.

WHAT TO SEE
GRAND FORKS COUNTY HISTORICAL SOCIETY

2405 Belmont Road, Grand Forks, 701-775-2216; www.grandforkshistory.com
This historical society maintains the Campbell House, the historic pioneer
cabin of agricultural innovator Tom Campbell. Original log cabin portion
dates from 1879. Also on the grounds are a log post office, one-room schoolhouse and Myra Carriage Museum, which houses a collection of late 19th-
and early 20th-century artifacts from surrounding area.
May-October, daily 1-5 p.m.

TURTLE RIVER STATE PARK

3084 Park Ave., Arvilla, 701-594-4445, 800-807-4723; www.parkrec.nd.gov

Located in a green valley carved out by the gently winding Turtle River, this 784-acre park is a big recreational draw in the Grand Forks area. Because the river is stocked with rainbow trout, angling is a popular pursuit, and there are hiking and biking trails, as well as cross-country ski routes and a sledding hill. For overnighters, a dozen duplex rental cabins, with running water but without kitchens, and 125 campsites are available.

UNIVERSITY OF NORTH DAKOTA

Grand Forks, west end of University Avenue, 701-777-3304, 800-225-5863;
www.und.edu

The Eternal Flame of Knowledge, an immense steel-girded sphere, commemorates Old Main and past presidents. Also here is the North Dakota Museum of Art and the Chester Fritz Library, both of which houses artwork. Tours.

WHERE TO STAY

★★BEST WESTERN TOWN HOUSE

710 First Ave., North, Grand Forks, 701-746-5411, 800-867-9797;
www.bestwestern.com

101 rooms. Restaurant, bar. Pool. Pets accepted. Casino. $61-150

★C'MON INN

3051 32nd Ave., Grand Forks, 701-775-3320, 800-255-2323; www.cmoninn.com

80 rooms. Complimentary breakfast. Fitness center. Pool. $61-150

★COMFORT INN

3251 30th Ave. South, Grand Forks, 701-775-7503, 800-424-6423;
www.comfortinn.com

65 rooms. Complimentary breakfast. Pool. Pets accepted. $61-150

★FAIRFIELD INN

3051 S. 34th St., Grand Forks, 701-775-7910, 800-228-2800; www.fairfieldinn.com

62 rooms. Complimentary breakfast. Pool. $61-150

★★HOLIDAY INN

1210 N. 43rd St., Grand Forks, 701-772-7131, 800-465-4329; www.holidayinn.com

148 rooms. Restaurant, bar. Fitness center. Pool. Casino. $61-150

★LAKEVIEW INNS AND SUITES GRAND FORKS

3350 S. 32nd Ave., Grand Forks, 701-775-5000, 877-355-3500;
www.lakeviewhotels.com

86 rooms. Complimentary breakfast. Pool. $61-150

★★RAMADA INN

1205 N. 43rd St., Grand Forks, 701-775-3951, 888-298-2054; www.ramada.com

100 rooms. Restaurant, bar. Business center. Fitness center. Pool. Pets accepted. Casino. $61-150

JAMESTOWN

See also Valley City

Settlers and businessmen arrived after soldiers and railroad workers established Jamestown as a transportation center guarded by Fort Seward. When
farmers discovered they could pay for their rich land with two years' worth
of crops, the area developed as a prosperous agricultural town. The James
River, the longest unnavigable river in the world, flows through the area. On
the northeastern edge of town is Jamestown College, founded in 1883.

WHAT TO SEE
FRONTIER VILLAGE

500 17th St., Southeast Jamestown, 701-252-8648 or 800-807-1511;
www.buffalomuseum.com

The big lure here is the "Worlds Largest Buffalo," a 60-ton concrete sculpture jutting out of the plains. The adjacent village is also a good place to get
a glimpse of North Dakota's pioneer past. About a dozen historic structures
were relocated here to spare them from the wrecking ball, including a one-
room schoolhouse, a barbershop and a train depot. Also onsite is the National
Buffalo Museum which houses the White Cloud, an albino buffalo.
May-September, daily.

WHITESTONE HILL BATTLEFIELD STATE HISTORIC SITE

Kulm, 701-396-7731

Probably triggered by the 1862 Sioux uprising in Minnesota, the September
1863 Battle of Whitestone Hill marked the beginning of a war between the
U.S. Cavalry and the Plains Sioux that lasted for more than 20 years.
Mid-May-mid-September, Thursday-Monday.

WHERE TO STAY
★COMFORT INN

811 S.W. 20th St., Jamestown, 701-252-7125; www.comfortinn.com
52 rooms. Complimentary breakfast. Pool. Pets accepted. $61-150

★★GLADSTONE INN AND SUITE

111 Second St. Northeast, Jamestown, 701-252-0700, 866-748-4466;
www.gladstoneinn.com
100 rooms. Restaurant, bar. Fitness center. Pool. Pets accepted. $61-150

★★QUALITY INN

Highway 281 S., Jamestown, 701-252-3611, 800-726-7924
120 rooms. Restaurant, bar. Pool. Pets accepted. $61-150

MANDAN

See also Bismarck

The Mandan tribe originally farmed this area, and today the agricultural tradition persists in the dairy and dry farms that surround the city. Lignite, a
soft coal, is mined in this region. Mandan has been an important railroad city
since tracks crossed the Missouri River the year the city was founded.

THE LITTLE MISSOURI BADLANDS

Medora sits at the base of the dramatic Little Missouri Badlands, a deeply eroded gorge that exposes millions of years of sedimentary deposits in colorful horizontal striations. Medora itself is a fascinating historical town—Teddy Roosevelt lived near here in the 1880s, as did the flamboyant Marquis de Mores, a French nobleman who journeyed to the Dakota Territory to live out his cowboy fantasies. Before setting out to explore bluffs that rise behind the town, be sure to visit the Chateau de More, the luxurious frontier home built by the Marquis. When it was constructed in 1883, this 26-room mansion was the finest and most modern private home for hundreds of miles.

The Maah Daah Hey Trail is 100 miles long and connects the northern and southern sections of the Theodore Roosevelt National Park, passing through the Little Missouri National Grassland. The following hike covers four miles at the trail's southern extreme and explores the scenic badlands above Medora, passing through the fascinating and ruggedly beautiful badlands ecosystem. The area is home to prairie wildlife including pronghorn antelope, coyotes, white-tail deer, prairie dogs and rattlesnakes.

Begin at Sully Creek State Park, two miles south of Medora (the Maah Daah Hey Trail is also popular with mountain bikers, so you'll share the trail). The trail crosses the Little Missouri River, which is ankle-deep and easily waded in summer, and follows the river valley through stands of cottonwood, willow and silver sage. The path then begins to climb up the face of a badland mesa, eventually reaching a plateau. From a rocky escarpment, enjoy a magnificent overlook onto Medora and the Little Missouri River breaks. Continue north on the trail through prairie grassland to a side path, the Canyon Trail, which drops steeply down a rugged canyon wall to a prairie dog town. Follow the trail north, through a self-closing gate, to where the Canyon Trail rejoins the Maah Daah Hey. From here, hikers can return to Medora along a gravel road or continue north through more badlands landscape to the South Unit of the Theodore Roosevelt National Park headquarters.

WHAT TO SEE
CROSS RANCH NATURE PRESERVE
The Nature Conservancy, 1401 River Road, Center, 701-794-8741

This 6,000-acre nature preserve has mixed grass prairies, Missouri River floodplain forest and upland woody draws. Bison herd. Hiking and self-guided nature trails.
Daily.

FORT ABRAHAM LINCOLN STATE PARK
4480 Fort Lincoln Road, Mandan, 701-667-6340; www.ndparks.com

This historic site marks the fort which Custer commanded prior to his "last stand." There are reconstructed fort buildings and Mandan earthlodge village along with a visitor center, amphitheater and museum which features interpretive programs in the summer. You can go fishing, hiking, cross-country skiing, snowmobiling and picnicking. There is a playground, concession stand and camping sites.
Tours: Memorial Day-Labor Day.

WHERE TO STAY
★★BEST WESTERN SEVEN SEAS INN & CONFERENCE CENTER
2611 Old Red Trail, Mandan, 701-663-7401, 800-597-7327; www.bestwestern.com

122 rooms. Restaurant, bar. Business center. Pool. Pets accepted. $61-150

MEDORA

This village is a living museum of two of the most colorful characters of the badlands frontier—young, bespectacled Theodore Roosevelt and the hot-blooded, visionary Marquis de Mores. The Marquis, a wealthy Frenchman, established the town and named it for his wife, daughter of a New York banker. He built a packing plant and icehouses, aiming to slaughter cattle on the range and ship them to metropolitan markets in refrigerated railroad cars. The plan fizzled, but not before the mustachioed Frenchman left his stamp on the community. Roosevelt came here in 1883 and won respect as part owner of the Maltese Cross and Elkhorn ranches and as organizer and first president of the Little Missouri Stockmen's Association.

WHAT TO SEE
CHATEAU DE MORES STATE HISTORIC SITE
612 E. Boulevard Ave., Bismarck, 701-623-4355
This site commemorates the life of Antoine de Vallombrosa, the Marquis de Mores. The Marquis dabbled with a stagecoach line, an experiment with refrigerated railroad cars, and a beef packing plant. Remaining are the ruins of a packing plant, a 26-room, two-story frame mansion filled with French furnishings, a library, servants' quarters and a relic room displaying the Marquis's saddles, guns, boots, coats and other possessions. An interpretive center is on the grounds.

THEODORE ROOSEVELT NATIONAL PARK

This national park is a monument to 26th president Theodore Roosevelt, who was the nation's champion of the conservation of natural resources. Roosevelt, who came to the Badlands in September 1883 to hunt buffalo and other big game, became interested in the open-range cattle industry and purchased an interest in the Maltese Cross Ranch near Medora. He returned the next year and established another ranch, the Elkhorn, about 35 miles north of Medora. The demands of his political career and failures at raising cattle eventually forced him to abandon his ranching ventures.

This park preserves the magnificent badlands landscape just as Roosevelt knew it. Wind and water have carved curiously sculptured formations, tablelands, buttes, canyons and rugged hills from a thick series of flat-lying sedimentary rocks. Thick, dark layers of lignite coal, which are sometimes fired by lightning and burn slowly for many years, are exposed in eroded hillsides. The fires often bake adjacent clay layers into a red, brick-like substance called scoria or clinker.

Elk and bison have been reintroduced and thrive here and can be easily seen throughout the park. There are several large prairie dog towns, and mule and whitetail deer are abundant. Wild horses can be seen in the South Unit, and the area is populated with hawks, falcons, eagles and other more common species.

The park is divided into three units. The South Unit is accessible from Interstate 94 (I-94) at Medora, where there is a visitor center and Roosevelt's Maltese Cross cabin. The Elkhorn Ranch Site on the Little Missouri River can be reached only by rough dirt roads, and visitors should check in with rangers at the Medora Visitor Center before venturing out (701-623-4466). The North Unit is accessible from US 85, near Watford City and has a visitor center. An additional visitor center is located at Painted Canyon Scenic Overlook on I-94 (April-October, daily). The park is open all year; visitor centers are closed on holidays.

Park headquarters: 701-623-4466; www.nps.gov/thro

Guided tours: mid-May-mid-September, daily; mid-September-mid-May, by appointment.

WHERE TO STAY
★AMERICINN MEDORA
75 E. River Road South, Medora, 701-623-4800; www.americinn.com
62 rooms. Complimentary breakfast. Pool. Pets accepted. $61-150

MINOT
Minot's advance from tepee and tarpaper to a supersonic-age city has been so vigorous that it calls itself the "Magic City." Where buffalo bones were once stacked by plainscombers stands a city rich from agriculture, lignite coal reserves, oil pools, industry and railroad yards on both sides of the Mouse River. Minot is the commercial center of a radius that sweeps into Canada. Minot State University is located here.

WHAT TO SEE
ROOSEVELT PARK AND ZOO
1219 Burdick Expressway E., Minot, 701-857-4166; www.rpzoo.com
Roosevelt Park and Zoo includes 90 acres of formal lawns and sunken gardens. On the grounds are a swimming pool, water slide and bathhouse. Late May-early September, daily.

SCANDINAVIAN HERITAGE CENTER
Broadway and 11th Ave., Minot, 701-852-9161; www.minotparkdistrict.org
This heritage center features a 230-year-old house from Sigdal, Norway; a Danish windmill; a flag display; and statues of famous Scandinavians. Memorial Day-Labor Day, Saturday-Sunday; Labor Day-Memorial Day, daily.

WHERE TO STAY
★BEST WESTERN KELLY INN
1510 26th Ave. S.W., Minot, 701-852-4400, 800-735-5868;
www.bestwesternminot.com
100 rooms. Bar. Complimentary breakfast. Pool. Pets accepted. $61-150

★COMFORT INN
1515 22nd Ave. S.W., Minot, 701-852-2201, 800-228-5150; www.comfortinn.com
140 rooms. Complimentary breakfast. Pool. Pets accepted. $61-150

★★HOLIDAY INN
2200 Burdick Expressway E., Minot, 701-852-2504, 800-465-4329;
www.holiday-inn.com
170 rooms. Restaurant, bar. Fitness center. Pool. Pets accepted. $61-150

VALLEY CITY
The railroad and the first settlers arrived here simultaneously to establish a community then known as Worthington. Later, as the seat of Barnes County,

this town in the deeply forested Sheyenne River Valley changed to its present name. The grain fields and dairy farms of the surrounding area are the town's main industry.

WHAT TO SEE
FORT RANSOM STATE PARK
5981 Walt Hjelle Parkway, Fort Ransom, 701-973-4331, 800-807-4723; www.ndparks.com

This former frontier Army post has a historic farm that re-creates the life of early homesteaders. The Sodbuster Days festival is held during the second weekends in July and September. An arts and crafts festival is the held during last weekend in September. There is also a downhill ski resort here along with camping, picnic areas, hiking, cross-country skiing and snowmobiling.

WHERE TO STAY
★WAGON WHEELS INN
455 Winter Show Road, Valley City, 701-845-5333; www.wagonwheelinn.com
88 rooms. Pool. $61-150

WHERE TO EAT
★DUTTON'S PARLOUR
256 Central Ave. N., Valley City, 701-845-3390; www.valleygallery.com
American menu. Breakfast, lunch. $61-150

WILLISTON
This city, which was first called Little Muddy, began as a small supply center for ranchers. As the area grew, farming and petroleum, discovered here in the early 1950s, had an impact on the local economy.

WHAT TO SEE
FORT BUFORD STATE HISTORIC SITE
15349 39th Lane N.W., Williston, 701-572-9034; www.nd.gov

Established in 1866 near the merging point of the Missouri and Yellowstone rivers, Fort Buford served as the distribution point for government annuities to peaceful natives in the vicinity. The fort was the site of the surrender of Sitting Bull in 1881. Original features include a stone powder magazine, the post cemetery and a museum.
Mid-May-mid-September, daily; mid-September-mid-May, by appointment.

FORT UNION TRADING POST NATIONAL HISTORIC SITE
15550 Highway 1804, Williston, 701-572-9083; www.nps.gov/fous

The American Fur Company built this fort in 1829 at the junction of the Yellowstone and Missouri Rivers. During the next three decades, it was one of the most important trading depots on the Western frontier. In 1867, the government bought the fort, dismantled it and used the materials to build Fort Buford two miles away. Much of the fort has been reconstructed. A National Park Service visitor center is located in the Bourgeois House. Guided tours and interpretive programs are available in the summer.
Daily.

LEWIS AND CLARK STATE PARK

4904 119th Road N.W., Williston, 701-859-3071; www.ndparks.com/parks/lcsp.htm

Situated on a northern bay in Lake Sakakawea—a man-made body of water created by damming the Missouri River—this state park is so named because the Lewis and Clark expedition camped nearby twice, on their 1805 westward journey in search of the fabled Northwest Passage and on the return trip east the next year. Today, the park is popular because of its marina, a jumping-off point for boaters and anglers. Of the fish lurking below, the most remarkable are immense paddlefish, prehistoric-looking beasts once thought to be extinct, and endangered pallid sturgeon, which grow up to six feet in length. A good trail system allows for hiking and cross-country skiing.

LEWIS AND CLARK TRAIL MUSEUM

Highway 85, Alexander, 701-828-3595

Located on the first leg of the Corps of Discovery's westward route (south of Williston and the Missouri River in Alexander), this museum covers not only Lewis and Clark but also early homesteaders in North Dakota. The most notable exhibit is a scale model of Fort Mandan, where the party stayed during the winter of 1804-1805.

Memorial Day-Labor Day, daily.

OKLAHOMA

PROBABLY EVERY STATE IS MISUNDERSTOOD IN ITS OWN WAY. BUT MAYBE OKLAHOMA HAS a special claim. Is it the vast dusty terrain from which impoverished farmers fled during the Great Depression? Is it the good-ol'boy land of *Okie from Muskogee* that Merle Haggard celebrated in song, or the romantic land of the stylized cowboy culture as sung about in the musical *Oklahoma!*? Is it Southern—bordered, as it is, by Arkansas on the east? Is it a northern annex of Texas? (The twang of the Lone Star state is certainly audible here.) Or does it belong to the West, with its neatly rectangular panhandle touching New Mexico and Colorado?

The area that was to become the state of Oklahoma was practically unknown to Americans at the time of the Louisiana Purchase of 1803. Believing those unsettled lands to be of little value, the government set them aside as "Indian Territory" in 1830, assigning a portion to each of the Five Civilized Tribes. Thousands of Creeks, Choctaws, Chickasaws, Seminoles and Cherokees were forced to leave the Southeastern U.S. and move to Oklahoma. About one-fourth of those forced west over this "Trail of Tears" died on the way of hunger, disease, cold and exhaustion. Today Oklahoma has the largest Native American population in the United States.

As the nation moved west, settlers squatted in the Indian Territory, wanting the land for development. On April 22, 1889, portions of the land were opened for settlement. In the next few years all unassigned Oklahoma land was opened by a series of six "runs." People who jumped the gun were called "Sooners," giving the state its nickname, the "Sooner State." Close to 17-million acres of land were settled in this way; the last lottery, a form of run, took place on August 16, 1901. Previously unsettled tracts became cities within eight hours.

Oklahoma produces millions of barrels of oil a year, and you might see churning derricks almost anywhere, including beside runways of the Oklahoma City airport. The state has vast expanses of lightly settled country forests and green fields in the eastern part, ranchland and prairie in the drier west. Some people would be surprised to learn that Oklahoma has mountains, but in the southeastern corner of the state (Kiamichi County), there are seven ranges. Northeast Oklahoma has both rolling hills and flat prairies, along with several large lakes and plenty of state parks. The southwestern part of the state is true Great Plains and Chisholm Trail territory and has several major museums that explore the region's heritage and history, which started with the Kiowa, Comanche, Apache, the original inhabitants and then saw the impact of settlers and clashes between newcomers and natives.

ALTUS

In the spring of 1891, a flood on Bitter Creek forced a group of settlers to flee to higher ground, taking with them what possessions they could. Gathered together to escape destruction, they founded a town and called it Altus because one of them said the word meant "high ground." On the border between the high plains and the southland, Altus lies between winter wheat on the north and cotton on the south. Nearby Altus Air Force Base is the home of the 97th Air Mobility Wing.

WHAT TO SEE
MUSEUM OF THE WESTERN PRAIRIE
1100 Memorial Drive, Altus, 580-482-1044;
www.okhistory.org/museums/westernprairie.html
Exhibits depict all aspects of pioneer living in Southwestern Oklahoma. Tuesday-Saturday.

SPECIAL EVENT
GREAT PLAINS STAMPEDE RODEO
Altus, Oklahoma, 580-482-0210; www.greatplainsstampederodeo.com
This is a Professional Rodeo Cowboys Association-sanctioned rodeo along with other special events.
Late August.

WHERE TO STAY
★BEST WESTERN ALTUS
2804 N. Main St., Altus, 580-482-9300, 888-537-1087; www.bestwestern.com
100 rooms. Complimentary breakfast. Business center. Fitness center. Pool. Pets accepted. $61-160

★★RAMADA INN
2515 E. Broadway St., Altus, 580-477-3000; www.motel6.com
20 rooms. Restaurant, bar. Pool. Pets accepted. $61-150

ALVA
Founded in 1893 as a land office for the largest land run in Oklahoma following the opening of the Cherokee strip, this small northwestern town is home to Northwestern Oklahoma State University.

WHAT TO SEE
ALABASTER CAVERNS
Highway 50A, Freedom, 580-621-3381; www.wildlifedepartment.com
On approximately 200 acres, Alabaster is said to be the largest known natural gypsum cavern in the world.
Tours: daily.

GREAT SALT PLAINS
Highway 38, Jet, 580-626-4731; www.greatsaltplains.com
The Great Salt Plains take up approximately 840 acres with a 9,300-acre lake. Enjoy wimming, fishing, boating, nature trails, a picnic area, a playground, camping areas and cabins here.
Daily.

LITTLE SAHARA
101 Main St., Alva, 580-824-1471; www.waynoka.com
This park makes up approximately 1,600 acres with sand dunes, picnicking areas, and a playground.

WHERE TO STAY
★RANGER INN

420 E. Oklahoma Blvd., Alva, 580-327-1981, 800-814-7402; www.rangerinnmotel.com
41 rooms. Pets accepted. $61-150

BARTLESVILLE

The Bartlesville area is proud of its Western and Native American heritage, which involves three tribes: the Cherokee, Delaware and Osage. Oklahoma's first electricity was produced here in 1876 when Jacob Bartles, an early settler, hitched a dynamo to the Caney River. Oil, first tapped in the area in 1897, is the economic base of the city. Bartlesville has become internationally known for its distinguished, modern architecture, a building trend initiated by the H. C. Price family, which made its fortune in oil. The town boasts a number of both public and private buildings by Frank Lloyd Wright and Bruce Goff.

WHAT TO SEE
FRANK PHILLIPS MANSION

1107 S. Cherokee Ave., Bartlesville, 918-336-2491; www.frankphillipshome.org
Built in 1909 by the founder of the Phillips Petroleum Company, this neoclassical house has been restored to the 1930s period. The interior includes imported woods, marble, Oriental rugs and original furnishings. This mansion is listed on the National Register of Historic Places.
Wednesday-Saturday 10 a.m.-5 p.m.; second Sunday of the month 1-5 p.m.

NELLIE JOHNSTONE OIL WELL

Johnstone Park, 300 N. Cherokee, Bartlesville
This is a replica of the first commercial oil well in the state. Also here is an 83-acre park with a low water dam on the Caney River where you can enjoy fishing, picnicking, playgrounds and children's rides.
Late May-Labor Day, daily. Park: daily.

PRICE TOWER

510 Dewey Ave., Bartlesville, 918-336-4949; www.pricetower.org
Designed by Frank Lloyd Wright, this 221-foot office building was built for pipeline construction pioneer H. C. Price as headquarters for his company. The building design is based on a diamond module of 30/60-degree triangles. Although Wright designed many skyscrapers, Price Tower was his only tall building to be completed.
Guided tours: Tuesday-Saturday.

TOM MIX MUSEUM

721 N. Delaware, Dewey, 918-534-1555
This museum features exhibits and memorabilia of silent movie star Tom Mix, the first "King of the Cowboys." There are displays of his cowboy gear and stills from his films.
Tuesday-Sunday.

WOOLAROC

Highway 123, Bartlesville, 918-336-0307; www.woolaroc.org

Complex covering 3,600 acres with wildlife preserve for herds of American bison, longhorn cattle, Scottish Highland cattle, elk, deer and other native wildlife. Paintings by Russell, Remington and other great Western artists are at the museum; exhibits on the development of America; artifacts of several Native American tribes, pioneers and cowboys. The Native American Heritage Center has multimedia shows, authentic Native American crafts, art displays, a picnic area and a nature trail.

Memorial Day-Labor Day, Tuesday-Sunday; Labor Day-Memorial Day, Wednesday-Sunday 10 a.m.-5 p.m.

WHERE TO STAY
★★BEST WESTERN WESTON INN

222 S.E. Washington Blvd., Bartlesville, 918-335-7755, 800-780-7234;
www.bestwestern.com

109 rooms. Restaurant. Complimentary breakfast. Pool. Pets accepted. $61-150

★★★INN AT PRICE TOWER

510 Dewey Ave., Bartlesville, 918-336-1000, 877-424-2424; www.innatpricetower.com

This contemporary hotel is located in the Frank Lloyd Wright-designed Price Tower. The tower suites, decorated in mid-century modern style, are two-story and offer views of the prairie.

19 rooms. Restaurant, bar. Complimentary breakfast. Business center. $251-350

WHERE TO EAT
★MURPHY'S ORIGINAL STEAK HOUSE

1625 S.W. Frank Phillips Blvd., Bartlesville, 918-336-4789

Steak. Lunch, dinner. Closed Monday. $16-35

★★STERLING'S GRILLE

2905 E. Frank Phillips Blvd., Bartlesville, 918-335-0707; www.sterlingsgrille.com

Seafood, steak. Lunch (Sunday-Friday), dinner. Outdoor seating. Children's menu. Bar. $16-35

BROKEN BOW

This Southeastern Oklahoma town is located near several state parks, including Broken Bow Lake. Timber and tourism are the area's main industries.

WHAT TO SEE
BEAVERS BEND RESORT STATE PARK

Highway 259A, Broken Bow, 580-494-6300; www.oklahomaparks.com

This 3,522-acre mountainous area is crossed by the Mountain Fork River and includes the Broken Bow Reservoir, and features swimming, a bathhouse, fishing, boating, a nature trail, picnic areas, a playground, grocery store, restaurant, camping and cabins.

Nature center. Daily.

EXPLORING OKLAHOMA'S STATE PARKS

Begin your tour of Southeastern and Eastern Oklahoma at the small town of Broken Bow, located at the edge of the Ouachita National Forest. About six miles east of town on Highway 70 is the 1880s home of Choctaw Chief Jefferson Gardner. Nearby Beavers Bend State Park is one of the most gorgeous places in this part of the country. Lake Broken Bow, at 14,200 acres, offers park visitors 180 miles of pretty, wooded shoreline, as well as bass fishing, paddle boating, canoeing and swimming. The park is also adjacent to Mountain Fork River, popular for its trout fishing and canoe trips; on land, you can try horseback riding, miniature golf and golf on Cedar Creek Golf Course. Stay overnight here or continue on for an overnight at Lake Wister.

Continue north on scenic Highway 259 through the tree-covered Kiamichi Mountains and you'll enter the Ouachita National Forest. If you turn west on Oklahoma Highway 1, you'll be on the spectacular Talimena Scenic Drive, which makes a 54-mile reach between Talihina, Oklahoma and Mena, Arkansas. Have the camera ready to capture the vistas from various lookout spots on the sides of the road; look to the north to see the beautiful Winding Stair Mountains. At Talihina, go four miles southwest on Highway 271 to Talimena State Park, a prime spot for picnicking. Back on Highway 259, continue north and pick up Highway 59 north to Lake Wister State Park, a pretty, wooded spread of 33,428 acres that showcase 4,000-acre Lake Wister. Some of the park's 15 cabins have fireplaces. Less than three miles northeast of Highway 59 and Highway 270, Heavener Runestone State Park features gigantic stone tablets carved with runic alphabet characters. Nobody knows how it happened, but the markings are thought to have been made by Vikings around A.D. 1012.

Finish a driving tour at Tahlequah, capital city of the Cherokee Nation. Destinations here include the Cherokee Heritage Center and the restored 1889 Cherokee National Female Seminary, at Northeastern State University.

WHERE TO STAY
★★THE CHARLES WESLEY MOTOR LODGE
302 N. Park Drive, Broken Bow, 580-584-3303; www.charleswesleymotorlodge.com
50 rooms. Restaurant. Pool. Pets accepted. $61-150

CHICKASHA

Established to serve as a passenger and freight division point for the Rock Island and Pacific Railroad in 1892, this town site was on land originally given to the Choctaw in 1820. It became part of the Chickasaw Nation in 1834. It was incorporated in 1907 when the Oklahoma and Indian territories were joined to form the 46th state.

WHAT TO SEE
LAKE CHICKASHA
Highway 62, Chickasha
Enjoy swimming, waterskiing, fishing, hunting, picnicking and camping here.

SPECIAL EVENTS
FESTIVAL OF LIGHT
Ninth Street, Chickasha, 405-224-9627; www.chickashafestivaloflight.com
This festival features lighted displays, a 16-story Christmas tree, Crystal Bridge and shopping.
Late November-December 31.

WHERE TO STAY
★★BEST WESTERN INN
2101 S. Fourth St., Chickasha, 405-224-4890, 877-489-0647; www.bestwestern.com
148 rooms. Restaurant, bar. Fitness center. Pool. Pets accepted. $61-150

CLAREMORE
See also Tulsa
Claremore is most famous for being the birthplace of Will Rogers. He was actually born about halfway between this city and Oologah but claimed Claremore as his home because, he said, "nobody but an Indian could pronounce Oologah." Rogers County, of which Claremore is the seat, was named not for Will Rogers but for his father, Clem.

WHAT TO SEE
LYNN RIGGS MEMORIAL
121 N. Chickasaw Ave., Claremore
Houses the author's personal belongings, sculpture of Riggs, original manuscripts and the original "surrey with the fringe on top" from *Oklahoma!* Monday-Friday.

WILL ROGERS BIRTHPLACE AND DOG IRON RANCH
9501 E. 380 Road, Oologah, 918-275-4201; www.willrogers.com
This is the home where the actor and cowboy, Will Rogers, was born on November 4, 1879.
Daily 8 a.m.-5 p.m.

WILL ROGERS MEMORIAL
1720 W. Will Rogers Blvd., Claremore, 918-341-0719, 800-324-9455;
www.willrogers.com
Located at this memorial, you'll find mementos, murals, a saddle collection, dioramas, theater, films, tapes and a research library. Jo Davidson's statue of Rogers stands in the foyer. The memorial is on 20 acres once owned by the humorist.
Daily 8 a.m.-5 p.m.

SPECIAL EVENT
WILL ROGERS STAMPEDE PRCA RODEO
Will Rogers Stampede Arena, Claremore, 918-798-3201; www.willrogersstampede.com
Late June.

WHERE TO STAY
★★WILL ROGERS INN CLAREMORE
940 S. Lynn Riggs Blvd., Claremore, 918-341-4410, 800-644-9455;
www.magnusonhotels.com
52 rooms. Restaurant, bar. Pool. Pets accepted. $61-150

WHERE TO EAT
★★HAMMETT HOUSE
1616 W. Will Rogers Blvd., Claremore, 918-341-7333; www.hammetthouse.com
American. Lunch, dinner. Closed Monday. Children's menu. $16-35

DUNCAN
See also Lawton
Once a cattle town on the old Chisholm Trail, Duncan has become an oil services and agricultural center. It was here that Erle P. Halliburton developed his oil well cementing business, which now operates all over the world.

WHAT TO SEE
CHISHOLM TRAIL MUSEUM
1000 N Chisholm Trail Parkway, Duncan, 580-252-6692; www.onthechisholmtrail.com
Interactive displays demonstrating the history of the Chisholm Trail.
Monday-Saturday 10 a.m.-5 p.m., Sunday 1-5 p.m.

STEPHENS COUNTY HISTORICAL MUSEUM
Fuqua Park, Highway 81 and Beech Avenue, Duncan, 580-252-0717
This museum houses pioneer and Native American artifacts, antique toys, gem and lapidary display as well as a Plains Indian exhibit.
Tuesday, Thursday-Saturday.

WHERE TO STAY
★★HOLIDAY INN
1015 N. Highway 81, Duncan, 580-252-1500; www.holiday-inn.com
138 rooms. Restaurant, bar. Fitness center. Pool. Pets accepted. $61-150

DURANT
See also Lake Texoma
Long a farm and livestock-producing town in Oklahoma's Red River Valley, Durant has become a recreation center since the completion of Lake Texoma. Home of Southeastern Oklahoma State University, Durant has many mansions, magnolia trees and gardens.

WHAT TO SEE
FORT WASHITA
Highway 199, Durant, 580-924-6502
Originally built in 1842 to protect the Five Civilized Tribes from the Plains Indians, this fort was used during the Civil War as a Confederate supply depot; remains of 48 buildings are visible.
Daily.

THREE VALLEY MUSEUM
401 W. Main St., Durant, 580-920-1907
This museum is housed in the Choctaw Nation Headquarters building and contains turn-of-the-century artifacts, art and beadwork.
Monday-Saturday, also by appointment.

SPECIAL EVENT
OKLAHOMA SHAKESPEAREAN FESTIVAL

Southeastern Oklahoma State University, Durant, 580-924-0121; www.se.edu
This festival features musicals; children's show, a teen cabaret and a dinner theater.
Late June-July.

WHERE TO STAY
★★BEST WESTERN MARKITA INN

2401 W. Main St., Durant, 580-924-7676, 800-780-7234; www.bestwestern.com
62 rooms. Restaurant. Pool. $61-150

★COMFORT INN

2112 W. Main St., Durant, 580-924-8881; www.choicehotels.com
62 rooms. Complimentary breakfast. Pets accepted. $61-150

ELK CITY

This was once a stopping point for cattlemen driving herds from Texas to railheads in Kansas. Centrally located on historic Route 66, Elk City lies near the center of the Anadarko Basin, where extensive natural gas exploration takes place.

WHAT TO SEE
OLD TOWN MUSEUM

2717 W. Third St., Elk City, 580-225-2207
Turn-of-the-century house has Victorian furnishings, Native American artifacts, Beutler Brothers Rodeo memorabilia and more.
Tuesday-Sunday.

WHERE TO STAY
★★HOLIDAY INN

101 Meadow Ridge, Elk City, 580-225-6637; www.holiday-inn.com
151 rooms. Restaurant, bar. Complimentary breakfast. Fitness center. Pool. Pets accepted. $61-150

WHERE TO EAT
★COUNTRY DOVE

610 W. Third St., Elk City, 580-225-7028
American. Lunch. Closed Sunday. $16-35

★LUPE'S

905 N. Main St., Elk City, 580-225-7109
American, Mexican. Lunch (Monday-Friday), dinner. Closed Sunday. Children's menu. Bar. $16-35

ENID

Like many Oklahoma cities, Enid was born of a land rush. When the Cherokee Outlet (more popularly known as the Cherokee Strip) was opened to settlement on September 16, 1893, a tent city sprang up. It is now a prosperous community and a center for farm marketing and oil processing. Just south of town is Vance Air Force Base, a training base for jet aircraft pilots.

WHAT TO SEE
HOMESTEADER'S SOD HOUSE
Highway 8, Cleo Springs, 580-463-2441
This two-room sod house built by Marshall McCully in 1894 is said to be the only original example of this type of structure still standing in Oklahoma. Here, you'll find period furnishings indoors and farm machinery outdoors. Tuesday-Sunday.

MUSEUM OF THE CHEROKEE STRIP
4125 W. Glarriot, Enid, 580-237-1907
Artifacts covering the Oklahoma history of the Plains Indians, the Land Run of 1893 and events from 1900-present.
Tuesday-Saturday.

WHERE TO STAY
★★BEST WESTERN INN
2818 S. Van Buren St., Enid, 580-242-7110, 800-378-6308; www.bestwestern.com
99 rooms. Restaurant, bar. Fitness center. Pool. Pets accepted. $61-150

★★DAYS INN
2901 S. Van Buren St., Enid, 580-237-6000, 800-329-7466; www.daysinn.com
100 rooms. Restaurant, bar. Complimentary breakfast. Fitness center. Pets accepted. $61-150

WHERE TO EAT
★★SAGE ROOM
1927 S. Van Buren St., Enid, 580-233-1212
Seafood. Dinner. Closed Sunday. Children's menu. $36-85

GROVE
This tourism-fueled community is located in the Ozark foothills on Grand Lake. The town got its start as a trading center for French fur trappers and as a community for resettled Cherokees.

WHAT TO SEE
HAR-BER VILLAGE
4404 W. 20th St., Grove, 918-786-3488; www.har-bervillage.com
Reconstructed village with 90 buildings and shops typical of a pioneer town. March-November, Monday-Saturday 9 a.m.-6 p.m., Sunday 12:30-5 p.m.

LENDONWOOD GARDENS
1308 W. 13th St., Grove, 918-786-2938; www.lendonwood.com
Houses one of the largest collections of chamaecyparis in the United States, plus rhododendrons, day lilies and azaleas. Gardens include the Display Garden, English Terrace Garden and Japanese Garden.
Daily.

WHERE TO STAY
★★SHANGRI-LA RESORT AND CONFERENCE CENTER
57401 E. Highway 125 S., Afton, 918-257-4204, 800-331-4060; www.shangrilaok.com
101 rooms. Restaurant, bar. Fitness center. Pool. Tennis. $61-150

GUTHRIE
See also Oklahoma City
Guthrie was founded in just a few hours during the great land rush. Prior to the run, only a small-frame railroad station and a partially completed land registration office stood on the site. A few hours later, perhaps 20,000 inhab-ited the tent city on the prairie. Oklahoma's territorial and first state capital, Guthrie now has the most complete collection of restored Victorian architec-ture in the United States, with 1,400 acres of the city listed on the National Register of Historic Places. Included are 160 buildings in the central busi-ness district and the center of town, and numerous Victorian mansions. The town is being restored to the 1907-1910 era, including the expansive Guthrie Railroad Hotel and the former opera house, the Pollard Theatre. Some who have called Guthrie home at one time or another are Tom Mix, Lon Chaney, Will Rogers, Carry Nation and O. Henry.

WHAT TO SEE
OKLAHOMA TERRITORIAL MUSEUM
406 E. Oklahoma Ave., Guthrie, 405-282-1889
Exhibits and displays of life in territorial Oklahoma during the turn of the century. Adjacent is the Carnegie Library, site of inaugurations of the last territorial and the first state governor.
Tuesday-Saturday 9 a.m.-5 p.m. Closed November-December.

SCOTTISH RITE MASONIC TEMPLE
900 E. Oklahoma Ave., Guthrie, 405-282-1281
This multimillion-dollar Classical Revival building is said to be the largest structure used for Masonic purposes. The building contains the original state capitol, 13 artistic rooms and 200 stained-glass windows. Surrounding it is a 10-acre park.
Monday-Friday 10 a.m. and 2 p.m.

STATE CAPITAL PUBLISHING MUSEUM
301 W. Harrison, Guthrie, 405-282-4123; www.guthrieok.com
Located in the four-story State Capital Publishing Company Building. Hous-es a collection of original furnishings, vintage letterpress equipment; exhib-its featuring the history of the first newspaper in the Oklahoma Territory and period printing technology.
Thursday-Saturday 9 a.m.-5 p.m.

SPECIAL EVENT
TERRITORIAL CHRISTMAS
Guthrie, 405-282-1947; www.guthrieok.com
Seven miles of lights outline architecture in the Historic District; streets are filled with persons clad in turn-of-the-century style clothes, horse-drawn ve-

hicles; window displays echo 1890-1920 era.
Friday after Thanksgiving-late December.

WHERE TO STAY
★★BEST WESTERN TERRITORIAL INN
2323 Territorial Trail, Guthrie, 405-282-8831, 800-780-7234; www.bestwestern.com
84 rooms. Restaurant, bar. Complimentary breakfast. Pool. Pets accepted.
$61-150

WHERE TO EAT
★STABLES CAFÉ
223 N. Division, Guthrie, 405-282-0893; www.stablescafe.com
American. Lunch, dinner. Closed holidays. Children's menu. $16-35

LAWTON
See also Duncan
Last of the many Oklahoma cities that sprang up overnight, Lawton had its
land rush on August 6, 1901. It is now the state's third-largest city. Much of
the city's prosperity is due to Fort Sill, established in 1869, and to the Good-
year Tire plant headquartered here, the world's largest. The Wichita Mountains provide a dramatic backdrop to the city.

WHAT TO SEE
FORT SILL MILITARY RESERVATION
Highway 277, Lawton, 580-442-2521; www.army.mil
A 94,268-acre army installation, U.S. Army Field Artillery Center and
School. Geronimo, war leader of the Apaches, spent his final years here and
is buried in the post's Apache cemetery.
Daily.

FORT SILL NATIONAL HISTORIC LANDMARK AND MUSEUM
437 Quanah Road, Fort Sill, 580-442-5123; www.army.mil
Forty-three buildings built of native stone during the 1870s, many of which
are still being used for their original purpose.
Monday-Saturday 8:30 a.m.-4:30 p.m.

OLD POST CHAPEL
N. Quanah Road, Fort Sill, Lawton, 580-442-5123; www.army.mil
One of the oldest houses of worship still in use in the state.
Monday-Saturday; services on Sunday.

MUSEUM OF THE GREAT PLAINS
Elmer Thomas Park, 601 Ferris Blvd., Lawton, 580-581-3460;
www.museumgreatplains.org
Displays on Native Americans, fur trade, exploration, cattle industry and
settlement of the area.
Monday-Saturday 10 a.m.-5 p.m., Sunday 1-5 p.m.

WICHITA MOUNTAINS WILDLIFE REFUGE
32 Refuge Headquarters, Indiahoma, 580-429-3222

This 59,060-acre refuge has 12 man-made lakes. Non-motorized boating permitted on four lakes, trolling motors on three lakes; picnicking, camping only at Doris Campground; limited backcountry camping by reservation only. Self-guided trails. Longhorn cattle, herds of buffalo, elk, deer and other wildlife can be viewed from several wildlife/scenic viewing areas.

Daily. Quanah Parker Visitor Center: March-November, Friday-Sunday.

WHERE TO STAY
★QUALITY INN
3110 N.W. Cache Road, Lawton, 580-353-3104; www.choicehotels.com

95 rooms. Complimentary breakfast. Pool. Pets accepted. $61-150

★★RAMADA INN
601 N. Second St., Lawton, 580-355-7155, 888-298-2054; www.ramada.com

98 rooms. Restaurant, bar. Pets accepted. $61-150

WHERE TO EAT
★★FISHERMEN'S COVE
Highway 49, Lawton, 580-529-2672; www.thefishermenscove.com

Seafood. Lunch Sunday only, dinner. Closed Monday-Tuesday. Children's menu. $16-35

★★SALAS
111 W. Lee Blvd., Lawton, 580-357-1600; www.salasrestaurant.com

Mexican, American. Lunch, dinner. Closed Monday-Tuesday. $16-35

MCALESTER

This town is named for James J. McAlester, who came to Indian Territory in 1870 armed with a geologist's notebook describing some coal deposits and a fine sense of commercial strategy. He set up a tent store where the heavily traveled Texas Road crossed the California Trail and later married a Native American woman, which made him a member of the Choctaw Nation with full rights. In 1911, he became lieutenant governor of the state.

WHAT TO SEE
MCALESTER SCOTTISH RITE TEMPLE
305 N. Second St., McAlester, 918-423-6360; www.mcalesterscottishrite.org

Unusual copper dome containing multicolored lenses makes this a landmark when lighted. One of its most illustrious members was Will Rogers who took degrees in 1908.

Tours: Monday-Friday 8 a.m.-5 p.m., by appointment.

ROBBER'S CAVE STATE PARK
2300 Park Cabin Road, McAlester, 918-465-2565; www.oklahomaparks.com

On approximately 8,200 acres, there are lakes, forests and an outlaw cave. Visit to go swimming, fishing, boating, hiking and horseback riding on many trails. There are also picnicking areas, a playground, a restaurant, a grocery

store, camping sites and cabins.
Daily.

WHERE TO STAY
★★BEST WESTERN INN OF MCALESTER
1215 George Nigh Expressway, McAlester, 918-426-0115, 800-780-7234;
www.bestwestern.com
61 rooms. Restaurant. Complimentary breakfast. Pool. Pets accepted. $61-150

★★HIWAY INN
1217 S. George Nigh Expressway, McAlester, 918-426-5050, 800-329-7466
100 rooms. Restaurant, bar. Pool. Pets accepted. $61-150

WHERE TO EAT
★GIACOMO'S
501 S. George Nigh Expressway, McAlester, 918-423-2662;
www.giacomositaliancuisine.com
American, Italian. Lunch, dinner. Closed Sunday-Monday. Children's menu.
$16-35

MUSKOGEE
Located near the confluence of the Verdigris, Grand and Arkansas rivers, Muskogee was a logical site for a trading center. Southward on the old Texas Road, over which families moved to Texas, and northward, over which cattle were driven to market, the town's location was commercially ideal. The railroad superseded the rivers in transportation importance, however, almost before the town was settled.

Today, Muskogee is a diversified agricultural and industrial center, a town dotted with 32 small parks and the gateway to the eastern lakes area. The port of Muskogee is part of the McClellan-Kerr Arkansas River Navigation System, handling barges that go through the inland waterway system from Pittsburgh and Minneapolis to Houston and New Orleans.

The area's surroundings made it a logical location for the U.S. Union Agency for the Five Civilized Tribes (Cherokee, Chickasaw, Choctaw, Creek and Seminole). The agency is in located in the Old Union Building.

WHAT TO SEE
FIVE CIVILIZED TRIBES MUSEUM
Honor Heights Park, 1101 Honor Heights Drive, Muskogee, 918-683-1701;
www.fivetribes.org
Art and artifacts of the Cherokees, Chickasaws, Choctaws, Creeks and Seminoles; displays relating to their history and culture.
March-December: daily; January-February, Tuesday-Saturday.

FORT GIBSON HISTORIC SITE
907 N. Garrison St., Fort Gibson, 918-478-4088; www.fortgibson.com
Established as the state's first military post in 1824, the park includes 12 reconstructed or restored buildings on a 55-acre site; period rooms depict

army life in the 1830s and 1870s. Fort Gibson National Cemetery is just over a mile east.

Mid-April-mid-October, Tuesday-Sunday 10 a.m.-5 p.m.; mid-October-mid-April, Thursday-Sunday 10 a.m.-5 p.m.

HONOR HEIGHTS PARK

North Honor Heights Drive Muskogee, 918-684-6302; www.muskogeeparks.com
This 120-acre park features azalea, rose and chrysanthemum gardens. There are nature walks, lakes, waterfalls and picnicking areas.
Daily.

WHERE TO STAY
★★AZALEA INN

800 S. 32nd St., Muskogee, 918-682-4341
142 rooms. Restaurant, bar. Fitness center. Pool. Pets accepted. $61-150

★DAYS INN

900 S. 32nd St., Muskogee, 918-683-3911, 800-329-7466; www.daysinn.com
43 rooms. Complimentary breakfast. Pool. Pets accepted. $61-150

WHERE TO EAT
★OKIES

219 S. 32nd St., Muskogee, 918-683-1056
American. Lunch, dinner. Children's menu. Bar. $16-35

NORMAN

Norman was founded on April 22, 1889, in the famous land rush known as the Oklahoma land run. The run opened what was once the Indian Territory to modern-day settlement. A year later, the University of Oklahoma was founded. The city now offers numerous restaurants, museums, shopping areas, parks and hotels, as well as convention, conference and symposium sites. The University of Oklahoma, once mostly known as a football powerhouse, has been transformed into a respected academic and research institution.

WHAT TO SEE
UNIVERSITY OF OKLAHOMA

1000 Asp Ave., Norman, 405-325-1188, 800-234-6868; www.ou.edu
This campus is home to 25,000 students and has more than 225 buildings. The University of Oklahoma Press is a distinguished publishing house. On campus are the Fred Jones Jr. Museum of Art (Tuesday-Sunday, 405-325-3272); Oklahoma Museum of Natural History (405-325-4712); and Rupel Jones Theater (405-325-4101).

WHERE TO EAT
★CAFÉ PLAID

333 W. Boyd St., Norman, 405-360-2233; www.cafeplaid.com
American, deli. Breakfast, lunch, brunch. Children's menu. $15 and under

★★★LEGEND'S
1313 W. Lindsey St., Norman, 405-329-8888; www.legendsrestaurant.com
Owner Joe Sparks has presided over this American-continental restaurant for 40 years. It's a favorite of university faculty. The intimate dining room is filled with original artwork and features a broad menu of pastas, steaks and daily seafood specials.
American. Lunch, dinner, Sunday brunch. Outdoor seating. Bar. $16-35

★VISTA SPORTS GRILL
111 N. Peters Ave., Norman, 405-447-0909; www.vistasportsgrill.com
American. Lunch, dinner. Children's menu. Bar. $16-35

OKLAHOMA CITY
See also Guthrie
What is now the site of Oklahoma's capital was barren prairie on the morning of April 22, 1889. Unassigned land was opened to settlement that day, and by nightfall the population numbered 10,000. No city was ever settled faster.
The city sits atop one of the nation's largest oil fields—there are even wells on the lawn of the Capitol. First discovered in 1928, the field was rapidly developed throughout the city. It still produces large quantities of high-gravity oil. Oil well equipment manufacturing became one of the city's major industries. Tinker Air Force Base is southeast of the city.

WHAT TO SEE
45TH INFANTRY DIVISION MUSEUM
2145 N.E. 36th St., Oklahoma City, 405-424-5313; www.45thdivisionmuseum.com
Exhibits showcase state military history from its beginnings in the early Oklahoma Territory through World War II and Korea to the present National Guard, including a Desert Storm exhibit; uniforms, vehicles, aircraft, artillery and an extensive military firearms collection with pieces dating from the American Revolution; and memorabilia and original cartoons by Bill Mauldin.
Tuesday-Friday 9 a.m.-4:15 p.m., Saturday 10 a.m.-4:15 p.m., Sunday 1-4:15 p.m.

AQUATICUS
2101 N.E. 50th, Oklahoma City, 405-424-3344
This marine life science facility contains a comprehensive collection of aquatic life; shark tank; adaptations and habitat exhibits; and underwater viewing.
Daily.

CIVIC CENTER MUSIC HALL
201 N. Walker Ave., Oklahoma City, 405-297-2584; www.okcciviccenter.org
Home of the Oklahoma City Philharmonic, Canterbury Choral Society, Ballet Oklahoma and Lyric Theatre of Oklahoma. Entertainment choices include Broadway shows and popular concerts.

FRONTIER CITY

11501 N.E. Expressway, Oklahoma City, 405-478-2412; www.frontiercity.com

A 65-acre Western theme park; including more than 75 rides, shows and attractions; entertainment; shops, restaurants.
Memorial Day-late August, daily; late March-Memorial Day and late August-October, Saturday-Sunday.

GARDEN EXHIBITION BUILDING AND HORTICULTURE GARDENS

3400 N.W. 36th St., Oklahoma City, 405-943-0827

These gardens feature azalea trails; a butterfly garden; rose, peony and iris gardens; and an arboretum. The conservatory has one of the country's largest cactus and succulent collections.

HARN HOMESTEAD AND 1889ERS MUSEUM

1721 N. Lincoln Blvd., Oklahoma City, 405-235-4058; www.harnhomestead.com

Historic homestead claimed in Land Run of 1889; 1904 farmhouse furnished with pre-statehood objects. Also here is a three-story stone and cedar barn; a one-room schoolhouse; and a working farm.
Monday-Friday.

INTERNATIONAL PHOTOGRAPHY HALL OF FAME AND MUSEUM

2100 N.E. 52nd St., Oklahoma City, 405-424-4055; www.iphf.org

This museum features permanent and traveling exhibits and one of world's largest photographic murals.
Monday-Friday 10 a.m.-5 p.m., Saturday 10 a.m.-6 p.m., Sunday 11 a.m.-6 p.m.

KIRKPATRICK SCIENCE AND AIR SPACE MUSEUM

2100 N.E. 52nd St., Oklahoma City, 405-602-6664, 800-532-7652; www.omniplex.org

This museum is hands-on featuring an Air Space Museum, Kirkpatrick Galleries, a gardens/greenhouse and the Kirkpatrick Planetarium (shows change quarterly).
Monday-Friday 9 a.m.-5 p.m., Saturday 9 a.m.-6 p.m., Sunday 11 a.m.-6 p.m.

MYRIAD BOTANICAL GARDENS

301 W. Reno Ave., Oklahoma City, 405-297-3995; www.myriadgardens.com

This 17-acre botanical garden is located in the heart of the city's redeveloping central business district. It features a lake, amphitheater, botanical gardens and seven-story Crystal Bridge Tropical Conservatory.
Monday-Saturday 9 a.m.-6 p.m., Sunday noon-6 p.m.

NATIONAL COWBOY HALL OF FAME AND WESTERN HERITAGE CENTER

1700 N.E. 63rd St., Oklahoma City, 405-478-2250; www.nationalcowboymuseum.org

This center features major art collections depicting America's Western heritage, a Rodeo Hall of Fame and landscaped gardens.
Daily 9 a.m.-5 p.m.

OKLAHOMA CITY MUSEUM OF ART

415 Coach Drive, Oklahoma City, 405-236-3100; www.okcmoa.com

This museum holds a permanent collection of 16th- to 20th-century European and American paintings, prints, drawings, photographs, sculpture and decorative arts.

Tuesday-Saturday 10 a.m.-5 p.m., Thursday 10 a.m.-9 p.m., Sunday noon-5 p.m.

OKLAHOMA CITY NATIONAL MEMORIAL

N.W. Fifth Street and North Robinson Avenue, Oklahoma City, 405-235-3313,

888-542-4673; www.oklahomacitynationalmemorial.org

A series of monuments honor the men, women and children killed by a bomb at the Murrah Federal Building on April 19, 1995. The Gates of Time memorial represents the moment of the blast; the Field of Empty Chairs pays tribute to the 168 lives lost in the bombing. The Survivor Tree is an American elm tree that withstood the blast.

Museum: Monday-Saturday 9 a.m.-6 p.m., Sunday afternoon 1-6 p.m.

OKLAHOMA CITY THEN AND NOW

Single-day events have shaped both the past and present of this settlement in the American heartland. Oklahoma City was born on April 22, 1889, when the area known as the Unassigned Lands in Oklahoma Territory was opened for settlement. A cannon was fired at noon that day, signaling a rush of thousands of settlers who raced into the two million acres of land to make their claims on the plains.

Just over a century later, the city was the site of the April 19, 1995 bombing of the Alfred P. Murrah Federal Building by American terrorist Timothy McVeigh. Today, this event is memorialized at the Oklahoma City National Memorial. Begin at the Gates of Time, twin monuments that frame the moment of destruction: 9:02 a.m. The east gate represents 9:01 a.m. and the west gate 9:03 a.m. The Field of Empty Chairs consists of 168 bronze-and-stone chairs arranged in nine rows, representing the lives lost and the floor each victim was on at the time of the blast. Smaller chairs memorialize the 19 children killed. The area also includes an orchard and reflecting pool.

OKLAHOMA CITY ZOO

2101 N.E. 50th St., Oklahoma City, 405-424-3344; www.okczoo.com

This zoo is home to more than 2,000 animals representing 500 species.

Daily 9 a.m.-6 p.m.

OKLAHOMA HISTORY CENTER

2401 N. Laird Ave., Oklahoma City, 405-522-5248; www.okhistorycenter.org

Located on 18 acres across from the capitol building, the History Center is a self-guided exploration of Oklahoma from past to present. Outside the museum, the Red River Journey offers visitors a walking tour of the Red River Valley. The grounds also include an outdoor oil field exhibit with drilling derricks, a portable derrick and machinery associated with Oklahoma oil explorations.

Monday-Saturday 9 a.m.-5 p.m., Sunday noon-5 p.m.

OKLAHOMA NATIONAL STOCKYARDS

2501 Exchange Ave., Oklahoma City, 405-235-8675; www.onsy.com

One of the world's largest cattle markets, this stockyard features auctions of cattle, hogs and sheep.

Monday-Tuesday.

STATE CAPITOL

2300 N. Lincoln Blvd., Oklahoma City, 405-521-3356; www.travelok.com

This Greco-Roman, Neoclassical building was designed by S. A. Layton and Wemyss Smith. An oil well beneath the Capitol building reaches 1 ¼ miles underground. After pumping oil from 1941 to 1986, it is now preserved as a monument. The legislature meets annually for 78 days beginning on the first Monday in February.

Tours: daily.

SPECIAL EVENTS
BALLET OKLAHOMA

7421 N. Classen Blvd., Oklahoma City, 405-843-9898; www.balletoklahoma.com

Enjoy ballet productions here, such as *The Nutcracker* and *The Legend of Sleepy Hollow.*

October-April.

FESTIVAL OF THE ARTS

Downtown, Hudson Ave., Oklahoma City, 405-270-4848; www.artscouncilokc.com

This festival features International foods, entertainment, a children's learning and play area; and a craft market. Artists from many states display their work here as well.

Late April.

INTERNATIONAL FINALS RODEO

State Fair Arena, Oklahoma City, 405-235-6540, 800-511-1552; www.iprarodeo.com

The International Pro Rodeo Association's top 15 cowboys and cowgirls compete in seven events to determine world championships.

Mid-January.

OKLAHOMA CITY PHILHARMONIC ORCHESTRA

Civic Center Music Hall, 201 N. Walker Ave., Oklahoma City, 405-297-2584;
www.okcciviccenter.org

Concerts are held weekly at the Civic Center.

Mid-September-May.

STATE FAIR OF OKLAHOMA

333 Gordon Cooper Blvd., Oklahoma City, 405-948-6700; www.okstatefair.com

The Oklahoma State Fair feature livestock, crafts, art exhibits, Native American ceremonial dances, a carnival and parades. There are also arena and grandstand attractions.

Mid-September.

WHERE TO STAY
★BAYMONT INN OKLAHOMA CITY SOUTH
8315 S. Interstate 35 Service Road, Oklahoma City, 405-631-8661, 877-229-6668;
www.baymontinns.com
122 rooms. Complimentary breakfast. Pool. $61-150

★★BEST WESTERN SADDLEBACK INN
4300 S.W. Third St., Oklahoma City, 405-947-7000, 800-228-3903;
www.bestwestern.com/saddlebackinn
220 rooms. Restaurant, bar. Complimentary breakfast. Business center. Fitness center. Pool. Pets accepted. $61-150

★★COURTYARD OKLAHOMA CITY DOWNTOWN
2 West Reno Ave., Oklahoma City, 405-232-2290, 800-217-9905; www.courtyard.com
225 rooms. Restaurant. Business center. Fitness center. Pool. $15 and under

---

MUSIC TO BROADWAY'S EARS: OKLAHOMA!

Oklahoma is lucky to have one of the most popular Broadway musicals celebrating its name in the title. *Oklahoma!*, the first musical collaboration between Richard Rodgers and Oscar Hammerstein II, was different. It had a plot. The songs and dances emerged logically from the plot and the thoughts and emotions of the characters helped carry the storyline, which, atypically for the time, had its share of dark moments and serious themes. The dancing was more folk-ballet style than kick-line. Even the rural setting of the play was unusual, as most musicals were set in urban confines, with sophisticated, affluent characters, not farmhands.

When it opened on Broadway in 1943, critics thought *Oklahoma!* wouldn't make it to a second performance. Scouts who saw the show in out-of-town tryouts were said to deliver a verdict along the lines of "No girls, no gags, no chance." In the tryout stage, the show had a different title: *Away We Go!* Rogers and Hammerstein changed the title to *Oklahoma!* and added the exuberant song of the same name as the show's closing number. The rousing song thrilled the audience, which gave a standing ovation. The next day, the once-doubting critics could not find enough praise for the show, and *Oklahoma!* was on its to theatrical immortality. It set a record of more than 2,000 performances over five years at St. James Theatre and is still performed at theaters across the country.

★★★CROWNE PLAZA HOTEL
2945 N.W. Expressway, Oklahoma City, 405-848-4811, 877-227-6963;
www.crowneplaza.com
Located in the business district of Oklahoma City, this hotel offers easy access to city attractions. Granite bathrooms with closets, dark wood furniture and club chairs with ottomans are found in guest rooms. The Spa Select bedding package includes an amenity bag of lavender linen spray, an eye pillow and a CD of soothing music.
215 rooms. Restaurant, bar. Business center. Fitness center. Pool. Pets accepted. $61-150

★★EMBASSY SUITES
1815 S. Meridian Ave., Oklahoma City, 405-682-6000, 800-362-2779;
www.embassysuites.com

236 rooms. Restaurant, bar. Complimentary breakfast. Business center. Fitness center. Pool. Pets accepted. $151-250

★GOVERNORS SUITES HOTEL

2308 S. Meridian Ave., Oklahoma City, 405-682-5299, 888-819-7575;
www.govsuitesokc.com

50 rooms. Complimentary breakfast. Fitness center. Pool. Spa. $61-150

★★★MARRIOTT WATERFORD

6300 Waterford Blvd., Oklahoma City, 405-848-4782, 800-992-2009; www.marriott.com

Located in Oklahoma City's tony Waterford community, the hotel is 15 minutes from downtown and the airport. Enjoy a drink in the waterfront lounge or take a swim in the outdoor pool. Volleyball and squash facilities are also available. Rooms feature pillow-top mattresses and crisp white linens, and the granite bathrooms have jetted tubs and Bath & Body Works amenities.

197 rooms. Restaurant, bar. Business center. Fitness center. Pool. Spa. $151-250

★★★RENAISSANCE OKLAHOMA CITY CONVENTION CENTER HOTEL

10 N. Broadway Ave., Oklahoma City, 405-228-8000, 800-468-3571;
www.renaissancehotels.com

Located in downtown Oklahoma City at the corner of Broadway and Sheridan, the Renaissance Oklahoma City is a 15-story tower that is connected to the adjacent Cox Convention Center by a sky bridge. It's close to the restored Bricktown area, with its shops, restaurants, amusements and River Walk. A 13-story atrium dominates the center of the hotel and the lobby is filled with lush landscaping that includes koi ponds and a waterfall.

311 rooms. Restaurant, bar. Business center. Fitness center. Pool. Spa. $151-250

★★★THE SHERATON OKLAHOMA CITY

1 N. Broadway Ave., Oklahoma City, 405-235-2780, 800-285-2780; www.sheraton.com

This downtown hotel is connected to the Cox Convention Center as well as many shops and businesses by an underground concourse. Contemporary styling is the theme, from the lobby with its leather sofas and modern art collection to the oversized guest rooms with long working desks with ergonomic chairs, black-and-white photographs and brown and black granite bathrooms. An outdoor pool, sun deck and fitness center are available, and pets are welcomed with bowls, treats and beds.

396 rooms. Restaurant, bar. Business center. Fitness center. Pool. Spa. Pets accepted. $151-250

WHERE TO EAT
★★ARIA GRILL

1 N. Broadway Ave., Oklahoma City, 405-235-2780; www.sheraton.com

American. Breakfast, lunch, dinner. Children's menu. Bar. $36-85

★★★BELLINI'S RISTORANTE & GRILL
6305 Waterford Blvd., Oklahoma City, 405-848-1065; www.bellinis.net

This casual restaurant has the ambience of an Italian piazza. Modern art hangs on the dark wood-paneled walls, and tables are set with black cloths. Everything from pizza to steak, seafood to pasta dishes, are featured on the extensive menu. It offers a view of lakeside sunset.

American, Italian. Lunch, dinner, Sunday brunch. Reservations recommended. Outdoor seating. Children's menu. Bar. $16-35

★BRICKTOWN BREWERY
1 N. Oklahoma Ave., Oklahoma City, 405-232-2739; www.bricktownbrewery.com

American. Lunch, dinner, late-night. Children's menu. Bar. $16-35

★★CAFÉ 501
501 S. Boulevard St., Edmond, 405-359-1501; www.my501cafe.com

International. Lunch, dinner. Saturday breakfast, Sunday brunch. Children's menu. $16-35

★★CASTLE FALLS
820 N. MacArthur Blvd., Oklahoma City, 405-942-6133; www.castlefalls.com

German. Dinner. Closed Monday-Wednesday, Sunday. Outdoor seating. Children's menu. Bar. $16-35

★★CATTLEMAN'S STEAKHOUSE
1309 S. Agnew St., Oklahoma City, 405-236-0416; www.cattlemensrestaurant.com

Steak. Breakfast, lunch, dinner, late-night, brunch. Children's menu. $16-35

★★★THE COACH HOUSE
6437 Avondale Drive, Oklahoma City, 405-842-1000; www.tch-ok.com

The seasonally changing menu at this restaurant features local produce and meats, with rack of lamb as a signature dish. The cuisine is supported by an extensive wine list. Subdued lighting, double-linen tablecloths, fine stemware and flatware and copper chargers give the restaurant an elegant, formal feel.

American. Lunch, dinner. Closed Sunday. Reservations recommended. Children's menu. $36-85

★COUNTY LINE
1226 N.E. 63rd St., Oklahoma City, 405-478-4955; www.countyline.com

Barbecue. Lunch, dinner. Children's menu. Bar. $16-35

★★DEEP FORK GRILL
5418 N. Western Ave., Oklahoma City, 405-848-7678; www.deepforkgrill.com

Steak, seafood. Lunch, dinner, brunch. Reservations recommended. Children's menu. Bar. $16-35

★GOPURAM TASTE OF INDIA
4559 N.W. 23rd St., Oklahoma City, 405-948-7373; www.gopuramtasteofindia.com

Indian. Lunch, dinner. Children's menu. $16-35

★★★JW'S STEAKHOUSE

3233 N.W. Expressway, Oklahoma City, 405-842-6633; www.marriott.com

This steakhouse in the Oklahoma City Marriott has dark wood paneling and red leather chairs and banquettes. Serving dinner only, JW's has the full steakhouse look and specializes in classics such as filet mignon and prime rib.

Steak. Dinner, late-night. Reservations recommended. Children's menu. $36-85

★★KONA RANCH STEAKHOUSE

2037 S. Meridian Ave., Oklahoma City, 405-681-1000; www.kona-ranch.com

Steak. Lunch, dinner. Children's menu. Bar. $16-35

★★★LA BAGUETTE BISTRO

7408 N. May Ave., Oklahoma City, 405-840-3047; www.labaguettebistro.com

Just northwest of downtown, this bistro offers an authentic experience. The owners/chefs hail from France and serve simple but authentic bistro fare (including baguette sandwiches) in an L-shaped dining room.

French. Breakfast, lunch, dinner, brunch. Bar. $16-35

★★LAS PALOMAS

2329 N. Meridian Ave., Oklahoma City, 405-949-9988

Mexican. Lunch, dinner. Children's menu. $15 and under

★★SUSHI NEKO

4318 N. Western Ave., Oklahoma City, 405-528-8862; www.sushineko.com

Japanese. Lunch, dinner, late-night. Closed Sunday. Reservations recommended. Outdoor seating. Children's menu. Bar. $16-35

PERRY

See also Stillwater

Settled during the opening of the Cherokee Outlet, this town was once called Hell's Half-Acre. It's home to a Carnegie library, a public library built with money donated by Andrew Carnegie.

WHAT TO SEE
CHEROKEE STRIP MUSEUM

2617 W. Fir Ave., Perry, 580-336-2405; www.cherokee-strip-museum.org

This museum includes a schoolhouse, pioneer artifacts and documents depicting the era of the 1893 land run.

Tuesday-Friday 9 a.m.-5 p.m., Saturday 10 a.m.-4 p.m. Closed Sunday-Monday.

SPECIAL EVENT
CHEROKEE STRIP CELEBRATION

4125 W. Glarriot, Perry, 580-336-4684

This festival commemorates the opening of the Cherokee Strip to settlers. Parade, entertainment, rodeo, contests, Noble County Fair. Mid-September.

WHERE TO STAY
★★BEST WESTERN CHEROKEE STRIP MOTEL
2903 Highway 77 W., Perry, 580-336-2218; www.bestwestern.com
88 rooms. Restaurant, bar. Pool. Pets accepted. $61-150

PONCA CITY
Ponca City was founded in a single day in the traditional Oklahoma land-rush manner. Although located in the Cherokee Strip, the town was named for the Ponca tribe. Ponca City is a modern industrial town surrounded by cattle and wheat country.

WHAT TO SEE
KAW LAKE
Highway 2, Ponca City, 580-762-5611; www.kawlake.com
Located on the Arkansas River, the shoreline of this lake covers 168 miles. Water sports, fishing, boating, hunting. Recreation and camping areas located one mile off Highway 60.
Daily.

MARLAND MANSION ESTATE
901 Monument Road, Ponca City, 580-767-0420; www.marlandmansion.com
A 55-room mansion built in 1928 by E. W. Marland, an oil baron, Oklahoma governor and philanthropist. Modeled after the Davanzati Palace in Florence, Italy, the estate features elaborate artwork and hand-painted ceilings.
Daily 10 a.m.-5 p.m., Sunday 1-5 p.m.

MARLAND'S GRAND HOME
1000 E. Grand Ave., Ponca City, 580-767-0427; www.marlandgrandhome.com
This structure houses an Indian Museum and a Daughters of the American Revolution Memorial Museum.
Tuesday-Saturday 10 a.m.-5 p.m.

WHERE TO STAY
★★HOLIDAY INN
2809 N.14th St., Ponca City, 580-762-8311, 800-465-4329; www.ihg.com
138 rooms. Restaurant, bar. Fitness center. Pool. Pets accepted. $61-150

SHAWNEE
The history of Shawnee is that of Oklahoma in miniature. In the center of the state, it stands on what was originally Sac and Fox land, which was also claimed at various times by Spain, France and England. It was opened by a land rush on September 22, 1891. Oil was struck in 1926. Shawnee is the home of Oklahoma Baptist University. Jim Thorpe, the great Native American athlete, and Dr. Brewster Higley, the physician who wrote, *Home on the Range*, lived here. Astronaut Gordon Cooper was born and raised in Shawnee.

WHAT TO SEE
MABEE-GERRER MUSEUM OF ART
1900 W. MacArthur Drive, Shawnee, 405-878-5300; www.mgmoa.org
This art gallery features works by 19th- and 20th-century European and American artists as well as works from the Middle Ages and the Renaissance. Museum features artifacts of Egyptian, Babylonian, Grecian, Roman, Persian, Chinese, African and Polynesian civilizations as well as North, Central and South American native civilizations.
Tuesday-Saturday 10 a.m.-5 p.m., Sunday 1-4 p.m.

SEMINOLE NATION MUSEUM
524 S. Wewoka Ave., Wewoka, 405-257-5580; www.theseminolenationmuseum.org
The museum traces the Seminoles' history from their removal from Florida via the Trail of Tears to the establishment of the capital in Oklahoma. Displays include a collection of Native American peace medals, replicas of a Chick (Florida Seminole house) and artifacts from the pioneer era through the oil boom days of the 1920s. Art gallery with Native American paintings and sculpture.
Monday-Saturday 10 a.m.-5 p.m. Closed January.

WHERE TO STAY
SUPER 8 SHAWNEE
4900 N. Harrison Blvd., Shawnee, 405-275-0089, 800-298-2054; www.ramada.com
106 rooms. Restaurant, bar. Pool. Pets accepted. $61-150

STILLWATER
See also Perry
Stillwater was born overnight in the great land run of 1889. The settlement was less than a year old when, on Christmas Day 1890, the territorial legislature established Oklahoma State University (formerly Oklahoma A & M).

WHAT TO SEE
LAKE CARL BLACKWELL
11000 W. Highway 51C, Stillwater, 405-372-5157; www.lcb.okstate.edu
A 19,364-acre recreation area operated by Oklahoma State University. Swimming, waterskiing, fishing, boating, sailing, hunting, picnic areas, campgrounds, cabins.

OKLAHOMA STATE UNIVERSITY
Washington Street and University Avenue, Stillwater, 405-744-9341;
www.osu.okstate.edu
On a campus of 840 acres with an additional 4,774 acres of experimental university farms statewide, this university has more than 20,000 students. The Noble Research Center for Agriculture and Renewable Natural Resources, an education/research complex with an emphasis on the biological sciences is on campus. Buildings include Old Central, the oldest collegiate building in the state built in 1894 of pink brick, and attractive modified Georgian buildings of red brick with slate roofs.

WHERE TO STAY
★★QUALITY INN

2515 W. Sixth Ave., Stillwater, 405-372-0800; www.qualityinn.com

139 rooms. Restaurant, bar. Complimentary breakfast. Business center. Fitness center. Pool. Pets accepted $61-150

★★STILLWATER PLAZA

600 E. McElroy Road., Stillwater, 405-377-7010, 800-353-6894; www.bestwestern.com

122 rooms. Restaurant, bar. Business center. Fitness center. Pool. Pets accepted. $61-150

TAHLEQUAH

See also Sequoyah State Park

Tribal branches of the Cherokee met here in 1839 to sign a new constitution forming the Cherokee Nation. They had been driven by the U.S. Army from North Carolina, Alabama, Tennessee and Georgia over the Trail of Tears. The Cherokee were the only tribe with a constitution and a body of law written in their own language, using a written alphabet, which had been created by Sequoyah. These talented people published the first newspaper in Indian Territory and in 1885 established the first commercial teleline in Oklahoma. The Southwestern Bell Telephone Company, to which it was later sold, established a monument to this remarkable enterprise on the Old Courthouse Square.

WHAT TO SEE
CHEROKEE HERITAGE CENTER

21192 S. Keeler Drive, Tahlequah, 918-456-6007, 888-999-6007;
www.cherokeeheritage.org

A National Museum of Cherokee artifacts, this center features a reconstructed rural village.

Monday-Saturday 10 a.m.-5 p.m., Sunday 1-5 p.m.

SPECIAL EVENTS
TRAIL OF TEARS

Tsa-La-Gi Amphitheater, Tahlequah, 918-456-6007

A professional cast presents a musical drama depicting the history of the Cherokee Tribe.

Mid-June-Labor Day.

CHEROKEE NATIONAL HOLIDAY

Tahlequah, 918-456-0671; www.holiday.cherokee.org

This celebration of Constitutional Convention includes a championship cornstalk bow and arrow shoot and a powwow.

Labor Day weekend.

ILLINOIS RIVER BALLOON FEST

Tahlequah City Municipal Airport, Tahlequah, 918-456-3742; www.okballoonfest.com

Thsi fest features a balloon race, balloon glow, arts and crafts, carnival, skydiving exhibition and plenty of food.

Mid-August.

WHERE TO STAY
★★TAHLEQUAH MOTOR LODGE
2501 S. Muskogee Ave., Tahlequah, 918-456-2350, 800-480-8705
53 rooms. Restaurant. Complimentary breakfast. Pool. Pets accepted. $61-150

TULSA
See also Claremore
No oil derricks are visible to visitors, yet Tulsa is an important energy city. Oil and gas fields surround it, and the offices of energy companies are prevalent: more than 600 energy firms employ 30,000 people. This is the second-largest city in Oklahoma and its atmosphere is cosmopolitan.

With the completion of the Arkansas River Navigation System, Tulsa gained a water route to the Great Lakes and the Gulf of Mexico. The Port of Catoosa, three miles from the city and located on the Verdigris River, is at the headwaters of the waterway and is now America's westernmost inland water port.

WHAT TO SEE
ARKANSAS RIVER HISTORICAL SOCIETY MUSEUM
Tulsa Port of Catoosa, 5350 Cimarron Road, Catoosa, 918-266-2291;
www.tulsaweb.com/port/museum.htm
Located in the Port Authority Building, this museum has pictorial displays and operating models that trace the history of the 1,450-mile Arkansas River and McClellan-Kerr Navigation System.
Monday-Friday 8 a.m.-4:30 p.m.

BELL'S AMUSEMENT PARK
3901 E. 21st St., Tulsa, 918-744-1991; www.teamled.com/bells/directions.htm
Rides include a large wooden roller coaster, a log ride, a sky ride and bumper boats, plus two miniature golf courses and an arcade.
June-August, daily; April-May and September, Saturday-Sunday.

BOSTON AVENUE UNITED METHODIST CHURCH
1301 S. Boston Ave., Tulsa, 918-583-5181; www.bostonavenue.org
Designed and built in 1929 by Adah Robinson, this structure was the first large-scale Art Deco church. It features a 225-foot tower and many lesser towers decorated with bas-relief pioneer figures. The sanctuary is ornamented with Italian mosaic reredos.
Tours after 11 a.m. Sunday services.

CREEK COUNCIL OAK TREE
18th Street and Cheyenne Avenue, Tulsa
A landscaped plot housing the Council Oak, this tree stands as a memorial to the Lochapokas Creek tribe.

GILCREASE MUSEUM
1400 Gilcrease Museum Road, Tulsa, 918-596-2700; www.gilcrease.org
Founded by Thomas Gilcrease, an oil man of Creek descent, this museum has

a collection of Native American art and artifacts from 12,000 years ago to the present. The library houses about 90,000 items, including the earliest known letter sent to Europe from the New World.
Tuesday-Sunday 10 a.m.-5 p.m.

OXLEY NATURE CENTER

6700 Mohawk Blvd., Tulsa, 918-669-6644; www.oxleynaturecenter.org
This 800-acre wildlife sanctuary has numerous nature trails.
Monday-Saturday 10 a.m.-4.30 p.m., Sunday noon-4.30 p.m.

PHILBROOK MUSEUM OF ART

2727 S. Rockford Road, Tulsa, 918-749-7941, 800-324-7941; www.philbrook.org
Exhibits here include Italian Renaissance, 19th-century English, American and Native American paintings; Native American baskets and pottery; Chinese jade and decorative material; Southeast Asian tradeware; African sculpture. Housed in an Italian Renaissance Revival villa on 23 acres; and a formal and sculpture gardens.
Tuesday-Sunday 10 a.m.-5 p.m., Thursday until 8 p.m.

SHERWIN MILLER MUSEUM OF JEWISH ART

2021 E. 71st St., Tulsa, 918-492-1818; www.jewishmuseum.net
The Southwest's largest collection of Judaica contains objects representative of Jewish history, art, ceremonial events and daily life from around the world.
Monday-Friday 10 a.m.-5 p.m., Sunday 1-5 p.m.

THE TULSA ZOO

6421 E. 36th St., Tulsa, 918-669-6600; www.tulsazoo.com
More than 200 varieties of animals are housed within 68 acres of landscaped grounds. The zoo features Native American artifacts, geological specimens, dinosaur replicas, live plants and animals.
Daily 9 a.m.-5 p.m.

UTICA SQUARE

21st and Utica streets, Tulsa, 918-742-5531; www.uticasquare.com
This upscale shopping district includes Saks Fifth Avenue, Coach and Williams-Sonoma. Set in a peaceful landscape that features manicured gardens, the area features many restaurants and cafés.

SPECIAL EVENT
DISCOVERYLAND! OUTDOOR THEATER

19501 W. 41st St., Tulsa, 918-245-6552; discoverylandusa.com
This theater presents Rodgers and Hammerstein's *Oklahoma!* in a 2,000-seat outdoor theater complex with a Western theme. Authentic Native American dancing, Western musical revue and barbecue dinner prior to performance.
Mid-June-late August, Monday-Friday.

WHERE TO STAY

★★BEST WESTERN TRADE WINDS CENTRAL INN

3141 E. Skelly Drive, Tulsa, 918-749-5561, 800-780-7234; www.bestwestern.com

164 rooms. Restaurant, bar. Complimentary breakfast. Business center. Fitness center. Pool. $61-150

★★★CROWNE PLAZA

100 E. Second St., Tulsa, 918-582-9000, 800-227-6963; www.crowneplaza.com

This hotel caters to business travelers with its central Tulsa location. A full-service spa, a restaurant, a lounge, a business center, an indoor and outdoor pool, a fitness room, and conference facilities are among the services.

460 rooms. Pets accepted. Restaurant, bar. Business center. Fitness center. Pool. Spa. $61-150

★★DOUBLETREE HOTEL

616 W. Seventh St., Tulsa, 918-587-8000, 800-222-8733; www.doubletree.com

417 rooms. Restaurant, bar. Business center. Fitness center. Pool. Pets accepted. $61-150

★★EMBASSY SUITES

3332 S. 79th E. Ave., Tulsa, 918-622-4000, 800-362-2779; www.embassysuites.com

244 rooms. Restaurant, bar. Complimentary breakfast. Business center. Fitness center. Pool. Pets accepted. $61-150

★HAMPTON INN

3209 S. 79th E. Ave., Tulsa, 918-663-1000, 800-426-7866; www.hamptoninn.com

148 rooms. Complimentary breakfast. Business center. Pool. Pets accepted. $61-150

★★★HILTON TULSA SOUTHERN HILLS

7902 S. Lewis St., Tulsa, 918-492-5000, 800-774-1500; www.hilton.com

Located in the Southern Hills area of Tulsa and across the street from Oral Roberts University, this hotel features spacious guest rooms with plush beds and Crabtree and Evelyn bath products. There's also complimentary wireless Internet access and a full fitness center.

282 rooms. Restaurant, bar. Business center. Fitness center. Pool. Pets accepted. $61-150

★LA QUINTA INN

6030 E. Skelly Drive, Tulsa, 918-665-2630, 800-447-0600; www.laquinta.com

105 rooms. Complimentary breakfast. Business center. Fitness center. Pool. Pets accepted. $61-150

★★★MARRIOTT TULSA SOUTHERN HILLS

1902 E. 71st St., Tulsa, 918-493-7000, 866-530-3760; www.marriott.com

Rising 11 stories in two connected wings, the Marriott Tulsa Southern Hills offers well-appointed guest rooms with full amenities. It is located near golf courses, tennis facilities, the Tulsa Zoo and other area attractions.

383 rooms. Restaurant, bar. Business center. Fitness center. Spa. Pool. $61-150

★PRESIDENTIAL SUITES TULSA

8338 E. 61 St. S., Tulsa, 918-254-0088, 888-627-1155;
www.presidentialsuitestulsa.com

52 rooms. Bar. Complimentary breakfast. Business center. Pool. Spa. Pets accepted. $61-150

★★★RADISSON HOTEL TULSA

10918 E. 41st St., Tulsa, 918-627-5000, 800-325-3535; www.radissontulsa.com

This hotel features an indoor water park. Located in the heart of southeast Tulsa, near the Tulsa International Airport and the Philbrook Museum, the hotel has rooms that are comfortable and spacious.

325 rooms. Restaurant, bar. Business center. Fitness center. Pool. Pets accepted. $61-150

WHERE TO EAT
★BAXTER'S INTERURBAN GRILL

717 S. Houston Ave., Tulsa, 918-585-3134; www.baxtersgrill.com

American. Lunch, dinner. Closed Sunday. Outdoor seating. Children's menu. Bar. $16-35

★★★BODEAN SEAFOOD

3323 E. 51st St., Tulsa, 918-749-1407; www.bodean.net

This popular restaurant serves creative seafood dishes—items are flown in twice daily—in a comfortable atmosphere that includes white linen-topped tables. A three-course prix fixe menu is available, and Tuesdays feature a four-course menu with three wines to match.

Seafood. Lunch, dinner. Bar. $16-35

★★CAMERELLI'S

1536 E. 15th St., Tulsa, 918-582-8900

Italian. Lunch, dinner, brunch. Reservations recommended. Bar. $36-85

★JAMIL'S

2833 E. 51st St., Tulsa, 918-742-9097; www.jamilsrestaurant.com

Seafood, steak. Dinner, Lunch. $16-35

★METRO DINER

3001 E. 11th St., Tulsa, 918-592-2616

American. Breakfast, lunch, dinner. Children's menu. $15 and under

★★★POLO GRILL

2038 Utica Square, Tulsa, 918-744-4280; www.pologrill.com

The creative American cuisine served at this restaurant features French, Southern and Southwest influences. Signature dishes include oven-roasted tomato bisque, tender leaf spinach and strawberry salad, crispy grit cakes, grilled steaks and baked fudge. There is a nine-course prix fixe tasting menu and an extensive wine list.

American. Lunch, dinner. Closed Sunday. Reservations recommended. Outdoor seating. Children's menu. Bar. $36-85

★RICARDOS
5629 E. 41st St., Tulsa, 918-622-2668; www.ricardostulsa.com
Mexican. Lunch, dinner. Closed Sunday. Children's menu. $15 and under

★★TI AMO ITALIAN RISTORANTE
6024A S. Sheridan Road, Tulsa, 918-499-1919; www.tiamotulsa.com
Italian. Lunch, dinner. Bar. $16-35

★★★WARREN DUCK CLUB
6110 S. Yale Ave., Tulsa, 918-495-1000; www.doubletree.com
This fine-dining restaurant is located inside the Doubletree Hotel. The menu features American classics such as grilled steaks, seafood and more.
American. Breakfast, lunch, dinner, late-night. Children's menu. Bar. $36-85

WEATHERFORD
See also Clinton
Weatherford is the home of Southwestern Oklahoma State University as well as Gemini and Apollo astronaut Thomas P. Stafford.

WHAT TO SEE
RED ROCK CANYON STATE PARK
Highway 281, Weatherford, 405-542-6344; www.touroklahoma.com
This park covers 310 acres and features a swimming pool and bathhouse. Hiking, picnicking and camping are also available.
Daily.

STAFFORD AIR AND SPACE CENTER
Stafford Field, 3000 E. Logan Road, Weatherford, 580-772-5871;
www.staffordspacecenter.com
This museum houses memorabilia of former astronaut Thomas Stafford, who flew on Gemini VI and IX as well as Apollo X.
Monday-Saturday 9 a.m.-5 p.m., Sunday 1-5 p.m.

WHERE TO STAY
★BEST WESTERN MARK MOTOR HOTEL
525 E. Main St., Weatherford, 580-772-3325, 800-780-7234; www.bestwestern.com
63 rooms. Complimentary breakfast. Pool. $61-150

WHERE TO EAT
★★T-BONE STEAK HOUSE
1805 E. Main St., Weatherford, 580-772-6329; www.tbonesteakhouse.com
Steak. Dinner. Children's menu. Bar. $16-35

SOUTH DAKOTA

THIS IS THE LAND OF THE PROUD AND MIGHTY SIOUX. IF YOUR ONLY PICTURE OF THIS TRIBE is from the 1990 film *Dances With Wolves*, a visit to South Dakota will reveal much about the fascinating history of this vast nation that ruled the plains, hunting buffalo by horseback. South Dakota Sioux are generally referred to as Lakota, Dakota or Nakota, and today there are more than 62,000 members of the tribes living in the state.

There are museums and monuments throughout the state where visitors can learn more about the Sioux, from the Crazy Horse Memorial and Indian Museum of North America in Custer, to the Cultural Heritage Center in the state capital of Pierre. Visit a powwow or tribal gathering with dancing and contests during the summer months in towns throughout the state. Or soak up the scenery with a drive along the Native American Scenic Byway, which stretches from Nebraska north through the center of South Dakota.

Beyond its rich Native American history, South Dakota is a quiet, sparsely filled space teeming with natural beauty. Each year, scores of tourists visit Badlands National Park, or trek a little further west to take a look at one of the country's most recognizable monuments, Mount Rushmore, a granite mountain carved with the visages of George Washington, Thomas Jefferson, Abraham Lincoln and Theodore Roosevelt.

South Dakota offers more than parks and presidential figures. It's one of the nation's richest archaeological dig sites. The largest and most complete Tyrannosaurus rex in the world, Sue (who now lives at Chicago's Field Museum) was discovered here, and mammoths, marine life and other creatures from the earth's past are found regularly. Join in an archeological dig during summer months with Rapid City's Archaeological Research Center, or any of the other organizations digging in the state. South Dakota tourism can provide tips on active digs.

Urbanites will find plenty to do in the state's big cities, from capital city Pierre in the center to Sioux Falls in the west.

Americana abounds in South Dakota, with roadside delights like the famously kitschy Corn Palace in Mitchell and more diners serving inexpensive, hearty meals and fantastic slices of fruit pie than any appetite can handle.

ABERDEEN

The roots of Aberdeen's commerce are the three railroads that converge here, giving it the nickname "Hub City." Alexander Mitchell, a railroader of the 19th century, named the town for his Scottish birthplace. German-Russian immigrants arrived in 1884. Hamlin Garland, author of Son of the Middle Border, and L. Frank Baum, author of The Wizard of Oz, lived here.

WHERE TO STAY
★★BEST WESTERN RAMKOTA HOTEL
1400 N.W. Eighth Ave., Aberdeen, 605-229-4040, 800-780-7234; www.ramkota.com
154 rooms. Restaurant, bar. Business center. Fitness center. Pool. Pets accepted. $61-150

★★RAMADA INN & CONVENTION CENTER

2727 S.E. Sixth Ave., Aberdeen, 605-225-3600, 800-272-6232; www.ramada.com
152 rooms. Restaurant, bar. Complimentary breakfast. Pool. Pets accepted. $61-150

WHERE TO EAT

★★FLAME RESTAURANT AND LOUNGE

2 S. Main St., Aberdeen, 605-225-2082
American. Lunch, dinner. Closed Sunday. Children's menu. Bar. $16-35

BROOKINGS

See also Madison, Watertown
Research done at South Dakota State University has helped make Brookings the agricultural capital of the state. It has developed diversified farming and manufacturing industries.

WHERE TO STAY

★★DAYS INN BROOKINGS

2500 E. Sixth St., Brookings, 605-692-9471, 877-831-1562; www.daysinn.com
125 rooms. Restaurant, bar. Complimentary breakfast. Business center. Fitness center. Pool. Pets accepted. $61-150

WHERE TO EAT
★★THE RAM & O'HARE'S
327 Main Ave., Brookings, 605-692-2485
American. Lunch, dinner. Closed Sunday. Children's menu. Bar. $16-35

CUSTER

See also Hill City, Hot Springs, Keystone, Rapid City

This is where a prospector with Lieutenant Colonel Custer's expedition of 1874 discovered gold, prompting the gold rush of 1875-1876. Main Street was laid out in the 1880s, wide enough for wagons pulled by teams of oxen to make U-turns. Custer is the seat of Custer County, headquarters of the Black Hills National Forest and center of an area of great mineral wealth. Gold, quartz, beryl, mica and gypsum are some of the minerals that are mined here. Custer is a popular area for winter sports activities.

WHERE TO STAY
★BAVARIAN INN
Highway 16 and 385 N., Custer, 605-673-2802, 800-657-4312; www.bavarianinnsd.com
65 rooms. Closed December-February. Complimentary breakfast. Pool. Pets accepted. $61-150

★★STATE GAME LODGE
Highway 16A, Custer, 605-255-4541, 800-658-3530; www.custerresorts.com
68 rooms. Closed October-April. Restaurant, bar. Pets accepted. $61-150

★★SYLVAN LAKE RESORT
24572 SD Highway 87 and Harney Peak, Custer, 605-574-2561, 800-658-3530; www.custerresorts.com
33 rooms. Closed November-April. Restaurant. Pets accepted. $61-150

WHERE TO EAT
★ELK CANYON STEAKHOUSE
511 Mount Rushmore Road, Custer, 605-673-4477
Steak. Breakfast, lunch, dinner, brunch. Children's menu. Bar. $16-35

CUSTER STATE PARK

See also Custer, Hill City, Hot Springs, Keystone

This is one of the largest state parks in the United States, measuring 73,000 acres. A mountain recreation area and game refuge, the park has one of the largest publicly owned herds of bison in the country (more than 1,400), as well as Rocky Mountain bighorn sheep, mountain goats, burros, deer, elk and other wildlife. Four man-made lakes and three streams provide excellent fishing and swimming. Near the park is the site of the original gold strike of 1874 and a replica of the Gordon stockade, built by the first gold rush party in 1874.

The Peter Norbeck Visitor Center (May-October, daily) has information about the park and naturalist programs, which are offered daily (May-September). Paddleboats; horseback riding, hiking, bicycle rentals, Jeep rides, camping, hayrides, chuck wagon cookouts. The Black Hills Playhouse, in

CRAZY HORSE MEMORIAL

This large sculpture, still being carved from the granite of Thunderhead Mountain, was the life work of Korczak Ziolkowski (1908-1982), who briefly assisted Gutzon Borglum on Mount Rushmore. With funds gained solely from admission fees and contributions, Ziolkowski worked alone on the memorial, refusing federal and state funding. The sculptor's wife and several of their children are continuing the work.

Crazy Horse—the stalwart Sioux chief who helped defeat Custer and the United States Seventh Cavalry—is depicted astride a magnificent horse in this nine-story carving. When completed in the round, the mountain carving will be 563 feet high and 641 feet long, the largest sculpture in the world. To date, 8.4 million tons of granite have been blasted off the mountain. Audiovisual programs and displays show how the mountain is being carved.

The Indian Museum of North America is located here and has almost 20,000 artifacts in three wings. A Native American educational and cultural center opened in 1997. Memorial Day, Memorial Day-Native American Day (October 13), 7 a.m.-dusk; Winter 8 a.m.-5 p.m.

Information: Avenue of the Chiefs, Crazy Horse, five miles north off Highway 16, 605-673-4681; www.crazyhorse.org

the heart of the park, is the scene of productions for 11 weeks (mid-June-late August, schedule varies; 605-255-4141).

DEADWOOD

See also Lead, Rapid City, Spearfish, Sturgis

This town is best known for gold and the famous Wild West characters such as Calamity Jane, Preacher Smith and Wild Bill Hickock who lived here. The main street runs through Deadwood Gulch. The rest of the town crawls up the steep canyon sides. A bust of Hickock by Korczak Ziolkowski—creator of the Crazy Horse Memorial—stands on Sherman Street. At the height of the 1876 gold rush, 25,000 people swarmed over the hillsides to dig gold. When gold was first struck at Deadwood, nearly the entire population of Custer rushed here. Predictably, at the height of a newer strike, nearly the entire population of Deadwood rushed to the town of Lead. Recently, legalized gambling has given Deadwood another boom.

WHAT TO SEE
MOUNT MORIAH CEMETERY

Deadwood, 605-578-2600

Graves of Wild Bill Hickock, Calamity Jane, Preacher Smith, Seth Bullock and others.

OLD STYLE SALOON #10

657 Main St., Deadwood, 605-578-3346; www.saloon10.com

Collection of Western artifacts, pictures, guns. This is the saloon in which Wild Bill Hickock was shot. There is entertainment (four shows per day, Memorial Day-Labor Day), gambling and a restaurant here. Daily.

WHERE TO STAY
★★BULLOCK HOTEL & CASINO
633 Main St., Deadwood, 605-578-1745, 800-336-1876; www.historicbullock.com
28 rooms. Restaurant, bar. Fitness center. Casino. $61-150

WHERE TO EAT
★★★JAKE'S ATOP THE MIDNIGHT STAR
677 Main St., Deadwood, 605-578-1555, 800-999-6482; www.themidnightstar.com
Located on the top floor of the Midnight Star Casino, this elegant dining room serves American favorites. Piano entertainment is provided five nights a week.
American. Dinner. Reservations recommended. Children's menu. Bar. $16-35

HILL CITY
See also Custer, Deadwood, Keystone, Rapid City
Hill City is a beautiful mountain town in the heart of the Black Hills. The Black Hills Institute of Geological Research and a Ranger District office of the Black Hills National Forest are located here.

WHERE TO STAY
★★BEST WESTERN GOLDEN SPIKE INN & SUITES
106 Main St., Hill City, 605-574-2577, 800-780-7234; www.hillcitysd.com
87 rooms. Closed mid-November-mid-March. Restaurant. Fitness center. Pool. Pets accepted. $61-150

WHERE TO EAT
★★ALPINE INN
225 Main St., Hill City, 605-574-2749; www.alpineinnhillcity.com
American, German. Lunch, dinner. Closed Sunday. $16-35

HOT SPRINGS
See also Custer, Keystone
Hot Springs, the seat of Fall River County, is on the southeast edge of the Black Hills National Forest. Many local buildings are made of pink, red and buff sandstone. A Ranger District office of the Nebraska National Forest is located here.

WHAT TO SEE
HOT SPRINGS HISTORIC DISTRICT
River Street, Hot Springs
The presence of underground springs catalyzed the development of Hot Springs in the 1880s, with River Street being the epicenter of the boom. The district includes 130 buildings on more than 3,000 acres, including 39 impressive Richardsonian-Romanesque structures made of locally quarried sandstone. Several are occupied by spas fed by the springs, while others house eateries and art galleries.

MAMMOTH SITE OF HOT SPRINGS
Hot Springs, 605-745-6017; www.mammothsite.com
Excavation of a remarkable concentration of mammoth skeletons; to date the remains of 51 mammoths, a camel and a giant short-faced bear have been unearthed.
Daily.

HURON
See also Brookings, Mitchell
Huron, the seat of Beadle County, is also the administrative center for a number of federal and state agencies. Twelve city parks feature swimming, picnicking, golf, tennis and ball fields. Nearby De Smet is famous for being the home of author Laura Ingalls Wilder.

WHAT TO SEE
GLADYS PYLE HISTORIC HOME
376 Idaho Ave. Southeast, Huron, 605-352-2528
This Queen Anne-style house, built in 1894, was the residence of the first elected female U.S. senator.
Daily.

HUBERT H. HUMPHREY DRUGSTORE
233 Dakota S., Huron, 605-352-4064; www.huronsd.com/livinginhuron.htm
Mid-1930s atmosphere; owned by the former senator and vice-president until his death; still owned by Humphrey family.
Monday-Saturday.

WHERE TO STAY
★★CROSSROADS HOTEL & CONVENTION CENTER
100 Fourth St. S.W., Huron, 605-352-3204, 800-876-5858; www.crossroadshotel.com
100 rooms. Restaurant, bar. Pool. Pets accepted. $61-150

KEYSTONE
See also Custer, Hill City, Rapid City
Sculptor Gutzon Borglum began drilling into the 6,200-foot Mount Rushmore in 1927. His carving took 14 years to complete and cost a mere $1 million, though it's now deemed priceless. Keystone is the entrance to Mount Rushmore and Custer State Park. A former mining town supplying miners for the Peerless, Hugo and the Holy Terror Gold Mine, it was also home to Carrie Ingalls (sister of Laura Ingalls Wilder) and the men who carved Mount Rushmore.

WHAT TO SEE
BORGLUM HISTORICAL CENTER
342 Winter St., Keystone, 605-666-4449, 800-888-4369
Born in Idaho, Gutzon Borglum won acclaim for his early paintings and was sent by patrons to study in Paris. After he returned to the United States, his lifelike sculptures generated a buzz in the national arts community. Sculpting success led Borglum in 1916 to propose carving the likeness of Robert E.

Lee into Stone Mountain in Georgia, a project that he left in 1925 after clashing with financiers. At the age of 60, he embarked on the work that immortalized his fame—carving presidents' faces on Mount Rushmore. Borglum died just before its completion and his son Lincoln finished the sculpture. The Borglum Historical Center tells the story of Gutzon's remarkable life, focusing on his Mount Rushmore days. The center's exhibits include a full-size replica of Lincoln's eye from the monument, assorted artworks by Borglum and a documentary about the Mount Rushmore project, narrated by former U.S. Senator (and South Dakotan) Tom Daschle.

May, September, daily 9 a.m.-5 p.m.; June-August, daily 8 a.m.-6 p.m.

RUSHMORE AERIAL TRAMWAY
203 Cemetery Road, Keystone, 605-666-4478
This 15-minute ride allows a view of the Black Hills and Mount Rushmore across the valley.
May-mid-September, daily.

WHERE TO STAY
★BEST WESTERN FOUR PRESIDENTS LODGE
24075 Highway 16A, Keystone, 605-666-4472, 800-780-7234; www.bestwestern.com
50 rooms. Closed November-March. Complimentary breakfast. Fitness center. Pool. Spa. Pets accepted. $61-150

LEAD
See also Deadwood, Rapid City, Spearfish, Sturgis
The chain of gold mines that began in Custer and spread through the Black Hills to Deadwood ended in Lead. The discovery of gold here in 1876 eventually led to the development of the Homestake Mine, one of the largest gold producers in this hemisphere. Lead is located on mountaintops with the Homestake Mine burrowing under the town.

WHERE TO STAY
★★GOLDEN HILLS RESORT
900 Miners Ave., Lead, 605-584-1800, 888-465-3080
100 rooms. Restaurant, bar. Complimentary breakfast. Pets accepted. $61-150

MITCHELL
This is a tree-shaded town in the James River Valley, where agriculture is celebrated with a colorful nine-day festival each September at the famous Corn Palace, a popular tourist attraction.

WHAT TO SEE
THE CORN PALACE
601 N. Main St., Mitchell, 605-996-6223; www.cornpalace.org
Mitchell dubs itself the Corn Capital of the World, a designation backed up by this one-of-a-kind community center. Each year since 1921, locals have decorated the exterior of the turreted, czarist Russia-style palace with different murals, but with a twist—the medium is not paint, but thousands of

bushels of corn and other South Dakota grains. The initial intent of the place was to prove the fertility of the South Dakota soil, but it has since evolved into a roadside tourist attraction. The Corn Palace Festival, held annually in September, celebrates the annual fall harvest with concerts, a carnival midway and other festivities. After the harvest, pigeons devour the palace's second skin, leaving the grand façade blank and ready for redecoration the following spring.

Daily 8 a.m.-5 p.m., until 9 p.m. in summer.

WHERE TO STAY
★COMFORT INN
2020 Highland Way, Mitchell, 605-990-2400; www.comfortinn.com
72 rooms. Complimentary breakfast. Business center. Fitness center. Pool. $61-150

★DAYS INN
1506 S. Burr St., Mitchell, 605-996-6208; www.daysinn.com
68 rooms. Complimentary breakfast.. Business center. Pool. Pets accepted. $61-150

★★RAMADA INN
1525 W. Havens St., Mitchell, 605-996-6501, 800-888-4702; www.ramada.com
153 rooms. Restaurant, bar. Fitness center. Pool. Pets accepted. $61-150

WHERE TO EAT
★★CHEF LOUIE'S
601 E. Havens St., Mitchell, 605-996-7565
Steak. Dinner. Closed Sunday. Children's menu. Bar. $16-35

PIERRE

Pierre is the capital of South Dakota, an honor for which it campaigned hard and won because of its central location, the geographic center of the state. The town grew thanks to cattle ranchers from the west, farmers from the east, local businesspeople and government officials.

WHAT TO SEE
CULTURAL HERITAGE CENTER
900 Governors Drive, Pierre, 605-773-3458, www.history.org
This historical museum north of the South Dakota State Capitol is home to collections of artifacts used by ranchers, miners and Native Americans. On display is the Verendrye Plate, buried by French brothers who explored this area in 1743 (making them the first Europeans to visit South Dakota), and more than 1,300 artifacts depicting the history of the Sioux tribes.
Monday-Friday 9 a.m.-4:30 p.m., Saturday-Sunday 1-4:30 p.m.

SOUTH DAKOTA DISCOVERY CENTER AND AQUARIUM
805 W. Sioux Ave., Pierre, 605-224-8295; www.sd-discovery.com
Visitors of all ages can encase themselves in a Body Bubble, explore a maze laden with displays about the lifestyles of wild animals or dismantle retired

appliances at the Take Apart Table. The modest aquarium houses fish native to South Dakota. Summer workshops allow kids to dig deeper into a science of their choosing.

Daily until 5 p.m.; opening time varies by season.

WHERE TO STAY
★★BEST WESTERN RAMKOTA HOTEL

920 W. Sioux Ave., Pierre, 605-224-6877, 800-780-7234; www.ramkotahotels.com

151 rooms. Restaurant, bar. Business center. Fitness center. Pool. Pets accepted. $61-150

★DAYS INN

520 W. Sioux Blvd., Pierre, 605-224-0411, 800-329-7466; www.daysinn.com

79 rooms. Complimentary breakfast. Fitness room. Pets accepted. $61-150

WHERE TO EAT
★★★LA MINESTRA

106 E. Dakota Ave., Pierre, 605-224-8090; www.laminestra.com

Set in Pierre's historic downtown in an 1896 building, the restaurant's dining room features original wainscoting and tin walls and ceilings. Upscale Italian fare is served here, including lobster tortellini and eggplant parmesan. Italian. Lunch (Monday-Friday), dinner. Closed Sunday. Bar. $36-85

RAPID CITY

See also Hill City, Keystone, Sturgis

In the last few decades, tourism has replaced gold mining as the main industry of Rapid City. Visitors come here to visit nearby Mount Rushmore or to learn about the many dinosaurs that once roamed the area (and even participate in dinosaur digs). Founded only two years after gold was discovered in the Black Hills, Rapid City is a boomtown that persevered. It is the seat of Pennington County, second-largest city in South Dakota, and home of Ellsworth Air Force Base.

WHAT TO SEE
BLACK HILLS PETRIFIED FOREST

8220 Elk Creek Road, Rapid City, 605-787-4560; www.elkresort.net

Visit the Black Hills Petrified Forest which includes an interpretive film on the Black Hills geology and petrification process; and a five-block walk-through area of logs ranging from 5-100 feet in length and up to 3-5 feet in diameter and stumps 3-5 feet in height. Self-guided tours are available as well as a rock, fossil and mineral museum; and gift and rock-lapidary shops.

Memorial Day-Labor Day, daily.

DINOSAUR PARK

940 Skyline Drive, Rapid City, www.dinosaurpark.net

This park has life-size steel and cement models of the dinosaurs once numerous in the area.

Daily 6 a.m.-10 p.m.

MOUNT RUSHMORE NATIONAL MEMORIAL

The faces of four great American presidents—Washington, Jefferson, Lincoln and Theodore Roosevelt—are carved onto a 5,675-foot mountain in the Black Hills of South Dakota, as grand and enduring as the contributions of the men they represent. Senator Peter Norbeck was instrumental in the realization of the monument. The original plan called for the presidents to be sculpted to the waist. It was a controversial project when sculptor Gutzon Borglum began his work on the carving in 1927. With crews often numbering 30 workers, he continued through 14 years of crisis and heartbreak and had almost finished by March, 1941, when he died. Lincoln Borglum, his son, brought the project to a close in October of that year. Today, the memorial is host to almost 3 million visitors a year. An orientation center, administrative and information headquarters and a snack bar (daily) are on the grounds as is the sculptor's studio museum. October-mid-May.

MUSEUM OF GEOLOGY

O'Harra Memorial Building, 501 E. St. Joseph, Rapid City, 605-394-2467;
www.sdsmt.edu
Exceptional display of minerals, fossils, gold samples and other geological material; first Tyrannosaurus Rex skull found in South Dakota.
Monday-Saturday, Sunday afternoons.

THUNDERHEAD UNDERGROUND FALLS

10940 W. Highway 44, Rapid City, 605-343-0081; www.thunderheadfalls.com
This tunnel, which dates to 1878, is one of the oldest gold mining tunnels in the Black Hills area. Stalactites and gold-bearing granite formations. Falls are 600 feet inside the mine.
May-October.

WHERE TO STAY
★★ALEX JOHNSON
523 Sixth St., Rapid City, 605-342-1210, 800-888-2539; www.alexjohnson.com
143 rooms. Restaurant, bar. Business center. Pets accepted. $61-150

★AMERICINN RAPID CITY
1632 Rapp St., Rapid City, 605-343-8424, 800-634-3444; www.americinn.com
64 rooms. Business center. Fitness center. Pool. Pets accepted. $61-150

★★BEST WESTERN RAMKOTA HOTEL
2111 N. Lacrosse St., Rapid City, 605-343-8550, 800-780-7234; www.ramkota.com
267 rooms. Restaurant,bar. Business center. Fitness center. Pool. Pets accepted. $61-150

★BEST WESTERN TOWN 'N COUNTRY
2505 Mount Rushmore Road, Rapid City, 605-343-5383, 877-666-5383;
www.bestwestern.com
99 rooms. Complimentary breakfast. Business center. Pool. $61-150

★DAYS INN
1570 Rapp St., Rapid City, 605-348-8410, 800-329-7466; www.daysinn.com
77 rooms. Complimentary breakfast. Fitness center. Pool. $61-150

BADLANDS NATIONAL PARK

This fantastic, painted landscape of steep canyons, spires and razor-edged ridges was made a national monument by President Franklin D. Roosevelt in 1939 and became a national park in 1978. Its stark and simple demonstration of geologic processes has an unusual beauty. Soft clays and sandstones deposited as sediments 26 to 37 million years ago by streams from the Black Hills created vast plains, which were inhabited by the saber-toothed cat, the rhinoceros-like brontothere, and ancestors of the present-day camel and horse. Their fossilized bones make the area an enormous prehistoric graveyard. Herds of bison roam the area again. Pronghorn antelope, mule deer, prairie dogs and Rocky Mountain bighorn sheep can also be seen.

The Ben Reifel Visitor Center, with exhibits and an audiovisual program, is open all year at Cedar Pass (daily). Evening programs and activities conducted by ranger-naturalists are offered during the summer. Camping is available at Cedar Pass and Sage Creek. The White River Visitor Center, 60 miles southwest of the Ben Reifel Visitor Center, features colorful displays on the history and culture of the Oglala Sioux.

★★HOLIDAY INN
505 N. Fifth St., Rapid City, 605-348-4000, 800-465-4329; www.holidayinn.com
205 rooms. Restaurant, bar. Business center. Fitness center. Pool. Pets accepted. $61-150

★★RAMADA INN
1721 N. Lacrosse St., Rapid City, 605-342-1300; www.grandgatewayhotel.com
139 rooms. Restaurant, bar. Business center. Fitness center. Pool. Pets accepted. $61-150

WHERE TO EAT
★FIREHOUSE BREWING CO.
610 Main St., Rapid City, 605-348-1915; www.firehousebrewing.com
American. Lunch, dinner. Outdoor seating. Children's menu. Bar. $16-35

★FLYING T. CHUCKWAGON SUPPER & SHOW
8971 S. Highway 16, Rapid City, 605-342-1905; www.flyingt.com
American. Dinner. Closed mid-September-late May. $15 and under

★★GREAT WALL
315 E. North St., Rapid City, 605-348-1060; www.greatwalltogo.com
Chinese. Lunch, dinner. Children's menu. $16-35

★★IMPERIAL
702 E. North St., Rapid City, 605-394-8888
Chinese. Lunch, dinner. Children's menu. $16-35

SIOUX FALLS

At the falls of the Sioux River, this city has developed at a constant pace since it was reestablished in 1865 (after being abandoned in 1862 following threats of a Lakota attack). Cattle are shipped from a three-state area, slaughtered and packed here, then shipped east. Manufactured goods from the East are distributed throughout much of South Dakota from Sioux Falls.

Sioux Falls is the center for EROS (Earth Resources Observation Systems), an international center for space and aircraft photography of the Earth.

WHAT TO SEE
GREAT PLAINS ZOO
805 S. Kiwanis Ave., Sioux Falls, 605-367-7003; www.gpzoo.org
The centerpiece of Sherman Park, the Great Plains Zoo focuses on animals native to places outside of South Dakota: black rhinos, red pandas and Galapagos tortoises are among the 400 residents (representing 100 species in all). The zoo replicates a variety of ecosystems, including the Australian Outback and the banks of the Nile River, to give visitors a better understanding of how the animals live in the wild. A seasonal train takes riders on a behind-the-scenes look at the African Savannah exhibit, and summertime shows give kids a closer look at some of the animals.
Daily; hours vary by season.

OLD COURTHOUSE MUSEUM
200 W. Sixth St., Sioux Falls, 605-367-4210; www.siouxlandmuseums.com
Restored Richardsonian-Romanesque quartzite stone courthouse from 1890 contains exhibits of Siouxland history, special exhibits on local culture.
Daily.

PETTIGREW HOME AND MUSEUM
131 N. Duluth Ave., Sioux Falls, 605-367-7097; www.siouxlandmuseums.com
This restored Queen Anne house from 1889 is furnished to show the life of state's first senator. The house features galleries of Native American items and the cultural history of the Sioux.
Daily.

USS SOUTH DAKOTA BATTLESHIP MEMORIAL
100, E. Sixth St., Sioux Falls, 605-367-7060; www.siouxfalls.org
The *USS South Dakota* was the first ship to fire on Japanese enemies in World War II and played a role in every major Pacific battle between 1942 and 1945. Located in Sherman Park, the memorial pays honor to the crew that served on the South Dakota and has the same dimensions as the ship, which was sold by the Navy in 1962, and features many items that were once onboard. A small museum is also on site.
Memorial Day-Labor Day, daily.

WHERE TO STAY
★AMERICINN
3508 S. Gateway Blvd., Sioux Falls, 605-361-3538, 800-634-3444; www.americinn.com
65 rooms. Complimentary breakfast. Pool. $61-150

★BAYMONT INN
3200 S. Meadow Ave., Sioux Falls, 605-362-0835, 877-229-6668; www.baymontinns.com
78 rooms. Complimentary breakfast. Business center. Fitness center. Pool. Pets accepted. $61-150

★★BEST WESTERN RAMKOTA HOTEL

3200 W. Maple St., Sioux Falls, 605-336-0650, 800-780-7234; www.ramkota.com
226 rooms. Restaurant, bar. Pool. Pets accepted. $61-150

★COMFORT INN

3216 S. Carolyn Ave., Sioux Falls, 605-361-2822, 800-252-7466; www.comfortinn.com
65 rooms. Pets accepted. Complimentary breakfast. Pool. $61-150

★COMFORT SUITES

3208 Carolyn Ave., Sioux Falls, 605-362-9711, 800-424-6423; www.comfortsuites.com
60 rooms. Complimentary breakfast. Business center. Fitness center. Pool. Pets accepted. $61-150

★★HOLIDAY INN

100 W. Eighth St., Sioux Falls, 605-339-2000, 800-465-4329; www.holiday-inn.com
299 rooms. Restaurant, bar. Business center. Fitness center. Pool. $61-150

★KELLY INN - SIOUX FALLS

3101 W. Russell, Sioux Falls, 605-338-6242, 800-635-3559; www.kellyinnsiouxfalls.com
43 rooms. Complimentary breakfast. Pool. Pets accepted. $61-150

★★RAMADA INN AND SUITES AIRPORT

1301 W. Russell St., Sioux Falls, 605-336-1020, 866-336-1020; www.ramada.com
153 rooms. Restaurant, bar. Business center. Fitness center. Pool. Pets accepted. $61-150

★★★SHERATON SIOUX FALLS AND CONVENTION CENTER

1211 N. West Ave., Sioux Falls, 605-331-0100, 800-325-3535;
www.starwoodhotels.com
The Sioux Falls Convention Center is attached to this hotel by an indoor walkway, while the hotel itself offers 97,400 square feet of meeting space. Rooms cater to the business travelers with amenities such as oversized desks, data ports and voicemail, as well as plasma TVs and plush beds. The hotel has an indoor heated pool, a whirlpool, a sauna, a fitness room and a sun deck. The Falling Waters Grille offers a menu of traditional American fare for breakfast, lunch and dinner, while the Waters Edge Lounge is a popular stop for cocktails.
184 rooms. Restaurant, bar. Business center. Fitness center. Pool. $61-150

WHERE TO EAT
★★★C.J. CALLAWAY'S

500 E. 69th St., Sioux Falls, 605-334-8888; www.cjcallaways.com
Overlooking Prairie Green Golf Course, this handsome, country-club-style restaurant offers creatively prepared regional fare.
American. Dinner. Closed Sunday. Reservations recommended. Outdoor seating. Children's menu. Bar. $16-35

SPEARFISH

See also Deadwood, Lead, Rapid City, Sturgis

The fertile valley in which Spearfish lies is at the mouth of Spearfish Canyon, famous for its scenery and fishing. A Ranger District office of the Black Hills National Forest is located here.

WHAT TO SEE
HIGH PLAINS WESTERN HERITAGE CENTER

825 Heritage Drive, Spearfish, 605-642-9378; www.westernheritagecenter.com

Covering pioneer life in the Dakotas, Montana, Wyoming and Nebraska, this history museum includes artwork, artifacts and snazzy custom saddles and Western furnishings. Among the exhibits is the original stagecoach that ran the Deadwood-to-Spearfish route and displays that cover mining, forestry and rodeo. Outside, there is a furnished log cabin, a one-room schoolhouse, a seasonal farm with small animals and pastures populated by bison and longhorn cattle year-round.

Daily 9 a.m.-5 p.m.

WHERE TO STAY
★BEST WESTERN BLACK HILLS LODGE

540 E. Jackson Blvd., Spearfish, 605-642-7795, 800-780-7234; www.bestwestern.com

50 rooms. Complimentary breakfast. Pool. Pets accepted. $61-150

★FAIRFIELD INN

2720 E. First Ave., Spearfish, 605-642-3500, 800-450-4442; www.fairfieldinn.com

57 rooms. Complimentary breakfast. Restaurants. Pool. $61-150

★★HOLIDAY INN

305 N. 27th St., Spearfish, 605-642-4683, 800-999-3541; www.holidayinn.com

145 rooms. Restaurant, bar. Fitness center. Pool. Pets accepted. $61-150

★★SPEARFISH CANYON RESORT

10619 Roughlock Falls Road, Spearfish, 605-584-3435, 877-975-6343; www.spfcanyon.com

54 rooms. Bar. Pets accepted. $61-150

STURGIS

See also Deadwood, Lead, Rapid City, Spearfish

Originally a "bullwhackers" (wagon drivers) stop on the way to Fort Meade, this was once known as "Scooptown" because soldiers who came in were "scooped" (cleaned out) by characters such as Poker Alice, a famed cigar-smoking scoop expert. Now Sturgis is a busy Black Hills trade center.

WHAT TO SEE
BEAR BUTTE STATE PARK

North Highway 79, Sturgis, 605-347-5240

Called Mato Paha (or Bear Mountain) by the Lakota people, the defining feature at this park is not actually a flat-topped butte, but a singular mountain (4,422 feet above sea level) rising from the plains. For generations, the mountain has been a spiritually significant site for the Lakota and Cheyenne people, and thousands of worshippers continue to visit the ceremonial area at its base every year. The 1.7-mile Summit Trail takes hikers on a steep path (gaining 1,253 feet) to the peak, where four states can be seen. The park also serves as the northern trailhead for the 111-mile Centennial Trail into the Black Hills. Bison roam free within the park's boundaries. The visitor center features displays on the area's ecology and history and there is a small campground and a lake with a boat ramp in the park.

Visitor center: May-early September, daily 8 a.m.-6 p.m. Park: daily 8 a.m.-7 p.m.

SPECIAL EVENT
STURGIS RALLY

Sturgis, 605-642-8166; www.sturgis-rally.com

The biggest motorcycle rally in the country isn't just for bikers anymore—it attracts lawyers, doctors and virtually everybody else who's ever revved a bike. The inaugural rally was held by the local motorcycle club, the Jackpine Gypsies, in 1938, and was quite modest: nine racers riding in front of a small audience. The annual August event has since snowballed into an extravaganza that draws in a crowd of more than 450,000. (More than 100 marriage licenses have been issued to attending couples in recent years.) During the rally, five blocks of Sturgis' historic Main Street are open to motorcycle traffic only, creating a wild atmosphere of wall-to-wall bikes and people. The schedule includes motorcycle races and tours, and there are hundreds of vendors selling everything from leather of all descriptions to exotic foods. Hotels, campgrounds and restaurants in Sturgis book up months before the bikes roar into town.

Mid-August.

WHERE TO STAY
★DAYS INN

2630 Lazelle St., Sturgis, 605-347-3027, 800-329-7466; www.daysinn.com

53 rooms. Complimentary breakfast. Pets accepted. $61-150

VERMILLION

Vermillion, the seat of Clay County, was located below the bluffs of the Missouri River until the flood of 1881 changed the river's course, forcing residents to higher ground. Located in a portion of the state that was claimed twice by France and once by Spain before being sold to the United States, Vermillion now prides itself on its rich farmland, good industrial climate and the University of South Dakota, which is located here.

WHAT TO SEE
UNIVERSITY OF SOUTH DAKOTA

414 E. Clark St., Vermillion, 605-677-5326, 877-269-6837; www.usd.edu

On campus is the DakotaDome, a physical education, recreation and athletic facility with an air-supported roof. Art galleries and theaters are located in the Warren M. Lee Center for the Fine Arts and Coyote Student Center.

WHERE TO STAY
★COMFORT INN

701 W. Cherry St., Vermillion, 605-624-8333, 800-228-5150; www.choicehotels.com

46 rooms. Complimentary breakfast. Fitness center. Pool. Pets accepted. $61-150

WALL

See also Rapid City

Established as a station on the Chicago & North Western Railroad in 1907, Wall is a gateway to Badlands National Park. The town is a trading center for local farmers and ranchers and is noted for its pure water, which is brought up from wells 3,200 feet deep. A Ranger District office of the Nebraska National Forest is located here.

WHAT TO SEE
WALL DRUG STORE

510 Main St., Wall, 605-279-2175; www.walldrug.com

Ted and Dorothy Hustead bought the Wall Drug pharmacy in 1931 during the Great Depression. Business was lukewarm for five years until Ted put up signs around town advertising free ice water. It worked and business boomed. Now in the hands of a third Hustead generation, Wall Drug is a sprawling tourist outpost that attracts nearly 20,000 visitors on hot summer days, pouring some 5,000 glasses of ice cold water in the process. The signs remain integral and thousands are in existence along I-90, in European cities like Amsterdam and London, and even in local homes. All this advertising has helped the Husteads build an empire that includes not just a drugstore, but also a shopping mall and a 500-seat restaurant. Studies have shown that about three-quarters of I-90s traffic exits at Wall.

Daily 6:30 a.m.-6 p.m.

WHERE TO STAY
★DAYS INN

210 10th Ave., Wall, 605-279-2000, 800-329-7466; www.daysinn.com

32 rooms. Complimentary breakfast. Fitness center. Pets accepted. $61-150

WHERE TO EAT
★WALL DRUG

510 Main St., Wall, 605-279-2175; www.walldrug.com

American. Breakfast, lunch, dinner. Children's menu. $61-150

WATERTOWN

See also Brookings

Originally called Waterville, this settlement owed its boom to the railroads. Two large lakes, Kampeska and Pelican, are on the edges of town.

WHAT TO SEE
MELLETTE HOUSE

421 Fifth Ave. N.W., Watertown, 605-886-4730; www.mellettehouse.org

This house was built in 1883 by Arthur C. Mellette, the last territorial and

WIND CAVE NATIONAL PARK

Wind Cave, one of many caves in the ring of limestone surrounding the Black Hills, is a maze of subterranean passages known to extend more than 79 miles. It's named for the strong currents of wind that blow in and out of its entrance according to the atmospheric pressure. (When the pressure decreases, the wind blows outward; when it increases, wind blows in.) It was the rushing sound of air coming out of the entrance that led to its discovery in 1881. The cave and surrounding area became a national park in 1903.

The temperature inside Wind Cave is a constant 53 F. Various one- to two-hour guided tours (daily) and four-hour tours (June-mid-August, daily). Tours are moderately strenuous.

On the surface are prairie grasslands, forests and a wildlife preserve the home of bison, pronghorn elk, deer, prairie dogs and other animals. The Centennial Trail, a 111-mile, multiuse trail, takes visitors from one end of the Black Hills to the other. The trail begins here and ends at Bear Butte State Park. Visitor center (daily).

Hours may vary throughout the year. Park (daily). 605-745-4600. www.nps.gov/wica

the first state governor of South Dakota. Original Victorian furnishings, heirlooms, family portraits.

May-September, Tuesday-Sunday.

REDLIN ART CENTER

1200 33rd St. S.E., Watertown, 605-882-3877; www.redlinart.com

This center houses more than 100 of artist Terry Redlin's original oil paintings. Center also includes the only planetarium in the state, an amphitheater, gift shop and Glacial Lakes and Prairie Tourism Association.

Daily.

WHERE TO STAY

★★BEST WESTERN RAMKOTA HOTEL

1901 S.W. Ninth Ave., Watertown, 605-886-8011, 800-780-7234;
www.watertown.ramkota.com

101 rooms. Restaurant, bar. Fitness center. Pool. Pets accepted. $61-150

INDEX

NUMBERS

1859 Marshal's Home And Jail Museum (Independence), *77*

36th Street Food & Drink Company (St. Joseph), *98*

45th Infantry Division Museum (Oklahoma City), *166*

A

Abilene & Smoky Valley Rail Road (Abilene), *44*

Adventureland Inn (Des Moines), *27*

Adventureland Park (Des Moines), *24*

Agate Fossil Beds National Monument (Scottsbluff), *136*

Ak-Sar-Ben Aquarium (Omaha), *131*

Alabaster Caverns (Alva), *153*

Albrecht-Kemper Museum of Art (St. Joseph), *97*

Alex Johnson (Rapid City), *191*

Allen-Lambe House Museum and Study Center (Wichita), *61*

Alley Rose (Kearney), *123*

Alpine Inn (Hill City), *186*

Amana Heritage Museum (Amana Colonies), *10*

Amana Heritage Sites (Amana Colonies), *9*

The American Restaurant (Kansas City), *85*

America's Best Value Inn (Fremont), *119*

Americinn Medora (Medora), *149*

Americinn Rapid City (Rapid City), *191*

Americinn (Fargo), *143*

Americinn (Sioux Falls), *193*

Ameristar Casino Hotel (Council Bluffs), *20*

Andre's Tearoom (Kansas City), *85*

Andy Williams Moon River Theater (Branson), *65*

Anheuser-Busch Brewery (St. Louis), *99*

Annie Gunn's (Chesterfield), *70*

Antique and Craft Extravaganza (Lexington), *123*

Anvil Saloon (Ste. Genevieve), *113*

Applejack Festival (Nebraska City), *127*

Aquaticus (Oklahoma City), *166*

Arabia Steamboat Museum (Kansas City), *80*

Arbor Day Celebration (Nebraska City), *127*

Arbor Lodge State Historical Park (Nebraska City), *127*

Aria Grill (Oklahoma City), *171*

Arkansas River Historical Society Museum (Tulsa), *177*

Arnolds Park Amusement Park (Okoboji), *39*

Arrowwood Resort and Conference Center by Clubhouse (Okoboji), *39*

Art and Design Center (Kansas City), *80*

Arthur Bryant's Barbeque (Kansas City), *85*

Ash Hollow State Historical Park (Ogallala), *129*

Auburn Inn (Auburn), *115*

Azalea Inn (Muskogee), *165*

B

Baldknobbers Jamboree (Branson), *65*

Ballet Oklahoma (Oklahoma City), *169*

Barbosa's Castillo (St. Joseph), *98*

Bass Pro Shops Outdoor World Showroom and Fish and Wildlife Museum (Springfield), *94*

Bavarian Inn (Custer), *184*

Baxter's Interurban Grill (Tulsa), *180*

Baymont Inn & Suites (Ames), *12*

Baymont Inn Oklahoma City South (Oklahoma City), *170*

W

Wagon Wheels Inn (Valley City), *150*

Wah-Shun-Gah Days (Council Grove), *45*

Wall Drug Store (Wall), *197*

Wall Drug (Wall), *197*

Ward Earthlodge Village Historic Site (Bismarck), *141*

Warren Duck Club (Tulsa), *181*

Washburn Sunflower Music Festival (Topeka), *59*

Washington University (St. Louis), *103*

Waterfront Seafood Market (Des Moines), *29*

Waterloo Community Playhouse (Waterloo), *41*

Waterloo Museum of Art (Waterloo), *42*

Watkins Woolen Mill State Park and State Historic Site (Excelsior Springs), *73*

Wells Fargo Bank of Iowa-Poweshiek County (Grinnell), *34*

West Nebraska Arts Center (Scottsbluff), *137*

Western Historic Trails Center (Council Bluffs), *19*

The Westin Crown Center (Kansas City), *85*

The Westin St. Louis (St. Louis), *107*

Westport (Kansas City), *80,*

Wheeler Inn (Auburn), *116*

Whitestone Hill Battlefield State Historic Site (Jamestown), *146*

Wichita Art Museum (Wichita), *62*

Wichita Center for the Arts (Wichita), *62*

Wichita Mountains Wildlife Refuge (Lawton), *163*

Wichita River Festival (Wichita), *62*

Wichita-Sedgwick County Historical Museum (Wichita), *62*

Wild West Festival (Hays), *49*

Wilderness Lodge and Comfort Center (Fremont), *119*

Wilderness Lodge (Pilot Knob), *91*

Wilder's Steakhouse (Joplin), *80*

Wildwood Historic Home (Nebraska City), *127*

Wildwood Lodge (Des Moines), *28*

Will Rogers Birthplace and Dog Iron Ranch (Claremore), *157*

Will Rogers Inn Claremore (Claremore), *157*

Will Rogers Memorial (Claremore), *157*

Will Rogers Stampede PRCA Rodeo (Claremore), *157*

Willa Cather State Historic Site (Hastings), *121*

Woodbury County Courthouse (Sioux City), *41*

Woodward Discovery Center (Dubuque), *32*

Woolaroc (Bartlesville), *155*

Worlds of Fun (Kansas City), *82*

Y

Yemanja Brasil (St. Louis), *112*

Yen Ching (Dubuque), *34*

Yia Yia (Lincoln), *56, 126*

Yia Yia's Eurobistro (Overland Park), *56*

Z

Zeno's Motel and Steak House (Rolla), *92*

Zia's (St. Louis), *112*

IOWA

KANSAS

NEBRASKA

MISSOURI

NORTH DAKOTA

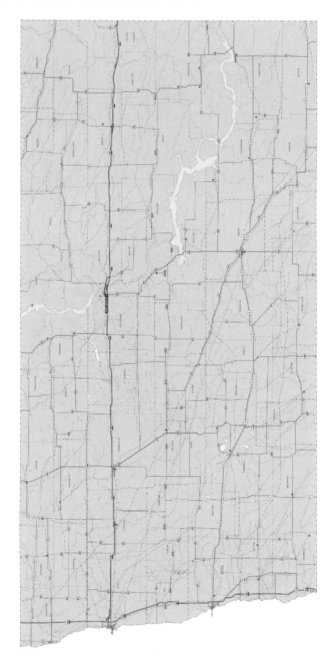